The Book of
CARD
GAMES

Peter Arnold

A & C BLACK · LONDON

HIPPOCRENE BOOKS · NEW YORK

Peter Arnold is an author and editor who specializes in sports and games. Many of his books have been concerned with card games, including *The Illustrated Book of Table Games*, *The Complete Book of Indoor Games* and *The Book of Games*. He has also written three books on gambling, one of which, *The Encyclopedia of Gambling*, was described by a New York author as 'the best history of gambling'. Many of his books have been published in the USA and in foreign-language editions.

Paperback reprinted 1995 for
A & C Black (Publishers) Limited
35 Bedford Row, London WC1R 4JH
ISBN 0-7136-4342-0

and simultaneously for
Hippocrene Books, Inc.
171 Madison Avenue, New York, N.Y. 10016
ISBN 0-7818-0418-3

First published 1988
Christopher Helm (Publishers) Ltd

© 1988 Peter Arnold

CIP catalogue records for this book
are available from the British Library
and the Library of Congress

Printed in the United States of America

CONTENTS

INTRODUCTION

Few inventions can have provided more hours of enjoyment for more people than the standard pack, or deck, of playing cards. An infinite number of games have been devised with them, yet the average person knows only a handful, and regularly plays only two or three. One reason is that while new games are readily learned from friends, it can be a daunting task to pick up the nuances of a game from the skeletal descriptions often set out in print, many of which assume readers are experienced players familiar with the terms used by experts.

In compiling this new book I have had this difficulty in mind, and have set out to describe games in non-technical language, explaining terms as they arise. By including example deals, by remarks on strategy intended to convey some of the nicer points of games, and by the use of simple, clear illustrations, I hope that the book will encourage readers to try new games, and that they will absorb them easily and find them rewarding. The short glossary of terms which follows this introduction is meant more as a checklist than as a sort of 'highway code' to be assimilated before one is competent to sit at the card-table.

I have thought it best to arrange the games in alphabetical order, and to provide indexes at the back of the book which classify them. There are two indexes. One is a simple index of names, which is necessary because many games are known by more than one name, and a reader searching for a game he knows as Double Pedro, for example, will not find it by looking at the Contents page, unless he is aware that the game is also known as Cinch.

The other index classifies games by the number of players wishing to play, since that is the main constraint when choosing a game. Given the number of players, this index lists firstly those games considered best for that number and secondly those other games which can be played satisfactorily by that number. Also listed separately are games for children, and gambling games, i.e. those games which would be pointless or impossible without the betting element.

The games included are those which demand inclusion because their popularity is such that it would be unthinkable to leave them out, and those which I consider are worth the trouble to learn.

Many games have similarities to other games, and indeed if one classified games into 'families' it would be possible to put 90 per cent of them into only three families: trick-taking games (like Whist), games of the stops variety (like Newmarket) and melding games (like Rummy). In this book, where two or more games are so similar that it would be a waste of space to run through separately all the common rules for each, they are coupled, one chosen as the 'parent' game and the others following as 'variants'. On the other hand, some games which might be thought of as variants are, in fact, sufficiently different or important to be described separately – thus, for example, Gin Rummy appears in its own right, not as a variant of Rummy, and Solo Whist is not considered a mere variant of Whist.

One standard convention has been used in the examples of trick-taking games which the reader might not be familiar with: in the summaries of deals the card that wins a trick is underlined (the player of that card leading to the next trick).

Finally, an acknowledgement, an apology and a hope. The acknowledgement is due to Matthew Macfadyen for supplying the example deal for Skat, he being a much better player of that game than I shall ever be. The apology is due to feminine readers who will notice that when a pronoun is required for a player 'he' is used. This, for the want of a satisfactory neutral pronoun, is to avoid 'he or she' dozens of times, which would be tedious. The hope is that readers, when they sit down to play with friends, will not now say, as they usually do: 'What can we all play?' but: 'Shall we try a new game?'

Peter Arnold, 1988

GLOSSARY

Available card   In patience or solitaire games, a card that can be moved or packed upon according to the rules.

Build   In patience or solitaire games, to play a card onto a *foundation card*.

Bundle   A group of two or more cards dealt to a player in one round of dealing.

Column   Two or more cards in a vertical line on the table, sometimes overlapping each other (as opposed to *row*).

Court Card   A King, Queen or Jack (also known as a *face card* or picture card).

Cut   To divide the pack into two parts and reverse their order. Also, when cutting for deal or partners, to take a number of cards from the top of the pack, exposing the bottom card of the packet taken.

Deal   To distribute the cards to the players. In some games this is done one card at a time, in others in *bundles* of two, three or four.

Discard   In trick-taking games, to play a card not of the *suit* led or of the *trump suit*. In games of the Rummy family, to lay aside a card to a *discard pile* when taking another. In other games, to lay aside cards in exchange for others. Cards so played are called *discards*.

Discard pile   Cards previously discarded. In games of the Rummy family, the pile from which a player may take a card in preference to drawing from *stock*.

Doubleton   A holding of two cards only of a particular suit.

Eldest hand   The player at the left of the dealer who, in most games, plays first. In two-player games he is *elder hand*.

Exposed card   In patience or solitaire games, a card at the foot of a column, right of a fan, or top of a *foundation pile* or *waste heap*, which may be played on or moved.

Face card   See *court card*.

Flush   A hand of cards all of the same suit.

Follow suit   To play a card of the same *suit* as the card led to a *trick*.

Foundation card   In patience or solitaire games, a card (usually, but not always, an Ace) upon which a complete suit or sequence has to be built in accordance with the object and rules of the game.

Foundation pile   The cards piled on a *foundation card*.

Hand   The collection of cards dealt to a player.

Honour cards   In Bridge, the Ace, King, Queen, Jack and 10 of the trump suit, or the four Aces in a no-trump contract. In games of the Whist family, the Ace, King, Queen and Jack of the trump suit.

Joker   An extra card supplied with the standard 52-card pack which is sometimes used as a *wild card*.

Kitty   See *pool*.

Lay-out   The arrangement of cards on the table for purposes of betting or, in patience or solitaire games, for moving or building on in accordance with the rules (also called *tableau*).

Lead   To play first to a *trick*, or the card so played.

Meld   To form cards into sets, usually of cards of the same *rank*, or cards of the same *suit* in *sequence*. Such collections of cards are called *melds*.

Pack   In patience or solitaire games, to place a card on an *exposed* card in the *layout* in a way in which conforms with the rules.

Pair   Two cards of the same *rank*.

Pair-royal   Three cards of the same rank (also called a *prial*).

Plain suit   A *suit* which is not the *trump* suit (also called a *side suit*).

Pool   The collective amount of money or chips in the centre of the table in gambling games (also called a *kitty* or a *pot*).

Pot   See *pool*.

Prial   Three cards of the same *rank* (also called a *pair-royal*).

Rank   The denomination or value of a card (i.e. Ace, King, Queen, Jack, 10, 9, 8, 7, 6, 5, 4, 3, 2) or the order in which they are valued.

Row   Two or more cards placed horizontally on the table, perhaps overlapping each other (as opposed to *column*).

Sequence   Two or more cards following one another in correct order (e.g. 9, 10, Jack). An ascending sequence is one from low to high (e.g. Ace to King), a descending sequence is one from high to low (e.g. King to Ace). A round-the-corner sequence is one in which the highest card is considered adjacent to the lowest (e.g. Q, K, A, 2, 3). A suit sequence is one in which the cards are in the same suit.

Shuffle   To mix the cards in the pack before dealing so that they are in random order.

Side suit   See *plain suit*.

Singleton   A holding of one card only of a particular suit.

Stake   The amount of money or chips put up in a bet.

Stock   The undealt part of the pack.

Suit   The four suits are spades, hearts, diamonds and clubs. In some games, some suits are ranked higher than others.

Tableau   In patience or solitaire games, the arrangement of the cards on the table at the beginning of the game, and subsequently as moves take place.

Talon   In patience or solitaire games, a *waste heap*, i.e. cards laid aside as not being immediately playable according to the rules; in games like piquet, cards laid aside for later use.

Trick   A round of cards, one being contributed by each player during play. Also such cards when collected together.

Trump suit   A designated suit which takes precedence over other suits in trick-taking games. To trump is to play a card from the trump suit.

Upcard   In trick-taking games, a card turned up to denote the *trump suit*; in games of the Rummy family, the card turned up to begin a *discard pile*.

Waste heap   A pile of cards laid aside as unwanted or unplayable (see *talon*).

Widow   Extra cards dealt to the table at the same time as the hands.

Wild card   A card which its holder can use to represent any card of his choice.

Younger hand   The dealer in two-player games like piquet (see also *eldest hand*).

ACCORDION ?

Accordion is one of the simplest of one-pack **patience** or **solitaire** games. It has no tableau.

The play
One pack is used. The cards are shuffled and turned over one at a time from hand. The first card is dealt to the top left of the space available. The second card is dealt to its right and rows of the cards from left to right are built up (but are to be considered, if necessary, as one long continuous line).

If a card matches its left-hand neighbour in suit or rank it can be packed upon it. Similarly, if it matches the card third to the left (i.e. jumping two) it can be packed upon it. Sometimes a card is dealt which can be packed in either of these places, when the player must choose which is more advantageous. Often one such move will make another possible. A move should always be made when possible.

The object is to finish the game with all of the cards in one pack. Sometimes the game can be frustrating, with a long line of single unmatching cards building up. Sometimes the number of piles never exceeds half a dozen or so. Sometimes the line goes backwards and forwards, like the accordion from which the game takes its name.

A game of Accordion in progress. If the next two cards are ♣J followed by ♣4 or ♠10 the piles will be reduced to one.

ALL FOURS

All Fours is an ancient game from which others have evolved. It is mentioned in *The Compleat Gamester* by Charles Cotton, published in 1674. In the United States the game is also known as Seven-up, High-Low-Jack or Old Sledge. It has been popular with both gamblers and middle-class society.

Players

The game is basically for two players, but can be played by three or four (see *Variants*).

Cards

The full pack of 52 is used, the cards ranking from Ace (high) to 2 (low).

Preliminaries

Cards are drawn to determine dealer, highest dealing. Dealer shuffles and the pack is cut by non-dealer.

Dealing

Six cards are dealt to each player, beginning with non-dealer, in bundles of three. The next card is turned up to indicate the trump suit. If it is a Jack, dealer immediately scores 1 point.

The play

It is necessary to understand the scoring from the beginning. The object is to gain 7 points. Four of them are scored in the following order at the end of the deal:

High is the highest trump in play, and is worth 1 point to the holder (i.e. to whom it was dealt).

Low is the lowest trump in play, and is worth 1 point to the holder. *Jack* is the Jack of trumps, and is worth 1 point to the player who takes it in a trick.

Game is worth 1 point and is scored by the player whose tricks won in play total the most, based on the scale of each Ace counting 4 points, each King 3, each Queen 2, each Jack 1 and each ten 10. Should the total won by each player be equal, non-dealer scores the point.

It is possible, of course, that the Jack of trumps will not be in play, in which case this point is not scored. Should there be only one trump in play, it scores the point for high and also that for low.

Begging Play begins with non-dealer either *standing* or *begging*. If he says 'I stand', he accepts the turned-up card as trumps and play begins. If he says 'I beg', he rejects the turned-up card. The dealer now has the option of either accepting or rejecting the turned-up card.

To accept he says 'Take one', and non-dealer immediately scores one point for *gift*. If the dealer does not like the trump suit he says 'I run the cards'. Naturally, if non-dealer is only one point short of game, the dealer must refuse the gift and run the cards.

When the dealer runs the cards the rejected turn-up is discarded face down, and he deals each player another bundle of three cards, turning up the next card. This card indicates trumps, i.e. it is not permitted to beg a second time. However, if the turn-up is the same suit as the original rejected card, it is discarded, and a further round of three cards each is dealt. This proceeds until the new trump suit is established. If a Jack is turned up while the dealer is running the cards, dealer scores one point, unless it is in the suit of the original rejected turn-up, in which case it is discarded as stated. Should the pack be exhausted before a trump suit is established, the deal is abandoned.

The play of the hands begins when the trump suit is established. If the cards have been run each player will hold nine, twelve or more cards, and so must first reduce his hand to six cards by discarding.

Non-dealer now leads to the first trick. In a departure from most trick-taking games, the second player is allowed to trump even if he is able to follow suit. He cannot discard, however, if holding a card in the suit led – he must either follow or trump. If unable to follow suit, he may trump or discard as preferred. If trumps are led, he must follow if able.

The deal for the hand of All Fours described in the text.

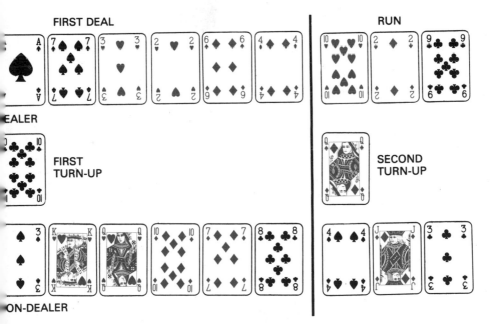

The winner of a trick leads to the next, and so on. When all six tricks are played the scores are calculated in the order stated. The first player to reach 7 points wins, even though his opponent is able to pass 7 on the same deal. For example, a player having the points for low, Jack and game will not score them if his opponent has reached 7 with a point for high. It sometimes happens that a player 'counts out' during a deal (e.g. if, needing one, he is dealt the Ace of trumps), in which case it is not customary to play out the deal.

The deal passes in rotation until one player reaches 7 points.

Example hand

Trumps are very important in All Fours, as they provide plenty of opportunities for strategy in the trick-taking phase of the game. In the specimen hand illustrated, with the ♣10 turned up, non-dealer begs, as his trump holding would be ♣8 only. Dealer refuses the gift, as his holding is nil, and announces he will run the cards. The cards dealt in the run are shown to the right of the line, and diamonds is turned up as the new trump suit.

Players now discard three cards each.

Non-dealer decides to discard ♠4 3 ♣3.
Dealer discards ♥3 2 ♣9.

Non-dealer's main object is to make the ♦J, worth a point to whoever takes it in a trick, and a secondary object is to make the ♦10, which will give him an excellent chance to make the point for game. He therefore decides to

lead his high hearts, on the grounds that he can afford to sacrifice them to dealer's trumps if it improves his chance of making the ♦J 10 himself. Dealer, with very small trumps only, and certain of a point for his ♦2, decides that his best chance of the point for game is to use his trumps if possible to take high cards in tricks, and to lead them in order to drive out his opponent's trumps so that he might make his ♠A. To make game it is essential he makes the ♥10, so when the ♥K is led, it confirms his policy of trumping and leading trumps back. The play goes as follows:

	Non-dealer	Dealer
1.	♥K	♦2
2.	♦J	♦4
3.	♥Q	♦6
4.	♦10	♠7
5.	♣8	♠A
6.	♦7	♥10

Dealer's strategy failed, and non-dealer's worked perfectly. As it happened, non-dealer's hand was too strong, and he was sure to make his ♦J 10 however dealer played. In the point for game, non-dealer won with tricks worth 25 points to dealer's five. Non-dealer also won the points for high, with the ♦J, and, of course, the point for jack, having won the trick containing the ♦J. Dealer made the point for low, with his ♦2.

After this deal, therefore, non-dealer led 3–1 and dealt the second hand.

Variants

Three-handed All Fours can be played with variants as follows. In the deal, only the dealer and the eldest hand (on dealer's left) may look at their cards. Eldest hand has the option of standing or begging, and the dealer of playing with the original trump or running the cards. Only when the trump is established does the third player pick up his cards. Play then proceeds as before.

In the count for game, should there be a tie between dealer and one of the non-dealers, non-dealer gets the point. If the two non-dealers tie, the point for game is not scored.

Four-handed All Fours is played in partnerships of two, partners sitting opposite each other. Only dealer and eldest hand partake in the determination of the trump suit by the standing or begging method. The other two players leave their hands face down on the table until the trick-taking phase begins. Since the partner's hands and tricks are combined from the point of view of scoring, the scoring is the same as in the two-handed game.

AUTHORS

Authors is a game played mainly by children up to an age of about fourteen. It is a game in which sets are collected, and it gets its name from a proprietory game in which the cards represent creations of famous authors, and a set is a collection of four of these relating to the same author.

Players

The game is best for four or five players, but any number from three to seven can play.

Cards

The full pack of 52 cards is used.

Dealing

All the cards are dealt one at a time, beginning with the player on dealer's left. Except with four players, some players will get more than others – it does not matter.

The play

The player on dealer's left begins by naming any other player and asking for a specific card. It must be a card in a rank of which the asker already holds a card. For example, a player might say: 'Mary, give me the nine of spades'. To do so he must already hold a nine. A player must not ask for a card which he holds himself.

A player asked for a card must give it up if he holds it. Should a player be successful in a request he has another turn, and continues asking for cards so long as he is successful. When his request fails, however, the turn passes to the player on his left. When a player obtains all four cards in a rank he must show them and place them face down on the table before him. Such a collection is called a *book*. A player who runs out of cards must wait till the end of the game. The player who has obtained the most books by the end of the game is the winner.

Variants

Two main variants are played to give the game more spice. In one it is not unethical for a player to ask for a card already in his hand. This might be considered a waste of turn but it has the value of misleading opponents and makes the game more interesting.

A second variant is that instead of the turn passing clockwise, it passes to the player who refuses a request. This convention ensures that a player gets a turn at asking for every time that he is asked himself, which some consider fairer.

BACCARAT

Baccarat is a name given to a family of casino gambling games. The basic game, described here, is more correctly known as Baccarat Banque, and is a game in which the casino usually holds the bank. It is also known as Baccarat à Deux Tableaux, since the table is in two halves, six players being seated in each half.

A later version of the game is known as Baccarat à Un Tableau, or Baccarat–Chemin de Fer, now commonly known as Chemin de Fer, and described later as a variant. A combination of the two games, Punto Banco, is sometimes called Baccarat–Chemin de Fer in United States' casinos, and is also described later.

Baccarat à Deux Tableaux was the game played for extremely high stakes in Deauville and elsewhere in France between the wars by the famous gambler Nico Zographos and the Greek Syndicate.

Players
Twelve players can sit round the table illustrated. A banker and a croupier sit in the middle.

Cards
Usually six full packs of 52 cards are used (sometimes three packs). The cards are shuffled together and placed in a *sabot*, a dealing shoe, and an indicator is placed between the tenth and eleventh cards at the back, these last few cards not being used.

All cards have their pip values, with court cards counting as ten and Aces as one.

Dealing
The banker deals two rounds of cards one at a time from the shoe, beginning with tableau un, and ending with himself, so that both tableaux and himself have hands of two cards.

The layout of the table on which Baccarat is played in a casino.

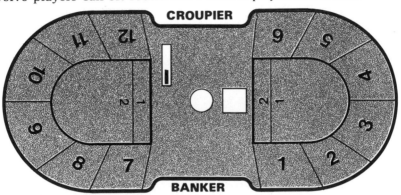

CROUPIER

BANKER

The play

Baccarat is purely a betting game. Players, wherever they are seated (or standing around the table) may bet that either tableau un or tableau deux, or both, will beat the bank.

Stakes, up to the limit of the bank, are placed by the players, if necessary helped by the croupier, in the spaces on the table marked 1 and 2. A stake on 1 is a bet that tableau un will win, on 2 that tableau deux will win. A stake on the line between 1 and 2 is a bet à cheval, which wins if both win, loses if both lose, and is void and returned to the player if the decision is split.

The object of the game is to obtain a pip count as near to 9 as possible, without exceeding 9. Only the last digit of the sum of the pips counts, thus a 7 and a 5, making 12, counts as 2. This number is called the *point*.

In certain circumstances, as will be explained, an extra card can be drawn to a baccarat hand, so that it consists of three cards. A three-card hand can never beat a two-card hand which totals 9 or 8, however. These are known to English or American players as 'naturals'. A two-card point of 9 is called *le grand*, and of 8 *le petit*.

When the three hands are dealt the players acting for tableaux un and deux, and the banker, look at their hands. If any of them have a point of 8 or 9 the hand is exposed, since it cannot be improved, and it wins immediately — unless of course both bank and a player hold a natural, in which case the point of 9 beats the point of 8. Equal hands are a stand-off, and the stake is returned to the player.

Should the banker not hold a natural, he must deal with the two hands in turn, beginning with tableau un. The player playing for that side of the table must either stand or draw a third card. As he is playing for all the players who have bet on that hand he has only one option, and must obey the following rules (which incidentally are the optimum play anyway). With a point of 0, 1, 2, 3, or 4, he must draw. With a point of 6 or 7 he must stand. His only option is with a point of 5, where he may stand or draw. These rules are called his 'Table of Play'. When a player draws, the third card is dealt to him face up. Otherwise he does not show the banker his hand.

Having dealt with tableau un, the banker deals similarly with tableau deux, and then deals with his own hand. He too has his Table of Play, which is more complicated, as it must take account of the cards dealt to the two tableaux. It is as follows:

Banker's Table of Play at Baccarat and Chemin de Fer

Banker's point	Banker draws if player draws	Banker stands if player draws	Banker has option if player draws
3	0,1,2,3,4,5,6,7	8	9
4	2,3,4,5,6,7	0,1,8,9	—
5	5,6,7	0,1,2,3,8,9	4
6	6,7	0,1,2,3,4,5,8,9	—

Note: If the player does not draw, the banker is advised to stand on 6 and draw on 3, 4 or 5. He always draws on 0, 1 or 2 and stands on 7.

The banker's Table of Play also gives him the optimum play, but for him it is only advisory, for the simple reason that he is playing against two opponents at once, and it is possible that the Table would indicate that he stand against one tableau and draw against the other. The banker must use his skill to make his choice. What he will usually do in practice, of course, is to assess which tableau is carrying the higher stake, and attempt to beat that tableau.

With all hands completed, they are exposed and the players are paid or lose their stakes according to whether their point is higher or not than the banker's. In ties, the player merely retains his stake.

Strategy

Since players have only one option, there is little room for strategy. However, there are two ways in which he can improve his prospects. On a point of 5, a player who draws has roughly a 20 per cent better chance of worsening his hand than improving it. It has been estimated that these odds, taken in conjunction with the banker's Table of Play, gives a player who stands about a $2\frac{1}{2}$ per cent advan-

tage over the bank. A player who draws still has a slight edge over the bank, but of only approximately 1 per cent. However, a player should not always stand (such a player is a *non-tireur*). He certainly should not always draw (a *tireur*). If the banker knows that a player always follows the same practice, he can use his own option in certain situations to improve his own chance. A player should therefore vary his play (a *douteur*), while perhaps favouring standing.

The other advantage a player can obtain lies in those cases mentioned where a banker must make his best play against that half of the table containing larger stake. It clearly pays to try to have one's bet on the other half.

Variants

Chemin de fer is the version of the game best suited for social play, since players hold the bank in rotation. It is played in casinos, where the casino will exact a commission, which varies from country to country and according to the

---

The layout of the table on which Chemin de Fer is played in a casino.

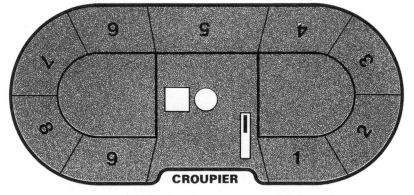

CROUPIER

stakes. A game found in Nevada casinos called Baccarat-Chemin de Fer is probably Punto Banco, which follows later.

Players Any number may play. In a casino they will sit at a table as illustrated.

Cards For friendly play for small stakes the normal pack is sufficient. From three to six packs of the same design shuffled together is better. In a casino six packs will usually be used in a *sabot*, or dealing shoe. It is the passing of the shoe round the table like a railway train which gives the game its name, the French for a railway. A marker card will be placed between the seventh and eighth cards from the back to indicate the end of the shoe.

Preliminaries The first banker is chosen either by lot or by auction, the player willing to put up the biggest bank being the banker. If the banker is chosen by lot he announces the amount of the bank. The banker places the amount of the bank before him, either in currency or chips.

The play There are only two hands, the banker's and the players'. The players first put up their stakes, beginning with the player on the banker's right, who may bet any amount up to the level of the bank. The next player then puts up his stake, and so on, until the amount in the bank is covered. If all players stake and the bank is not covered, the excess is removed. There are three preferential calls. A player may call '*Banco*', which means he is willing to bet the whole amount of the bank himself. If two players wish to call 'Banco', preference

goes to the player nearer banker's right.

There is one call which takes precedence over 'Banco' but this occurs only after a player has called 'Banco' and lost. He is entitled to call '*Banco suivi*', which allows him to bet the total amount of the bank again.

The third preferential call, ranking below those above, is '*Avec la table*' in which a player states his intention to bet half the value of the bank.

When the bets are made, the player with the highest stake holds the cards for the players. Banker deals two cards to the active player and two cards to himself, one at a time face down.

The object, as in Baccarat, is to obtain the closest point to 9. The two sides examine their hands and if either holds a natural 8 or 9, as described in Baccarat, he exposes it and bets are settled. Otherwise the player stands or draws as in Baccarat, i.e. with 0, 1, 2, 3 or 4 he must draw, with 6 or 7 he must stand and with 5 he has the option. The banker must also follow the Table of Play as set out above under Baccarat – the player thus has one option, the banker two.

Some casinos might allow *faux tirages*, or false draws, and social players must decide if they will allow them. This convention allows both player and banker to draw at his discretion – but it is only allowed for either when the player has called 'Banco' or 'Banco suivi'. In other words, the player and banker may make false draws when only they alone are involved – when other players'

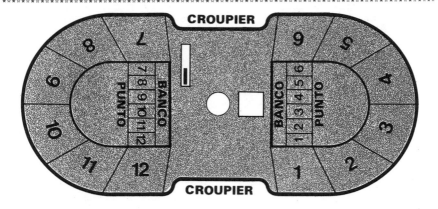

The layout of the table on which Punto Banco is played in a casino.

stakes are also involved, each must follow the Table of Play.

As in Baccarat, when each hand is complete, they are compared and the players are paid from the bank, or their stakes are added to the bank, doubling it.

While the banker retains the bank he is not allowed to withdraw any of it (unless, in a casino, it exceeds the casino limit). However, at any time he can pass the bank to the player on his right, withdrawing his own bank plus winnings. The bank also passes to the right when the players win and the amount in the bank is reduced to nil.

Punto Banco This version of Baccarat is a simplified Chemin de Fer. It is a casino game and is becoming the most popular version of Baccarat in casinos. Any number can play, on a table as illustrated. The cards and dealing arrangements are as for Chemin de Fer.

All players in rotation are given the opportunity to play the bank's hand, and a croupier plays the players' hand. The names 'bank' and 'players' therefore do not have the usual significance, and in fact all bets are made against the casino. Players are not required to put up a bank.

The game is a two-handed game, and each player may bet any amount between the casino's limits on either the 'bank' or 'players' hands. A player may bet on the players' hand by placing a stake in front of him in the space marked 'punto' (on some tables it is actually marked 'players'). He may bet on the bank hand by placing his stake in the small box which is numbered to correspond with his position at the table. These are marked 'banco' or 'bank'.

A croupier deals two cards to each of the croupier, playing the players' hand, and the player, playing the bank's. Neither has any options whatever, and must expose their cards, stand or draw according to the Table of Play as follows:

Player	Point		
	0, 1, 2, 3, 4, 5	draws	
	6, 7	stands	
	8, 9	exposes cards	
Banker	Point	Draws if player draws	Stands if
	0, 1, 2	0, 1, 2, 3, 4, 5, 6, 7, 8, 9	player draws
	3	0, 1, 2, 3, 4, 5, 6, 7, 9	8
	4	2, 3, 4, 5, 6, 7	0, 1, 8, 9
	5	4, 5, 6, 7	0, 1, 2, 3, 8, 9
	6	6, 7	0, 1, 2, 3, 4, 5, 8, 9
	7	Stands	
	8, 9	Exposes cards	

When both hands are complete bets are settled. If 'players' wins, winning bets are settled at odds of 1–1. If 'bank' wins, the casino settles at odds of 19–20, i.e. 5 per cent less (on winnings) than 1–1.

It has been estimated that the 'bank' hand has an advantage of 1.34 per cent over 'players', so by this deduction the casino enjoys a 1.34 per cent edge on those who bet on 'players' and a 1.20 per cent edge on those who back 'bank', making this slightly the better bet.

_____

Examples of the banker's play in Punto Banco. He must stand in the top instance with a point of 3, and draw in the lower instance with a point of 6.

PLAYER   BANKER

STANDS

DRAWS

BELEAGUERED CASTLE

Beleaguered Castle is a one-pack **patience** or **solitaire** game of skill, with a pleasing tableau. It can be a very frustrating game and often ends early, but with a good disposition of cards can be interesting.

The play

The four Aces are placed in a column at the centre of the layout. These are the foundations. The remaining cards are shuffled and a column of four is dealt to the extreme left of the layout, then a column to the right of the Aces. A second column is then dealt to the left overlapping the first column, then a similar column to the right etc. until all the cards are laid out as in the illustration. The cards to the left of the Aces are called the *left wing*, those to the right the *right wing*.

The object is to build all the cards in correct suit sequence on the foundations up to the Kings. The cards available for play are those uppermost in each row, i.e. the eight cards which are on the

---

The deal for the game of Beleaguered Castle described in the text.

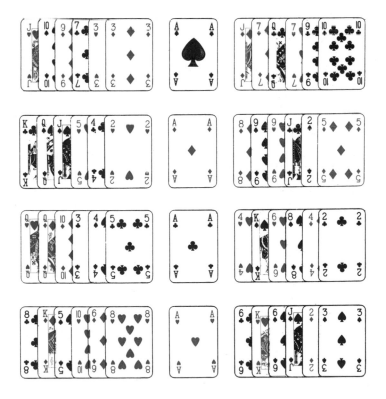

right of each row. They can be built onto the foundations or onto another available card in descending order of rank, irrespective of suit, e.g. any 5 can be built on any 6. Should one of the rows become empty, the space can be filled by any available card, so there are always eight available cards.

Example deal

In the deal illustrated the ♥2 and ♣2 can immediately be played to the foundations, a good start. The ♠3 can now be played on the ♣4, allowing the ♦2 to be played to its foundation, followed by the ♦3 and ♥3. The ♦4 5, and the ♠2 3 can also be played to the foundations. The ♣10 can now be played to the ♣J, followed by the ♣9. The ♥8 can be played on the ♣9, the ♥7 on the ♥8, and the ♣5 on the ♦6. This releases the ♠4 to its foundation, and the ♣3 4 5 and the ♦6. The top row of the left wing can now be cleared: ♣7 on ♠8, ♦9 on ♦10, ♠10 on ♠J, ♥J on ♣Q. Now the ♥10 can be played to the ♥J, releasing the ♠5 for its foundation. The ♦K can fill the blank space. And so on. The game can proceed a little further, but the ♥4 will be a problem.

The game rewards careful play. Blocks occur when high cards overlap low ones, particularly if they are in the same suit. Kings near the top of rows should be played to spaces as soon as possible, as clearly they block all the cards below them. It is best to build the foundations as evenly as possible, which helps the transfer of cards from row to row.

LA BELLE LUCIE

La Belle Lucie is a one-pack **patience** or **solitaire** game in which all the cards are visible in numerous fan layouts. It has little scope for skill but grants the satisfaction of allowing two re-deals. It is also called Fan, Clover Leaf (presumably because the fans are of three) and Midnight Oil.

The play

The entire pack is laid out in fans of three, with the odd card forming a 'fan' of its own, as illustrated. The cards available for play are those at the end or 'top' of a fan, so there are 18 cards available immediately after the deal. When Aces become available they are played to a foundation row. The object is to build up the foundations from Ace to King in ascending suit sequences. Available cards can be played to the foundation, or to the end of another fan on a card of the same suit and next high in sequence. A space created by playing off a whole fan is not filled.

When all available cards have been played after the first deal, those remaining in fans are collected up, shuffled and re-dealt in fans of three, any odd card or cards forming a fan of its own, and the game proceeds. When this play comes to a standstill a third deal is allowed. If the game is not resolved on this deal, a final play is allowed, the *merci*. One buried card, i.e. not available for play, can be pulled out and played.

Example deal

In the layout illustrated, the ♥A is played to the foundation row, and the ♥2 built upon it. The ♦8 is played to the ♦9, releasing the ♦A for its foundation. The ♦2 can be played upon it. The ♦7 can be played to the ♦8, allowing the ♥3 to be played to the foundation. The ♥4 can now be played to its foundation, and the ♥7 to the ♥8. The ♣9 can now be played to the ♣10 and the ♣5 to the ♣6, releasing the ♣A for its foundation. The ♦Q can now be played to the ♦K, allowing the ♣2 3 4 5 6 to be played to the foundation. The ♦3 4 can be played to the foundation, and the ♣4 can be played to the ♣5. The ♥5 goes to the foundation, allowing the ♠5 and ♦J to be played to fans, releasing the ♦5 to its foundation. This is as far as the game can go at this stage, so the remaining fans are collected and re-dealt.

First deals are not always as successful as this. Frequently the game moves quicker on the second deal. Few games are won without the merci. In the final deal a King above a card of the same suit automatically blocks the game, and the merci should be used to free such a card.

Cards should always be played to a foundation when available. It does not help to hold them back.

Variants

The game can be played to allow sequences to be built both upwards and downwards on fans. This clearly makes the game much easier, so re-deals and merci are not allowed.

The deal for the game of La Belle Lucie
described in the text.

BÉZIQUE

Popular in France in the nineteenth century, Bézique came to Britain in the 1860s, where it enjoyed a vogue when Queen Victoria's son, later Edward VII, showed a liking for it. In the United States it has largely been superseded by Pinochle, which is derived from it and described later in this book.

Players
Bézique is principally a game for two players, as described here, but can be played by three or four players, as described under *Variants*.

Cards
Two packs of cards are required, from which the 6s, 5s, 4s, 3s, and 2s are removed, making a 64-card pack. The cards rank in order: Ace, 10, King, Queen, Jack, 9, 8, 7.

Under *Variants* are described versions of the game using six and eight packs.

Preliminaries
The cards are cut by each player, and the player with the lower card deals. The dealer shuffles and non-dealer cuts the pack.

Dealing
The dealer deals eight cards to each player, a bundle of three to each player, then two, then three, non-dealer receiving first. The next card is turned up to denote the trump suit. The rest of the cards form the stock, are placed face down beside the trump indicator. If the turn-up is a 7 dealer scores 10 points for it.

Object
The object is to score an agreed number of points, 2,000 being the most common. The game is a trick-taking game, and points are scored in various ways. Each Ace or 10 taken in a trick counts 10 points to the holder at the end of the game. These cards are known as *brisques*. Either player, on winning a trick, may exchange a 7 of trumps for the trump card, and score 10 points, or he may declare a 7 of trumps (see below) and score 10 points. The winner of the last trick scores 10 points. Points are also scored for making *declarations*. Upon winning a trick a player may place on the table in front of him combinations of cards which score points as follows:

double bézique (♠Q, ♦J, ♠Q, ♦J)	500
bézique (♠Q, ♦J)	40
sequence in trumps (A, 10, K, Q, J)	250
any four Aces	100
any four Kings	80
any four Queens	60
any four Jacks	40
royal marriage (K, Q of trumps)	40
common marriage (K, Q of plain suit)	20
dix (pronounced 'deece') (7 of trumps)	10

Declarations can be made only one at a time – a player holding two must win two tricks to declare them both.

A card may be used in two or more different declarations, but not twice in the same declaration. For example, if a marriage of ♠K Q is declared, it is possible later to add ♦J to the ♠Q and declare bézique. However, if ♠K Q is declared as a marriage, and the King subsequently played, it is not permitted to add a second ♠K later and declare a second marriage.

A double bézique scores 500 only if all four cards are declared together. However, it is possible to score a bézique for 40, and later a second bézique for 40, and if all four cards remain on the table, score 500 for a double bézique on the next trick won.

Similarly, the score of 250 for a trump sequence includes the points for a royal marriage, but if the royal marriage is declared first, for 40, the other three cards may be added on a further declaration for 250. Cards laid down in declarations remain part of the hand, and can be played at any time.

The play
Non-dealer leads to the first trick, and dealer plays any card he likes. There is no need to follow suit. The trick is won by the higher trump, or if no trumps are played, by the higher card in the suit led. If two identical cards are played the card led wins the trick.

The winner of the trick can declare any of the point-scoring combinations mentioned above before leading to the next trick. The main value of winning tricks is the opportunity it offers to make declarations. The tricks themselves are of no value, except for any brisques they may contain, and the tricks won are just piled in front of the player – there is no need to keep each trick separate from the others.

The player who wins a trick takes the top card of the stock into his hand, the other player taking the next card. Both players' hands therefore continue to contain eight cards, although some of these cards, perhaps as many as six or seven, might be laid on the table in declarations.

Eventually, as tricks are played, the stage will be reached in which there are only two cards in the centre of the table – the upturned trump card (which by now is usually the 7 exchanged for the original card) and the last card of the stock. The winner of the previous trick now takes the last card of the stock into his hand and the loser the turn-up.

The last eight tricks are now played in what is sometimes called the 'play-off' or 'end-game'. The rules are now different. No further declarations can be made, and the players pick up any cards in declarations and play the last eight tricks from their hands.

It is now obligatory to follow suit, and to win the trick if possible. If one cannot follow suit one must trump, if able. The second player can only lose a trick legitimately in this stage by playing a lower card in the suit led if he hasn't a higher one, or by discarding if he has neither a card in the suit led nor a trump.

The player who takes the last trick of all scores 10 points for *last*, and the two players then add up their brisques (there are 160 points to be shared for brisques) and add them to the points scored in declarations.

Example hand
Cards are dealt to players North and South as in the illustration,

NORTH

SOUTH

UPCARD

The deal for the hand of Bézique described in the text.

---

with ♣8 turned up to denote trumps. South dealt, so North led to the first trick.

The feature of North's hand is the three Aces, which should earn some brisques, and the common marriage, but no trumps. South has three 10s and an Ace, also good for brisques, and the ♣Q 10 as a start for a sequence of trumps, and the ♦J as a possible bézique.

The first tricks and the draw were as follows:

	Cards played		Cards drawn	
	North	South	North	South
1.	♥J	♠7	♥9	♥9
2.	♥9	♥9	♠7	♠9
3.	♣7	♣8	♣Q	♣7

North now has three Queens as a possibility towards a quartet of Queens and the ♠Q as a possibility towards a bézique. South has a trump 7, for which he will accept 10 points on his next winning trick.

4.	♥J	♠9

Before drawing, South exchanges ♣7 for ♣8, scoring 10 points.

4.		♥Q	♣Q

Both players are now in some difficulty. South has nothing to declare but does not wish to lead a brisque (he might if he knew North had no trumps). North on the other hand needs to win a trick to begin declaring, as he now holds four Queens as well as a common marriage. When South leads his ♣8 he decides to sacrifice his common marriage.

5.	♥K	♣8	♠J	♠8
6.	♠J	♣8		

North now declares his four Queens for 60 points. He will now play them, keeping his ♠Q as long as he can for a possible bézique.

6.			♠K	♠10
7.	♥Q	♥A	♠10	♦K
8.	♠Q	♦K	♠8	♣J
9.	♦8	♦J	♠Q	♥7
10.	♥Q	♥7	♠9	♣K

At last North has a trump. South only needs the Ace of trumps for a trump sequence. North decides to lead his ♠Q from the table, as he has another for a possible bézique. South does not want to concede a brisque, so plays his spare ♣Q.

11. ♠Q	♣Q	♠J	♣J
12. ♠J	♣J̲	♦J	♣A

Both players now have declarations to make – South a sequence and North bézique. South wishes he did not have the lead. He leads ♦10 which North takes to ensure 20 for brisques.

13. ♦A	♦10

North declares his bézique for 40 points.

13.		♦9	♣10
14. ♦9	♦10̲		

South now declares his sequence for 250 points.

14.		♦7	♥10
15. ♦7	♣J	♦9	♦8
16. ♦9	♦8		

North now puts his ♠K on the table and declares a common marriage.

16.		♣K	♥8
17. ♦J	♣10	♣7	♦10
18. ♣7	♥8		

North scores 10 for playing the ♣7.

18.		♦7	♠K
19. ♦7	♦Q	♥8	♦A
20. ♥8	♠K̲	♥A	♦K
21. ♠Q	♦K̲	♠9	♣8

There are now only three tricks left. North is anxious to draw another Ace. South is now marshalling his hand for the end-play, when he hopes to make his brisques.

22. ♠9	♣8	♥K	♥7
23. ♠K	♥7̲	♣9	♥10

South has no chance of a further declaration, and suspecting that North might be on the edge of a final declaration plays ♣A to ensure winning this trick.

24. ♥K	♣A	♣7	♣A

South's lead was excellent, as it prevented North scoring 100 points for four Aces.

The players now pick up the cards from the table and South leads to the first of the tricks of the end-play. He knows he can make his Ace, 10, King of trumps and decides to make these to reduce North's holding of trumps before sacrificing his ♦A as an exit card. He knows that North would have to use a fourth trump to beat it, which should give him his best chance of making at least one of his ♥10s.

North	South
♣7	♣A
♣9	♣10
♣9	♣K
♣K	♦A
♠A	♠10
♠A	♣Q
♥A	♥10
♠10	♥10

North makes 10 points for last trick.

During the play North has made 140 points, and South 260 thanks to his trump sequence. North scores 90 for brisques and South 70. The final score for the hand is thus North 230 and South 330.

North now deals for the second hand, and play continues until one player passes the target score. If both pass the target on the same hand, higher wins.

Strategy

Decide early on which combinations to go for, and memorize which cards have been played, so that no time is wasted in waiting for cards that are no longer available. A sequence of trumps is particularly difficult as there are only two cards of each of five components. A quartet of four, however, requires no more than any four cards from a possible eight.

It is as well to have a useless card or two in the hand to throw on unwanted tricks. In the example hand both players suffered from not having a card with which they wished to part.

With strong trumps in the endgame it is often a good policy to lead them to draw the opponent's trumps, although in the example hand it did not quite work for South.

Variants

The main variant on the standard game concerns the combinations of bézique and double bézique, should spades or diamonds be the trump suit. If spades is the trump suit, in this variation bézique is ♣Q and ♦J. If diamonds is the trump suit bézique is ♠Q and ♥J. Double bézique follows the same convention. Sometimes ♣Q and ♥J is regarded as bézique if either spades or diamonds are trumps.

A second variant is Bézique without a trump. In this variation a trump card is not turned over and there are no trumps until a marriage is declared. The suit of the first marriage thereafter becomes the trump suit.

Bézique for three players Bézique for three players is played with three packs of cards (i.e. 96 cards). All players play against each other, and play and deal rotate to the left. The winner of a trick draws first from stock and the player on his left second. There is a new combination, triple bézique, which scores 1,500 points. Game of 2,000 points is the most popular.

Bézique for four players There are two ways to play Bézique with four players. One is a version of Rubicon Bézique and is described after that game. Described here is the simpler version.

Four packs are used (i.e. 128 cards). Each player plays for himself, as in Bézique for three players. A quadruple bézique scores 1,500 points, as does triple bézique (a player can, of course, score them in separate declarations).

If players wish to play in partnership, partners sit opposite each other. A player taking a trick may offer his partner the privilege of making a declaration. However, the partners may not consult. The trick-winner must either declare or offer. A player, on winning a trick, may make a declaration by combining a card or cards from his hand to cards his partner has on the table (although retaining them himself for play, of course). However, he is not allowed to make a combination which would be illegal for his partner to make. The target for game can again be 2,000 points.

Rubicon bézique This is a game for two players using four packs of cards (i.e. 128 cards).

Differences from the standard game are as follows:

a) Nine cards are dealt to each

player, not eight. They are dealt in three bundles of three.

b) There is no turn-up to indicate trumps. There are no trumps until the first marriage is declared, the suit of the marriage becoming trumps. A player can, of course, establish trumps with a sequence, since a sequence includes a marriage, but this is very rare. There is no peculiar value attached to the 7 of trumps.

c) There are differences from or additions to the scoring as follows:

Carte blanche A player dealt a hand which does not contain a court (or face) card (i.e. it is composed entirely of Aces, 10s, 9s, 8s and 7s) may show it to his opponent and score 50 points for carte blanche. Thereafter at each draw he may claim another 50 points if not drawing a court card by showing the drawn card to his opponent. Once he has drawn a court card, however, he cannot claim carte blanche again.

triple bézique (Three of ♠Q, ♦J) scores 1,500 points
quadruple bézique (four of ♠Q, ♦J) scores 4,500 points
plain-suit sequence (A, 10, K, Q, J in a plain suit) scores 150 points

d) There are differences in the play as follows:

1. Tricks are left in the middle of the table until a brisque is scored, when the winner will take all the cards. Thereafter tricks are gathered in the usual way.
2. A player who declares a combination, and later plays a card from the combination may subsequently play a replacement card to the same combination and score in full for it again.
3. Following on from this, a player who declares two marriages in the same suit may on subsequent declarations transpose the Queens to score two more marriages.
4. The winner of the last trick scores 50 points.

e) The game is complete in one deal.

f) Brisques are not scored, except to break a tie or to prevent a player from being *rubiconed*.

g) At the end of the deal, each player rounds his points down to the nearest 100 (e.g. 1,660 becomes 1,600). If both totals reach 1,000 (the *rubicon*) the winner scores the difference in the two totals plus 500 bonus. If rounding down produces a tie the scores for brisques (at 10 points per brisque) are added to the original totals, which are then rounded down again. If this again produces a tie the player with the higher total counts the difference as 100 and therefore wins by 600 points.

If the loser's rounded down total does not reach 1,000, both players add on their brisques to see if the loser can reach 1,000. If not he is rubiconed. His original rounded down total is now added to the winner's total, whose game bonus is now 1,000 (not 500) and he moreover counts another 300 'for *brisques*'. For example, player A has 1,250, rounded down to 1,200. Player B has 670, rounded down to 600. Player B cannot reach the rubicon even with his brisques, so Player A wins by the addition of the two scores (1,800) plus 1,000 for game, plus 300 for brisques, making 3,100 points.

If both players are rubiconed the winner is not penalized for failing to reach 1,000, and still scores the addition of the points, plus 1,300.

Casual players rather than gamblers might decide, of course, to play each game for its own sake and not bother about calculating the margin of victory.

Rubicon Bézique for four players
This version of the game is played with six packs (i.e. 192 cards). Two pairs play in partnership.

The dealer, after the cards are shuffled and cut, places 24 cards face down on the table with a marker above to warn players when the stock is nearing exhaustion. After dealing four hands of nine cards to each player in bundles of three, he then places the remainder of the stock above the marker.

Play follows the rules described in Rubicon Bézique above except for differences in scoring and declaring. The points scores are as follows:

carte blanche	100
double carte blanche (i.e. neither partner being dealt a court card):	500
quintuple bézique	13,500
sextuple bézique (practically impossible)	40,500
any four Aces	1,000
any four 10s	900
any four Kings	800
any four Queens	600
any four Jacks	400

The game bonus is 1,000 points, and the rubicon is 2,500 points. Brisques are never counted. Otherwise the scoring is the same as

in Rubicon Bézique, with the following additions arising from the partnership principle.

A player winning a trick may offer the opportunity to declare to his partner, but must not consult with him first and cannot claim the right back should his partner decline. Secondly, a player may declare a combination which includes cards already declared by his partner (it will be noticed that quintuple or septuple bézique can only be scored thus, since a player has only nine cards of his own).

Each deal is a game in itself, and the play and deal rotate to the left.

Six-pack Bézique Six-pack Bézique is sometimes known as Chinese Bézique. It is for two players, and is probably the most popular version of the game. Sir Winston Churchill was a good and keen player.

Six packs (192 cards) are required. Players cut for choice of deal; higher has choice, and for this cut only 10 takes its normal place in precedence. It is advisable for the winner to pass the deal, as non-dealer has a slight advantage. The dealer has the option of shuffling last, and non-dealer cuts the pack.

The dealer does not hold all the pack when dealing. He takes a few from the top, trying, without counting, to gauge the 24 he will need. Non-dealer guesses how many he has. Dealer then deals 12 cards to each hand, one at a time. If it transpires he took exactly 24 cards he scores 250 points. If non-dealer's guess was correct, he scores 150 points.

There is no turn-up. The trump suit is determined, as in Rubicon

Bézique, by the first marriage or sequence declared by either player.

In Six-pack Bézique, the usual convention is that the declaration of bézique consists of the Queen of the trump suit with a Jack as follows:

♠Q and ♦J; ♦Q and ♠J
♣Q and ♥J; ♥Q and ♣J

However, some prefer to retain ♠Q and ♦J as bézique whatever the trump suit – it is something to be agreed in advance. With a variable bézique, of course, nobody can declare bézique before the trump suit is established.

The points for declarations are as follows:

carte blanche	250
(plus another 250 for each time it is declared)	
four Aces in trumps	1,000
four 10s in trumps	900
four Kings in trumps	800
four Queens in trumps	600
four Jacks in trumps	400
any four Aces	100
any four Kings	80
any four Queens	60
any four Jacks	40
sequence in trumps	250
sequence in plain suit	150
royal marriage	40
common marriage	20
bézique	40
double bézique	500
triple bézique	1,500
quadruple bézique	4,500

There are no special scores for quintuple or sextuple bézique.

As in the parent game, in the first phase of the trick-taking game, it is not necessary to follow suit. Only the winner of a trick may make a declaration. Winner takes the top card from stock and loser the next. Brisques are never counted, and it is customary to leave the tricks piled up in the centre of the table face up, as they are not required again.

Declarations can be repeated with replacement cards, as in Rubicon Bézique (this is different from the standard game).

When the last two cards of the stock have been drawn no further declarations are allowed, and the players pick up any declared cards and play out the last eight tricks. The rules for this end-game are as for the standard game: a player must follow suit, if he can, and if he cannot follow suit to trump if he can; he *must* win the trick if he can. The winner of the last trick makes 250 points.

Each deal constitutes a game. The player with most points wins the difference between the scores plus 1,000 points. Fractions of 100 points are disregarded except to determine the winner. If the loser has not reached 3,000 points he is rubiconed, and the winner scores the sum of the points of both players, plus 1,000.

Eight-pack Bézique Eight-pack Bézique is played exactly as Six-pack Bézique with the following exceptions:

a) eight packs (256 cards) are used
b) each player is dealt 15 cards
c) the points scores for béziques are:

bézique	50
double bézique	500
triple bézique	1,500
quadruple bézique	4,500
quintuple bézique	9,000

d) In the trump suit the points scores are:

five Aces	2,000
five 10s	1,800
five Kings	1,600
five Queens	1,200
five Jacks	800

There are no points for quartets in the trump suit.

e) A player is rubiconed if he fails to score 5,000 points.

Fildinski (Polish Bézique) Fildinski is for two players with the usual two packs (64 cards). There is one vital difference to the standard game of Bézique, and that is that declarations are made not from cards in the hand but from cards won in tricks. Advocates of Fildinski claim that this improves the game and adds to its skill factor.

The deal, determination of the trump suit and the value of the combinations (including *dix*) are the same as for standard Bézique.

Brisques are valued in the same way, but are scored immediately they are won in tricks, rather than at the end of the play.

The cards in a player's hand are never used in declarations. They are played to tricks as usual. When a player wins a trick containing a card or cards which might form a part of a combination (i.e. any Aces, Kings, Queens or Jacks, and the 10 and 7 of trumps) he places these cards before him on the table. Other cards played to tricks are put aside face down.

A player winning a trick may use a card or both cards from it to add to a card or cards in front of him on the table to make a declaration or declarations. He may not use any of the cards in his hand, which after the draw always remain at eight cards.

Declared cards remain face up on the table till the end of the game. Unlike standard Bézique, Fildinski does not allow a player to use a card in more than one combination, even if the combinations are of a different class.

Cards on the table are not part of the hand, of course, as in Bézique, and are not played again to tricks. In Fildinski the cards on the table are for possible declarations, the cards in the hand for trick-taking only.

The play in the end-game, i.e. the last eight tricks, follows that of standard Bézique, in that a player must follow suit or trump, and win if possible. However, players may continue to declare combinations right up to the final trick. If the 7 of trumps has been exchanged for the turn-up the player drawing it on the last trick cannot declare it as dix. The player who takes the last trick scores 10 for *last*.

The winning target can be set by agreement. If the winner is first to 2,000 points, the game will be quicker than Bézique, as scores per deal are generally higher, since all 'combination' cards remain available to one or other player throughout the game.

BISLEY

This **patience** or **solitaire** game is played with the full pack.

The play

The four Aces are removed from the pack and dealt in a row face upwards on the table. The remaining cards are shuffled and then nine are dealt face up to the right of the Aces, completing a row of 13 cards. The remaining cards are then dealt face up in three rows below them. This forms the tableau. A sample deal is shown in the illustration.

Cards available for play are those on the bottom of a column.

The deal for the game of Bisley described in the text.

When a King becomes available for play it is placed in a position above its corresponding Ace.

The object of the game is to pack all the cards in suit sequence on their Ace or King foundations, upwards on the Aces and downwards on the Kings.

In addition to packing cards on Aces and Kings, the bottom card of a column may be packed on the bottom card of another column, in either ascending or descending order to suit the player. A space left vacant in the layout is not filled – the playing of a card automatically releases the one above it for play.

In the layout the ♠K is played to its foundation, which releases the ♥K to be played there also. There

are also three 2s at the bottom of columns, which can be built on their Aces: the ♣2, ♥ 2 and ♦ 2. The ♥ 3 and the ♣3 can now follow, also the ♣4.

The ♦ J can now be packed on the ♦ Q, which allows the ♠5 to be packed on the ♠6. The ♥ 7 can now be packed on the ♥ 8, and the ♥ 6 on the ♥ 7. Now the ♦ 7 can be packed on the ♦ 8, followed by the ♦ 6 and ♦ 5. This allows the ♣6 to be packed on the ♣7, releasing the ♣K for its place above the Ace. The ♣Q can be packed on it, and the ♠2 becomes free to be played to its foundation. The ♠3 and ♠4 follow it, then the ♠5 6 7.

The ♣10 can be packed on the ♣J, followed by the ♣9, allowing the ♥ Q and ♥ J to be played to the foundation King. The ♥ 10 follows, and the ♠8 and ♠9 can be played to the foundation, allowing the ♦ K to go to its place above the Ace.

The game proceeds until all cards are packed on either the Ace or King foundations, when the game is won, or until no further moves are possible, when the game is lost. This example game is shortly doomed to failure, but Bisley is won more often than many one-player games.

BLACKJACK

Blackjack is a gambling game played in casinos, where it is often the only card game. Its immediate predecessor is the French game Vingt-et-un, played in Britain as Pontoon. An American casino, popularizing the game, offered a bonus to any player holding Ace of spades with a Jack of spades or clubs, a hand which became known as a 'blackjack', which ultimately became the name of the game. The game described here is that found in most American casinos. The more interesting social version for playing at home is described under Vingt-et-un.

Players

Seven may play on the table as illustrated, sitting at the appropriate spaces, with the dealer, who is operating for the casino, facing them. If space is available a player

---

The layout of the table in which Blackjack is played in a casino.

may play at two spaces if he wishes, but each hand is separate and he must play the hand to his right first.

Cards

Four standard packs are used, shuffled by the dealer, and cut by a player using an indicator card. The pack is combined and a second indicator is placed some 50 cards from the bottom of the pack. The pack is placed face down in a dealing shoe, and the indicator is to show where the shoe ends – the last few cards will not be used. All cards have their pip value, with King, Queen and Jack all counting as ten, except the Ace which when held by the player has a value of one or eleven at his discretion. It also has these values when held by the dealer, but subject to restrictions, as will be seen.

The play

Before the deal, each player puts up a stake in the betting space

before him. Stakes will be subject to the casino's minimum and maximum limits.

The first card dealt from the shoe is 'burnt', i.e. is discarded without its value being revealed. The dealer then deals a card to each player, in turn, starting on his left, and one to himself. All these cards are face up. He then deals a second card to all the players face up, and a second card to himself, face down.

The object of the game, from the player's point of view, is to obtain a total card count, with the two cards dealt or with the addition of others, higher than that of the dealer, but not exceeding a maximum of 21. Should his count exceed 21 he has 'busted' and loses his stake.

A count of 21 with two cards (i.e. an Ace and a ten-count card) is known as a *natural* or *blackjack* and beats any other hand (blackjack now means any Ace and ten-count card). When a player wins with a blackjack the dealer pays him at odds of 3–2, as is indicated on the table layout. All other bets are settled at odds of 1–1, and all ties are a stand-off, i.e. the player retains his stake.

When the dealer has a blackjack he wins all the stakes, except from a player who also has a blackjack, in which case that bet is a stand-off. If the dealer's face-up card is an Ace, he must ask all players if they wish to insure against him holding a blackjack. This is achieved by any player putting up a premium of half his stake.

The dealer then looks at his face-down card, and if it is a ten-count, he declares it. Players who insured are paid at odds of 2–1 on their premium, so in effect save their stake and neither win nor lose on the deal. Players who did not insure lose their stakes.

The dealer also looks at his face-down card if his face-up card is a ten-count, and should he have a blackjack he immediately declares it and settles all bets. In this case, however, insurance does not arise.

When dealer does not have a blackjack he leaves his second card face-down, so as not to reveal his total count, and deals with all players in turn, beginning with the player on his left.

The player has four options. The first is to stand. If he is satisfied with his count (as he should be with 19, 20 or 21) he will stand.

His second option is to draw another card. This choice is governed by his two-card total and the face-up card that the dealer holds. An optimum strategy is given later. Any additional card dealt to the player is given face-up. The player may continue asking for cards until he is satisfied with his count. If he should 'bust', i.e. exceed 21, the dealer will collect his stake immediately and dispose of his cards.

A third option open to the player occurs when his two cards are of the same rank. In this respect all ten-count cards are regarded as of the same rank. The player is allowed to 'split his pairs'. In effect each card becomes the first card of two separate hands. The player puts a stake equal to his original stake on the second hand. The dealer then deals him a second card to each hand, whereupon the player plays the hands in turn, beginning with the one on his right. Should the second card in a split hand again form a pair, he may split them again, and so on.

If a player splits a pair of Aces, he may not draw a third card to either hand. The second card dealt to each hand completes it (unless it is another Ace, when he may split again). A blackjack scored with a split hand wins, of course, but is paid at 1–1 and not at the special odds of 3–2.

The player's fourth option is to double down. This allows him to double his stake and receive a third card face down. This card completes the hand and remains face down until the dealer faces it when settling.

When the dealer has dealt with each player, and any remain who have not busted, he faces his second card so that his hand is exposed. He has no options in playing his hand. If his count is 16 or less he must draw, and continue to do so until his count becomes 17, 18, 19, 20 or 21, when he must stand. Should he bust, he pays all players still in the game.

An Ace may still count as one or eleven for the dealer, but should his total reach one of the numbers on which he must stand, i.e. 17–21, then he must. For example, if he has 6-Ace, then he must stand on 17, and cannot draw to 7, as the player

probably would. A count which uses an Ace as eleven, as the above example, is known as a 'soft' count. When an Ace is used as one, or when no Ace is held, the count is 'hard'.

When the dealer stands he pays all players with a count higher than him, and collects the stakes of those with a lower. Where counts are equal, the player retains his stake.

Strategy

At one time with only one pack used, it was possible to get an occasional edge over the casino at Blackjack by 'counting' the cards played, i.e. noting their values. Nowadays, with four packs in the shoe and up to 50 cards not used, this edge has virtually disappeared.

The player has all the options in the game, and receives the bonus payment for a blackjack, but the casino, or dealer, has one advantage which pays for all – he plays second. The player always loses when he busts. However, when the dealer busts he loses only to those hands still remaining. If four have busted already he will win four hands and lose three. Thus it is not true to say that all ties are a stand-off. However, because the player has the other advantages, if he plays well, the house edge is very small – less than 1 per cent.

A player's main choice is whether to stand, hit or double down. Experts have differed in some details in working out the optimum play, but the following table is a good consensus of opinion (when the game is played as described).

☆

Player's optimum play at Blackjack

Player holds	Dealer's face-up card									
	2	3	4	5	6	7	8	9	10	A
17	S	S	S	S	S	S	S	S	S	S
16	S	S	S	S	S	H	H	H	S	S
Hard 15	S	S	S	S	S	H	H	H	H	H
2-card 14	S	S	S	S	S	H	H	H	H	H
total 13	S	S	S	S	S	H	H	H	H	H
12	H	H	S	S	S	H	H	H	H	H
11	D	D	D	D	D	D	D	D	D	D
10	D	D	D	D	D	D	D	D	H	H
9	D	D	D	D	D	H	H	H	H	H

	Dealer's face-up card									
19	S	S	S	S	S	S	S	S	S	S
18	S	S	S	S	S	S	H	H	H	H
Soft 17	D	D	D	D	D	H	H	H	H	H
2-card 16	H	H	H	H	D	H	H	H	H	H
total 15	H	H	H	H	D	H	H	H	H	H
14	H	H	H	H	D	H	H	H	H	H
13	H	H	H	H	D	H	H	H	H	H

Note: Always stand on hard hands of 17 or more and soft hands of 19 and 20.

S = stand, H = hit, D – double down.

Another choice involves when to split pairs. The following table gives the most accepted guidance (again with the proviso that the above rules apply).

Advisability of splitting pairs

Player's pair	Dealer's face-up card									
	2	3	4	5	6	7	8	9	10	A
A	S	S	S	S	S	S	S	S	S	S
10	X	X	X	X	X	X	X	X	X	X
9	S	S	S	S	S	X	X	X	X	X
8	S	S	S	S	S	S	S	X	X	S
7	S	S	S	S	S	S	X	X	X	X
6	S	S	S	S	S	X	X	X	X	X
5	X	X	X	X	X	X	X	X	X	X
4	X	X	X	X	X	X	X	X	X	X
3	S	S	S	S	S	S	X	X	X	X
2	S	S	S	S	S	S	X	X	X	X

S = split, X = do not split.

Whether or not to take insurance is clear cut. Insurance is really a misnomer. When dealer has a face-up Ace the insurance 'premium' is really a bet that the face-down card is a ten-count. As the proportion of ten-counts in the pack is 16 to 36, the odds should be 9 to 4, not 2 to 1, giving a house edge of over 7 per cent. The bet should always be declined, therefore.

Variants

The commonest variations to the above are as follows:

a) dealers will draw on soft 17. This will be a rule, not an option, and will be printed on the table;
b) casinos will not offer insurance;
c) the players' initial two cards will be dealt face down. This does not affect the play. As the dealer has no options in his play, it does not matter whether or not the players' hands are exposed;
d) doubling down will be restricted, perhaps to hands of 9, 10, 11 or to 10, 11 or to 11 only.

When gambling was legalized in Great Britain, the Gaming Board introduced restrictions to protect players. Where these are observed:

e) splitting pairs of 4, 5 or 10 will be barred;
f) doubling down will be restricted to 9, 10 or 11;
g) insurance will be offered only to a player holding blackjack himself.

These are harmless. However one variant, known as the 'London deal', is controversial. To prevent cheating by collusion between the dealer and a player, the dealer deals only one card to himself in the opening round, his second card being dealt after the players have completed their betting. Players might therefore increase their stakes when the dealer ultimately deals himself a natural or blackjack. When the London deal operates, it is advisable to ignore the tables of strategy above when dealer's faced card is an Ace or ten-count, to eschew doubling-down altogether and to split Aces only.

BLACK MARIA

This game is a form of Hearts (q.v.), sometimes known as Black Lady and occasionally as Slippery Anne.

Players

Black Maria is the form of Hearts best suited for three players, and is regarded as one of the best games for three. It can also be played by four, five or six players, as noted under *Variants*. The three-player version is described.

Cards

The full pack is used, from which is removed the ♣2, leaving 51 cards. Cards rank from Ace (high) to 2 (low). There is no trump suit.

Dealing

The dealer is determined by any agreed method, and the deal passes in rotation clockwise. Dealer deals 17 cards, one at a time, to each player beginning on his left.

The play

Each player begins by looking at his cards and passing three on, face down, to the player on his right. He must not look at the cards he is receiving from his left-hand opponent until he has passed on cards himself.

The game is a trick-taking game, and the three players play against each other. The object is to avoid winning tricks containing penalty cards. These cards and their penalty points are as follows:

The deal for the hand of Black Maria described in the text.

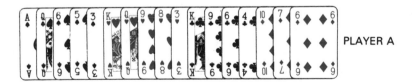

PLAYER A

PLAYER B

PLAYER C

every card in the heart suit	1
Ace of spades	7
King of spades	10
Queen of spades (Black Maria)	13

The player to dealer's left leads to the first trick. Players must follow suit if possible; if not they may play any card they like. The winner of a trick leads to the next.

Each player collects the tricks made by himself, and at the end of the hand sorts out from his cards those carrying penalties and totals them. For checking purposes, there is a total of 43 penalty points in each deal. The winner is the player with the lowest score after an agreed number of rounds, e.g. nine, three deals for each player.

Example hand
An example hand can include points on strategy. The three

The hands after each player has passed three cards to his right.

hands are dealt as in the illustration.

When it comes to passing cards on, high hearts and spades are not necessarily the best to pass. In fact a player holding them can often control when they're played, to his advantage. The best suits to hold are long suits with plenty of low cards, even in hearts. A void suit is a big asset – as soon as it is led penalty cards can be parked on opponents' tricks. However, in passing on cards to create a void suit a player faces the danger that higher cards in the same suit will be passed to him, and the void suddenly becomes a suit in which he must take penalties.

This is the problem with A, the dealer, who could create a void in diamonds. He is happy with his spades, but not keen on his two high hearts or King of clubs. Nevertheless, he takes a chance by passing to the player on his right his three diamonds.

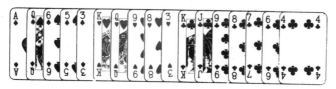

PLAYER A

PLAYER B

PLAYER C

Player B has a similar problem, and decides to pass on his three biggest clubs. With the lead, he can lead the fourth and create a void.

Player C has problems: he is vulnerable in both clubs and diamonds, although the ♣3 and ♦2 both give him certain exit cards. He decides to pass on his three big clubs.

So far as their new cards are concerned, player A does not mind the clubs too much, but he lacks the 3,2 and must beware that he is not given the lead when he is the only player with clubs left, or he will collect all the remaining penalty cards.

Player B's strategy has been wrecked, as he collects worse clubs than he passed on.

Player C's danger is that he realizes that Player B probably has most of the diamonds with him, so he must keep his ♦2 as long as possible, as he will probably find ♦5 4 3 led through him.

The new hands are as in the second illustration. Player B has the lead, and decides to discover the state of the diamond suit, leading his ♦5. Play proceeds as follows:

	A	B	C
1.	♠Q	♦5	♦2

Player C has a difficult choice. He knew that it was probable A had no diamonds. He also knew by playing the ♦2 he was vulnerable when Player B next had the lead — another diamond would be led which he would have to take. His decision to play the ♦2 was correct, and Player B collected the Black Maria. Player A decided to

unload his ♠Q as he is nervous about his clubs, and wants to pass on penalty cards while he can.

	A	B	C
2.	♥K	♦3	♦K

Player A is happier with his ♠A than his big hearts. Player C decides to keep his ♣3 for emergencies and not to lead it.

	A	B	C
3.	♠6	♠10	♠9

Player B does not want to lead ♦4 now, as he will then be at the mercy of Player C in this suit, so leads ♠J.

	A	B	C
4.	♠5	♠J	♠8
5.	♠3	♠4	♠7

Player C knows now that the only spade against him is the Ace, and that he can safely lead ♠K and saddle an opponent, almost certainly Player A, with both ♠A K. Player A might have been advised to have taken his Ace on trick 5 (or better still to have thrown it on trick 2) — he has made two wrong decisions.

	A	B	C
6.	♠A	♥A	♠K
7.	♣6	♣A	♣3
8.	♥3	♥2	♥4
9.	♥Q	♥6	♥5
10.	♣4	♣Q	♥J
11.	♥9	♥7	♥10
12.	♥8	♦4	♦6

All penalty cards have now been played, so the players do not play out the final tricks. The players have collected penalties as follows: Player A 21 points; Player B 14 points; Player C 8 points.

With only three players, it is not long before each player has a good idea of the other players' hands,

PLAYER A

PLAYER C   PLAYER B

The three-card ending discussed in the text.

and this can be used near the end of the game to give one opponent or the other the penalty points. The second illustration shows such a three-card ending.

With A on lead he should know that by leading his ♠2 he will give C all 11 of the remaining penalty points, whereas by leading♥ 5 he will give them all to B.

Variants

Black Maria for four can be played as above by not removing the ♣2 from the pack, and dealing each player 13 cards. Players can play as individuals or in pairs.

Black Maria for five is played by removing the ♣2 and♦ 2 from the pack, each player being dealt ten cards and playing for himself. It is possible for more players to play, but the game loses some appeal with more players.

Passing variants After the deal some players prefer to pass on three cards to the left rather than to the right. This enables players to lead through the known weakness of their left-hand opponents, but is considered to detract from the skill factor.

Scoring variants There are many variants in scoring, most designed to even out the imbalance in the penalties (in the standard game the ♠Q is worth equal to all the hearts). The main variants are:

a) the penalty cards are ♠Q (13 points) and all hearts (1 point each). Total penalties: 26 points;

b) the penalty cards are ♠Q (13 points), ♥A (5 points), ♥K (4 points), ♥Q (3 points), ♥J (2 points), all other hearts (1 point each). Total penalties: 36 points;

c) the penalty cards are ♠Q (13 points),♥Q (13 points), all other hearts (1 point each). Total penalties: 38 points. In this version of the game the ♥Q is called the Pink Lady.

d) *Hitting the Moon* This is an optional rule by which a player with a poor hand who is doomed to collect a lot of penalties can attempt to get all of them. He need not declare such an intention, and indeed is unlikely to succeed except by stealth. A player who collects all the penalties has the total in credit rather than in debit, e.g. in the standard game described his penalty score would be reduced by 43 rather than this total being added to it. It is, of course, a dangerous play, and one that is usually attempted only by a player who has already gathered most of the penalties, and therefore has a lot to gain and little to lose by trying to get the remainder.

BRAG

Brag is probably derived from the Spanish game of Primero, which was very popular in Tudor England. In turn Brag became the main ancestor of Poker (q.v.). Brag is still very popular, and is constantly incorporating new features, many from Poker, and is rarely played nowadays in its original form. However that is described first. It is purely a gambling game.

Players
Any number from four to eight can play.

Cards
The standard pack of 52 is used, cards ranking from Ace (high) to 2.

Preliminaries
As Brag is a staking game, a maximum and minimum stake must be agreed. It is a fairer game if all players have an equal bank, so it is a good idea if all players begin with an agreed total of stakes before them. The length of the game should also be agreed, as those losing rarely want to stop. It should be agreed that play ends at a specified time, or after an agreed number of deals or when a player loses his entire stakes. It should also be agreed as to whether there will be a shuffle between hands, and if so whether it be light or heavy.

Dealing
Players cut for deal, highest dealing. Dealer shuffles and the player to his right cuts. After each hand the deal passes to the left, where the new dealer will shuffle or not as agreed beforehand. The cards should be cut between each deal.

Before dealing the dealer puts up an initial stake between the agreed limits. He then deals three cards to each player, one at a time, starting on his left.

The play
The object of the game is to have the best hand remaining at the showdown, which hand wins all the stakes. Players cannot improve their hands so the game is a simple one of betting.

There are three classes of hand: the *pair-royal*, which is three cards of the same rank, the pair, which is two cards of the same rank, and *high card*, by which the hand is ranked by its highest ranking card. However, there are three *braggers*, or wild cards, and as a hand without a bragger beats one with, there might be said to be five classes of hand. The wild cards are:

$$\diamondsuit A \quad \clubsuit J \quad \diamondsuit 9$$

These can represent any card the holder wishes. When they represent their actual rank, they are not considered as braggers. The classes of hand in order of value are:

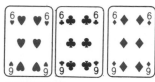

PAIR-ROYAL

PAIR-ROYAL WITH BRAGGER

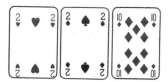

PAIR

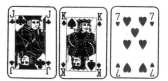

PAIR WITH BRAGGER

HIGH CARD

The classes of hand in traditional Brag.

---

pair-royal: three cards of the same rank

pair-royal with bragger: two cards of the same rank with a bragger (or one card with two braggers)

pair: two cards of the same rank with a spare card

pair with bragger: one card with a bragger to form a pair, with a third card

high-card: three odd cards, valued by the highest in rank

Examples of each hand are in the illustration.

Pairs-royal and pairs of higher-ranking cards beat those of lower ranking cards. Where pairs are equal, the rank of the spare card decides the higher hand. With high-card hands, if the highest cards are equal, the second card decides, then the third. Where hands are exactly equal, the winning hand is that held by the player nearest the dealer's left, i.e. the one to stake first.

When the dealer has staked and dealt, the players in turn, beginning with the player on dealer's left, must do one of the following:

a) put in a stake equal to that of the dealer;

b) raise the stake by equalling the dealer's stake and adding an extra stake, without exceeding the maximum;

c) throw in his hand.

Once a player has raised the stake, the following players must equal it to remain in the game, and when the turn comes round again to those who have already staked, they must increase their stake to the new amount or drop out, in which case they lose the stakes they have already put in. The turn continues to circulate, and provided the stake has not reached the maximum any player may increase it on his turn. Betting continues until all players have either dropped out or all stakes are equal. Should only one player be left in, he collects all the stakes, and does not need to show his hand. If two or more players are left in, they all turn over their hands and the highest wins the stakes.

If the dealer makes his opening stake and all players drop out, nobody reveals their cards, the dealer retrieves his stake, and is paid a previously agreed sum by each player (perhaps the minimum stake).

Three-stake Brag In this variant, each player including dealer puts up three stakes (of an agreed amount) before the deal. Each hand, in effect, is three separate games, and the three stakes are for separate purposes.

The dealer deals three cards each to each player as before, but the third card is dealt face up. This card determines the first stake. The player with the highest face-up card wins the stakes. In this respect, the braggers (♦ A, ♣J,♦ 9) represent their proper ranks. Should two or more players tie with cards of the highest rank, the tying player nearest the dealer's left wins the stakes.

The second round is a game of Brag, with players betting in the usual way, raising or dropping out until all stakes are equal, with the winner taking the stakes at the showdown. Every player is deemed to have made a stake with the initial stake put in before the deal, so if nobody raises, then all hands are shown and the best hand takes the stakes.

The third stakes are won by the player whose hand, with or without a draw, is nearest to a pip count of 31. Braggers again take their natural value. All court or face cards (K, Q, J) have a value of ten, and Aces count one or 11 as their holders wish.

All hands are faced so that each player can see the total to beat. Beginning with the player on dealer's left, each player may draw an extra card or cards to bring his total nearer to 31, and can stand when he is satisfied. A player whose total exceeds 31, however, is 'bust' and automatically loses. Should two or more hands be equal, the stakes are won by the player nearest the dealer's left. The first player to stand with exactly 31 must automatically win therefore.

Modern Brag The traditional game of brag, as described, has been largely superseded by a modern version which recognizes runs (equivalent to Poker's straights) and flushes.

There are six classes of hand, valued as follows:

Prial: three cards of the same rank. Prials rank from Aces down to 2s, except that a prial of 3s is the highest hand of all.
Running flush: three cards of the same suit in sequence. An Ace can be part of two runs, A 2 3 or A K Q. The highest run is A 2 3, and the others rank from A K Q down to 4 3 2.
Run: three cards in sequence, but not of the same suit. The Ace can again be used with K Q or 2 3, and A 2 3 is the highest run, with A K Q next down to 4 3 2.
Flush: three cards of the same suit,

PRIAL

RUNNING FLUSH

RUN

FLUSH

PAIR

HIGH CARD

The classes of hand in modern Brag.

not in sequence. Of two flushes, the one containing the highest ranking card takes precedence, if equal the next highest and so on.

Pair: two cards of the same rank. A pair of higher rank beats a pair of lower rank. Where the rank of pairs are equal, the rank of the odd card decides the winner.

High card: a hand including none of the above combinations. Of two hands of this type, the one containing the highest ranking card takes precedence, if this is equal the next highest and so on.

The play proceeds as in the traditional game, with players betting, raising or dropping out in the same way, and with the highest hand remaining when the stakes are equal being the winner.

Variants on Modern Brag Some players prefer not to recognise a prial of 3s as the best hand and relegate it to its natural place between the prials of 4 and 2. Similarly they do not recognize A 2 3 as being a higher run, or running flush, than A K Q and relegate it to lowest place after 4 3 2.

The other main variant is in the use of wild cards. If used they are not the traditional braggers, and are not called such. The most popular wild cards are the black 2s, while some players prefer all 2s to be wild. The use of a wild card does not reduce the value of a hand, as it does in traditional Brag.

Seven-card Brag Seven-card Brag is based on Modern Brag. There is no progressive betting.

It can be played by any number up to seven players. The deal passes to the left as before. Before each deal each player places an agreed stake in the pool. All players are dealt seven cards, from which they discard one face down to the centre of the table. From the remaining six cards they make their two best Brag hands, according to the illustration for Modern Brag. Wild cards must, of course, be agreed in advance.

When a player has arranged his cards into two hands he places the two hands face down before him. When all are ready each player reveals his better hand. When the best hand is determined, each player reveals his second hand. If the same player wins both he takes the pool. Otherwise the pool remains for the next deal, and is augmented by each player adding a second stake. Thus with each deal which passes in which no player wins both hands, the pool increases in size. The more players there are, the harder the pool is to win, and the more rapidly it grows.

A player is not obliged to make his first hand the best possible. For example, should he be dealt ♥A, ♦A, ♣A, ♥K, ♥Q, ♣3, ♦2, he would be best advised not to use his prial of Aces, which would leave him a second hand of King high, but to discard the ♣A and hold two hands of ♥A, ♥K, ♥Q and ♦A, ♦2, ♣3.

Each player's better hand should remain exposed when the second hands are being considered so that all players can ver-ify that each player has played his two hands in the correct order.

Strategy

Skill at Brag depends upon two things: a working knowledge of the probability of being dealt certain hands in order to assess how good a hand is, and the ability to bluff and judge when others are bluffing.

The value of the various hands (i.e. the probability that a hand will be dealt) can be seen from the table, which assumes no wild cards.

Hand	Total in pack	Probability (per cent)
Prial	52	0.2+
Running flush	48	0.2+
Run	720	3.2
Flush	1096	5.0
Pair	3744	17.0
High card	16440	74.4
	22100	100.0

Notice that over 90 per cent of hands are no better than a pair. It can be worked out from this table that with five players a run will be good enough to win more than four deals out of five, and a flush more than three deals out of five.

So far as bluffing is concerned, a player with a good hand will probably not raise too rapidly for fear of scaring off his opponents, while a player trying to win a pot with a poor hand will raise sufficiently to force his opponents to drop out. The best strategy is to vary one's own tactics and to try to work out one's opponents'.

BRIDGE

When Bridge is referred to today almost always it is Contract Bridge that is meant. The game which was first called Bridge began its life in London in the 1890s, and it is possible that its name arose from a pamphlet published there in 1889 about *Biritch*, or Russian Whist. Its main differences to Whist were that the trump suit was not chosen at random – it was the dealer's advantage to select it – and that the hand was played with a dummy.

Auction Bridge followed in the early years of the century. The introduction of the auction meant that every player could bid for the right to name the trump suit. Contract Bridge dates from the 1920s, when Harold S. Vanderbilt of New York was given the credit for amendments which led to the elaborate scoring table that is used today.

Ely Culbertson, who won a famous marathon match in the 1930s, became a prolific writer on the strategy of the game, and he has been followed by hundreds of others. Bridge has become the most popular card game ever invented, with a vast literature in many languages. Books are devoted to one aspect of the game. Here it is thought best to give a brief outline of the game, then to give the procedure relating to each aspect in more detail, then to outline some of the niceties of the game under the general heading *Strategy*.

Brief outline
Bridge is a trick-taking game played by four players in partnership. After the deal there is an auction in which each partnership bids to name the trump suit, by promising to make a certain number of tricks with the trump suit of their choice. For the successful side, that promise becomes a *contract*. It is the bidding which most newcomers to the game find the most mysterious aspect of Bridge, and which leads to the most post-mortems afterwards. During the bidding each bid made by a player conveys something to each of the other players. After a well-contested auction each player should have knowledge about all four hands.

The object of the bidding so far as a partnership is concerned is to arrive at the best contract, i.e. to undertake to make the correct number of tricks with the correct suit as trumps. If their opponents happen to hold the balance of power, and a partnership is destined to become *defenders* (i.e. their task will be to try to defeat their opponents' contract), then the bidding can still sometimes be used to convey information to each other about the way to achieve this. Partners might regard the bidding as a conversation between them, in which they develop their plan for the game. If they misunderstand each other they will pay the consequences.

When the contract has been decided one of the contracting side becomes the *declarer*. His partner lays his hand on the table (it becomes the *dummy*) and in effect takes no further part in the deal. The declarer then attempts to make his contract in the normal way of trick-taking games, while his opponents try to stop him.

This is the essence of the game which will now be described in detail.

Players
Bridge is for four players, playing in partnerships of two.

Cards
The standard pack of 52 cards is used. The cards rank from Ace (high) to 2 (low). The Ace, King, Queen, Jack and 10 of each suit are known as its *honour* cards. For bidding and scoring purposes the suits rank in the order: spades, hearts, diamonds, clubs. Spades and hearts are known as *major* suits and diamonds and clubs as *minor* suits. It is customary where possible to use two packs, one being shuffled by dealer's partner during the deal and placed to his right for the next deal.

Preliminaries
A pack is spreadeagled on the table, and each player draws a card to determine partners. The highest two become partners, and the highest of these, dealer. If two players draw the same rank of card, precedence is determined by the suit order given above. Partners sit opposite each other. The pack is shuffled by the player on dealer's left and dealer then places it to be cut by the player on his right. The deal passes clockwise to dealer's left.

Dealing
The dealer deals the pack one at a time clockwise to each player beginning on his left, so each has 13 cards.

The auction
Each player studies his cards and, beginning with the dealer, makes a *call* in rotation to the left.

A player may pass, bid, double or redouble, and passing does not bar a player from making any of the other calls when his turn comes round again.

Pass A player who does not wish to bid, double or redouble may pass. He usually says 'pass', 'no bid', or 'no'.

Bid A bid is an undertaking to make the majority of the tricks, either with a named suit as trumps or with no trumps. The bidder states the number of tricks in excess of six he promises to make and the denomination. The suits rank as stated above, and a bid with no trumps as the denomination ranks above spades. The lowest bid available is therefore 'one club', which is followed by 'one diamond', 'one heart', 'one spade', 'one no-trump', 'two clubs' and so on up to 'seven no-trumps', the highest bid possible.

Each bid must be higher than a previous bid, i.e. it must be either for more tricks or for the same number in a superior denomination. This is called over-calling.

Double A player on his turn may double the preceding bid if it was made by an opponent. It does not affect the contract, which will still be played by the opponents at the level stated – its effect is to increase the points at stake in the hand. It does not affect the required level of the next bid, e.g. if four hearts is doubled, the next bidder may make any bid of four spades or higher. A player cannot double his own side's bid.

Redouble When a side has been doubled it may redouble, provided there have been no intervening bids. The effect is to increase further the points at stake. Like a double, it does not affect the required level of a subsequent bid.

A double or redouble applies only to the highest bid at the time it is made. If a subsequent bid is made the double or redouble is cancelled, although, of course, any succeeding bid can also be doubled and redoubled in its turn.

The auction ends when three players pass consecutively. The last bid becomes the contract and determines which suit is trumps or whether the contract is to be played with no trumps. The player on the contracting side who first named the trump suit becomes the declarer (who is not necessarily the player who made the last bid). If all players pass without a bid being made, the hand is abandoned and the deal passes.

At no time in the bidding may information be passed by signals, inflection of voice, displays of enthusiasm, eagerness in responding to a bid, exaggerated pauses for consideration, etc. These are cheating.

To get some more of the terminology out of the way, the player who makes the first bid is said to open the bidding and is often called the opening bidder or opener. A player making a second bid is often said to rebid. A con-

tract at the six level (i.e. an undertaking to make 12 tricks) is called a small slam, and a contract at the seven level (to make all the tricks) is a grand slam. These terms do not affect the understanding of the game, but they are used in Bridge literature, as is the convention that the players are known by the four points of the compass. Here is an example of bidding, NT meaning 'no trumps':

South	West	North	East
1♣	Pass	1♥	1♠
1 NT	2♠	3♣	Pass
3 NT	Pass	Pass	Double
4♣	Pass	5♣	Double
Redouble	Pass	Pass	Pass

The contract is thus five clubs, and South is declarer, because although it was North who bid five clubs, South was the first to bid clubs. The contract is redoubled, which means there are lots of points at stake.

The play

When the bidding ends the player to the left of declarer leads to the first trick by playing a card to the centre of the table. This is called the opening lead. The declarer's partner then lays down his hand on the table, arranged in suits, with the trumps on his right, i.e. declarer's left. This hand, and the player, are called the dummy. Except that he has the right to warn the declarer of some irregularities, like leading from the wrong hand, dummy takes no further part in the play. The dummy is played by the declarer.

The usual trick-taking principles apply. Players must follow suit to the card led when able, and if they cannot may trump or discard. The highest trump in a trick wins it, and if there is none, the highest card in the suit led. The player (or dummy) who wins the trick leads to the next.

One member of each side keeps the tricks won by his side, squaring up the cards and keeping the tricks separate face down, so that all can see how many each side has. The tricks may not be looked at during play, except that a player may look at the last trick provided his side has not played to the next.

The object, of course, is for the declarer to make at least as many tricks as named in the contract, and for the defenders to prevent him.

Scoring

Pads of score-sheets are printed for Bridge. One can easily make one's own. Ideally, one player on each side should keep score and the two players should agree on the scores they are entering, but of course one scorer should be adequate among friends.

A score-sheet for a game in progress is shown in the illustration. The most important thing about it is the horizontal line which divides it in two. Certain scores are entered *below the line* and certain scores *above the line*.

When a declarer makes his contract the score for it is entered below the line. All other scores are entered above the line. Only scores entered below the line count in determining who wins a game. The other scores are in the nature of bonus scores. They count in the final settlement, and could total

more than the scores of the team which won the game.

A score-sheet of a game of Bridge in progress.
  Notes:
1. We bid 4♠ and were one short
2. They made 3NT
3. We made 2♥
4. We made 6♦
5. The bonus for the small slam
6. We were 2 down on 4♥ doubled (vulnerable)
7. They were 1 down in 3NT (vulnerable)
8. We made 4♠
9. The bonus for the rubber
The final score: 1400–650.

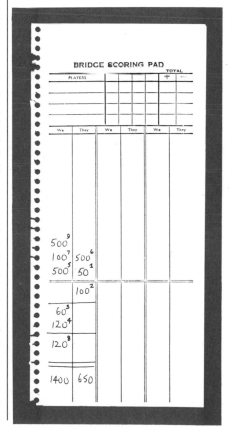

A game is won when a partnership scores 100 points below the line, either in one or more deals. A score of less than 100 below the line is said to be a *part-score*. Another part-score at least is required to score game. When a partnership wins a game, a fresh horizontal line is drawn below the scores, and each side begins the next game with nothing below the line. Bridge is played in *rubbers*, a rubber consisting of the best of three games, so the object is to win two games, and win the rubber either by 2−1 or 2−0. There is a bonus for winning the rubber.

A side which has won a game is said to be *vulnerable*, and is subject to higher bonus scores and higher penalties on subsequent contracts.

The actual points entered on the score-sheet are as follows:

1. If a side makes its contract it scores:

a) in no-trumps, 40 points for the first trick and 30 points for subsequent tricks;
b) in spades and hearts, 30 points for each trick;
c) in diamonds and clubs, 20 points for each trick. These points are doubled if the contract has been doubled, and quadrupled if it has been redoubled.

2. If a side makes its contract with tricks in excess of its contract (called *over-tricks*) it scores:

a) if undoubled, the value for each trick as above;
b) if doubled, 100 points for each trick if not vulnerable; 200 points

for each trick if vulnerable;
c) if redoubled, 200 points for each trick if not vulnerable; 400 points for each trick if vulnerable.

3. If a side fails to make its contract, the opponents score:

a) if undoubled, 50 points for each short trick (now called an *under-trick*) if the contracting side is not vulnerable; 100 points for each trick if the contracting side is vulnerable;
b) if doubled, 100 points for the first trick and 200 points for each subsequent trick if the contracting side is not vulnerable; 200 points for the first trick and 300 points for each subsequent trick if the contracting side is vulnerable;
c) if redoubled, 200 points for the first trick and 400 points for each subsequent trick if the contracting side is not vulnerable; 400 points for the first trick and 600 points for each subsequent trick if the contracting side is vulnerable.

4. If a side wins a rubber it scores:

a) if it wins in three games, 500 points;
b) if it wins in two games, 700 points.

5. A side scores other bonuses as follows:

a) for bidding and making a grand slam, 1,000 points if not vulnerable and 1,500 points if vulnerable;
b) for bidding and making a small slam, 500 points if not vulnerable and 750 points if vulnerable;
c) if either partner holds all four

Aces in a no-trump contract, or all five honours in a suit contract, 150 points;

d) if either partner holds any four honours in a suit contract, 150 points;

e) for making a doubled or redoubled contract, 50 points (sometimes said to be for the *insult*).

Strategy

In Bridge literature, the bidding probably receives more attention than the play. The play can be analysed much more exactly; the bidding is more a question of intuition, particularly when both sides are bidding.

There are no rules; each player may bid what he likes. But of course the main purpose of bidding is to reach the right contract, which involves partners discovering something about each other's hands. Many systems of bidding have been invented, and all modern partnerships will use some bids, called *conventional* bids, to convey information to each other.

The first task is to value the hand. Most modern players use the *Work count* named after Milton Work, who first proposed it. It is very simple. It involves counting the hand on the basis of the number of Aces, Kings, Queens and Jacks it contains, on this scale: four points for an Ace, three for a King, two for a Queen and one for a Jack. It is also called the *point count*.

Some players develop this further, adding half-points for 10s, points for voids and singletons (called *distribution* values), etc.

The simplest point count is obviously very rough. A player holding A K Q J in one suit and no other card over 10 has ten points, but he is clearly very strong in that suit and his side would probably make the majority of tricks if that suit were trumps. On the other hand, a player holding four Kings has 12 points, but might not make a single trick with them.

But the simple point count is a good basic guide to the strength of the hand, provided a player does not become a slave to it. 'I had 13 points, so I had to bid' is not a remark of a good player. The point count should be used with the knowledge that a hand might be a 'good' 12 points or a 'weak' 12 points. And the value of a hand tends to change when partner bids, as we will see.

Opening bid The number of points in a pack, based on the point count described, is 40. It follows that an average hand has 10. Most players would make an opening bid with 12 or 13. They might make an opening bid with fewer, but must bear in mind that they are giving information to partner. If a player makes an opening bid his partner will expect him to have, usually, at least 12 points, and he can thus immediately get a lead on the balance of power between the two sides.

There is also the negative side to consider. A partnership might decide that a player will *always* open the bidding with 13 points. It follows that if a player does not open, his partner knows that he has fewer than 13 points.

A player's trump strength will affect his decision about opening.

The fewer points he holds, the stronger will need to be his trump holding. For example, a player holding five good cards in a suit might open with 11 points, whereas if his suit distribution is 4–3–3–3, and the points evenly

spread, he might consider 12 points not enough to open.

All hands must have at least one suit containing at least four cards. A player should open the bidding with his longest suit, which automatically promises partner at least four cards in that suit. At the same time, an opening bidder should consider what rebid he can make over a *response* from partner. A

Four Bridge hands discussed in the text.

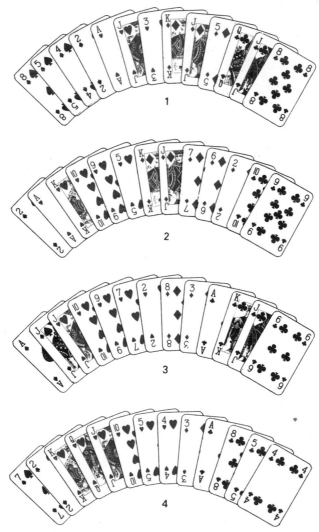

partner will generally expect that if he responds, the opening bidder will make a further bid.

The four hands in the illustration on page 48 indicate some of the points to consider in opening the bidding.

With hand 1, a player should pass. He has 12 points, but none of his suits is strong enough to open.

If he did open, one spade would be the only bid he could make, and the spades are very weak. With hand 2, there are only 11 points, but a player should open one

Hands which should be opened with a bid at the two level: the first and third with two hearts, the second with two spades and the fourth with two clubs.

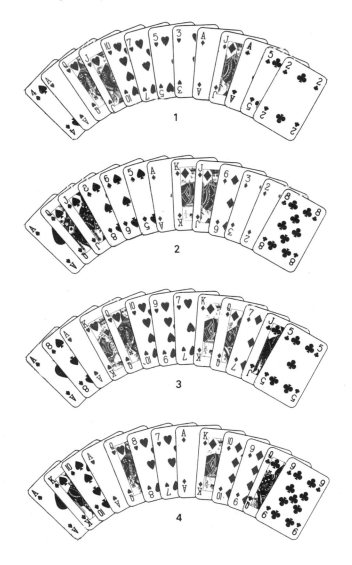

heart. He has an ideal rebid over anything partner might respond in his diamond suit. With suits of equal length, it is better to bid the higher. If, in this example, partner responds with one spade or two clubs, the rebid of two diamonds keeps the bidding fairly low. If the player with hand 2 opens one diamond, his rebid would be two hearts, so that if his partner then wanted to show he had backing for the hearts, he would have to bid three rather than two.

With hand 3, with 14 points, one should open one heart, although it is headed only by the Jack, because it is the longest suit, not one club where most of the points are.

With hand 4, there are only 10 points but a very strong heart suit, so a bid of one heart is in order. For a rebid the player would have to repeat the hearts, which tells partner that he has little apart from hearts and giving partner the choice of stopping there or continuing.

A player can show he is strong, i.e. has a much better hand than the minimum needed to open, by bidding two in a suit. This should be made on a hand with a very strong major suit (six cards headed by at least A Q), or a hand with a strong major suit backed up by a second good suit, or on a hand with about 18–20 points. Examples are shown in the illustration on page 49.

A bid of two in a suit is regarded as *forcing* for one round. That is to say that partner must respond, and not let the bidding die immediately. Another bid of two introduces a new idea, the *conventional* bid. A conventional bid is

one which conveys a precise meaning, not logically connected with the cards held. It is also called an *artificial* bid. One of the most widely used is a bid of two clubs. It does not mean that the bidder is very strong in clubs – he might not hold a single card in the suit. It conveys to partner that the bidder holds a very good hand, containing 22 points or more. It is, of course, forcing, and is, with one exception, *forcing to game*. This means that neither partner should cease bidding until they reach a contract with enough points for a game. The exception is when partner's hand is so weak that he does not hold 7 points, which he conveys by the conventional response of two diamonds (this is called a *negative* response). If the opener has no particular strong suit, and cannot bid anything stronger than two no-trumps, his partner may then allow the bidding to end there. For example:

West	East
♠A K 6	♠5 4 3
♥K J 5 4	♥8 6 3
♦A Q 3	♦J 5 4 2
♣K Q 7	♣J 6 2

West is strong enough for two clubs, East responds two diamonds (holding only two points), West can bid only two no-trumps, and East passes.

An opening bid of three in a suit is tactical. It is made with a weak hand which contains a long suit. The type of hand is shown in the illustration. This hand has only 8 points, but if a bid of three spades is made it is unlikely to be defeated by more than a trick or two even if partner has practically

A hand suitable for a pre-emptive bid of three spades.

nothing. If partner has a strong hand he can bid because he has a very good idea of bidder's hand. This is called a pre-emptive bid.

A pre-emptive bid acknowledges that it is likely that the opponents might have the balance of power, and it restricts their space for bidding. In the example given, the opponents have to start bidding at three no-trumps or four of a suit, and more often than not they pass, frequently missing a contract they could have made.

Occasionally a player might open with a bid of four of a suit. This is also pre-emptive, and the sort of hand that it might be bid on is the one in the previous illustration, with perhaps the ♠10 instead of a red card. All partner needs for game is an Ace and ♣K, so the opening bidder risks bidding game immediately.

No-trump opening There are two schools of thought on opening bids of one no-trump. Some players prefer what is called a *weak no-trump*, in which a bid of one no-trump conveys a balanced hand of 12−14 points. Others prefer a *strong no-trump*, which presupposes 16−18 points. Whichever is used, partners must be clear and consistent.

An opening bid of two no-trumps requires 20−22 points.

Both these opening bids, of one or two no-trumps, should be made on balanced hands, ideally 4−3−3−3 in the various suits, but possibly 4−4−3−2. The point count is particularly important in no-trump contracts. It is generally estimated that a contract worth game (e.g. three no-trumps, worth 100 points) will usually be made if the point count of the two partners' hands is 25 or more (a small slam requires 33, a grand slam 37). So if a player hears his partner open one or two no-trumps, and has the points to see that the combined total is 25 or more, he can, if he wishes, immediately bid three no-trumps.

An opening bid of three no-trumps is tactical. It is made with a hand consisting of a long minor suit with all the top cards (such a suit is called *solid*) and a card or two outside which could obtain the lead. It is a hand which might not make game in a suit contract, but should make nine tricks in no-trumps (i.e. a game) if partner has a card or two to help. The illustration shows three hands which could be opened with no-trump bids.

Responses When a player's partner has made an opening bid of

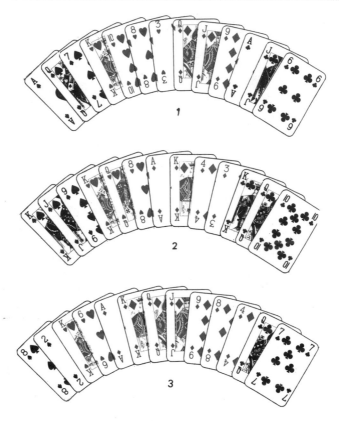

1

2

3

Suitable hands for no-trump opening bids. They might be opened one, two and three no-trumps respectively.

---

one in a suit, his first question is whether he himself can bid at all. A player with fewer than 6 points, unless he has length in his partner's suit, should pass. It is likely that the two hands between them lack the power to make a game, and to bid on could well lead to giving away penalties.

Assuming a reasonable hand, the next question is can partner's suit be supported? If partner has bid one spade, and the response is two spades, partner will expect

support of at least four spades, or at the very worst three, headed by Ace or King or both Queen and Jack.

Otherwise one should bid one's own strongest suit. By doing so one is denying that one holds support for partner's suit, but giving him the information about one's own, which should be preferably of at least five cards, or at worst four headed by some honours.

If one has support for one's partner but also has a strong suit of one's own, one can show the strong suit first, and support partner's suit next time round. For example:

West	East
♠9 2	♠8 7
♥A K 8 7 3	♥Q J 9 6
♦A Q 8 7	♦4 2
♣J 3	♣A K 10 8 2

Bidding	Bidding
1♥	2♣
2♦	2♥

Each partner now has an idea of the other's hand, and they should reach, and make, a contract of four hearts.

If a player holds a strong hand with which he would have opened the bidding himself, and partner opens before him, he can tell him the good news by a *jump* bid. This is raising the bidding by a step more than is necessary, and it is forcing to game. For example:

West	East
♠9 7 2	♠A Q J 10 4 3
♥A 8	♥K 6 3
♦A K 8 7 6	♦5 3
♣Q J 6	♣A 2

Bidding	Bidding
1♦	2♠

East could have shown his spade suit by bidding one spade, but by bidding two spades he has shown not only his spade suit but told partner that he has at least 12 points of his own. The opener can see that his side almost certainly have the values for game, possibly even a slam, and the subsequent bidding will be used to discover the correct contract.

Responses to a no-trump opening are slightly different. When a strong no-trump is being played responder knows that the opener has at least 16 points. With nine points himself he can jump to three no-trumps. With a good five-card suit he can jump to three no-trumps with 8 points. For example:

West	East
♠A 10 5 4	♠J 8 6
♥K J 2	♥A 10 8 7 3
♦A 8 7	♦Q 5
♣K Q 3	♣J 9 7

Bidding	Bidding
1 NT	3 NT

The above hand should make three no-trumps, but normally with 7 or 8 points, a responder will bid two no-trumps after his partner has opened one. The opener can then proceed to three no-trumps if he had opened with the maximum but stop at two if he had opened with the minimum.

If the responder is weak, i.e. he has less than 7 points, he should name his best suit at the next level. For example:

West	East
♠A 10 5 4	♠8 6 2
♥K J 2	♥A 10 8 7 3
♦A 8 7	♦5 4
♣K Q 3	♣J 9 7

Bidding	Bidding
1 NT	2♥

In this case West will now pass. The response of two hearts shows weakness. West will know that if his partner has four or five hearts and little else, two hearts is the highest contract his side should be in.

If responder has a hand which might be more suitable for play in a major suit than in three no-trumps, he puts the choice to his partner by a jump bid in his suit. For example:

West	East
♠A 10 5 4	♠K J 8 6 3
♥K J 2	♥Q 7
♦A 8 7	♦Q J 4 2
♣K Q 3	♣7 5

Bidding	Bidding
1 NT	3♠

East in this case is effectively saying to West: 'I have the points necessary for three no-trumps, but my strength is a spade suit. You choose whether you'd like to play in four spades or three no-trumps'. In this case West will bid four spades and probably make them, whereas three no-trumps might have foundered on a club lead.

Another artificial bid is found useful by many players responding to one no-trump. It is called the Stayman convention. It is a bid of two clubs over one no-trump, or three clubs over two no-trumps, and it is used by a responder with two good major suits. It is asking the opener to bid his better major suit, or to bid three diamonds if he doesn't hold a four-card major suit. This is an example:

West	East
♠A 10 5 4	♠K Q J 6
♥K J 2	♥A 10 9 7
♦A 8 7	♦6 4
♣K Q 3	♣J 8 2

Bidding	Bidding
1 NT	2♣
2♠	

East will now bid four spades, confident that his partner has four, probably headed by the Ace. It is a better contract than three no-trumps, which would be threatened by a diamond lead.

Rebidding When a player is making a second bid he is said to be rebidding. To rebid one's initial suit is a sign of weakness. For example:

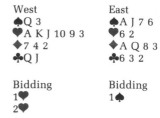

West	East
♠Q 3	♠A J 7 6
♥A K J 10 9 3	♥6 2
♦7 4 2	♦A Q 8 3
♣Q J	♣6 3 2

Bidding	Bidding
1♥	1♠
2♥	

West is telling partner that he has no other suits worth mentioning. East should pass. Should East try three diamonds, West could only say three hearts. With such sequences it is best to stop as low as one can.

Where the bidder has a good second suit he should mention it over partner's response. For example:

West	East
♠Q 7	♠5
♥A K 10 5	♥9 6
♦A Q 10 9	♦K 8 4 3 2
♣9 7 6	♣A K Q 8 5

Bidding	Bidding
1♥	2♣
2♦	

East here will agree diamonds by bidding three, and the pair will have the tricky task of deciding whether or not to bid on to six diamonds.

Sometimes the opener will want to force with his rebid, and can do so, in the same manner as described before for the responder, by a jump bid. For example:

West	East
♠K Q 6 4	♠A J 7 2
♥A K 10 6 2	♥9 8
♦—	♦8 7 6
♣A J 10 9	♣K Q 7 3

Bidding	Bidding
1♥	1♠
3♣	

West's rebid is forcing to game. He could agree partner's spades immediately, but with his 17 points he has the room to explore further. His jump not only forces East to bid again, but alerts East to the possibilities. East will agree clubs on his turn, and with luck the partnership might reach and make a small slam.

Sometimes the forcing situation arises out of the logic of the bidding. For example:

West	East
♣K Q 10 9 7	♠8 6 5 3
♥A J 10 5	♥K Q 6 2
♦7	♦Q 8 7
♣A 6 3	♣4 2

Bidding	Bidding
1♠	2♠
3♥	

West has here got a weak response from East, who with only 7 points feels he can do no more than let his partner know he has four spades in support. But by introducing a new suit (hearts) West is saying, in effect; 'We can make three spades, how are you on hearts?' With weak hearts, East would have replied with three spades, and the bidding would end. But in the example East, whose hearts are very strong, should bid four hearts, which is a good contract.

Responder can also force in this manner. For example:

West's jump to two no-trumps suggests a hand of at least 15 points (just short of a no-trump opening bid) and that his hand is probably 4–3–3–3 or 4–4–3–2, with four hearts. East knows, because he has 11 points, that they probably have the hands for three no-trumps. His agreement of West's initial heart bid is now, in effect, saying to West: 'We have the values for game. Decide whether it is to be no-trumps or hearts'. West, with his club weakness, will probably bid four hearts.

When a partnership has clearly established that it has the balance of power, a useful device is the cue bid. The cue bid is an artificial bid that does not show strength in the suit (by the time it is used the partners know they haven't strength in the suit), but it shows first-round control of the suit. For example:

West	East
♠K 10 9 5	♠A Q 8 7 2
♥A K 10 9 2	♥8 6 4
♦A 9	♦7 6 5 3
♣8 7	♣A

West	North	East	South
1♥	2♣	2♠	3♣
3♠	Pass	4♣	

East clearly has no power in clubs as both opponents have bid the suit. The bid shows West first round control of clubs, and West might well explore the possibility of a slam.

When the bidding suggests that a side might have slam prospects another useful artificial bid is the Blackwood convention. It is a bid of four no-trumps which asks partner to state how many Aces he holds by the following responses: five clubs for no Aces or all four, five diamonds for one Ace, five hearts for two Aces, five spades for three Aces. He might then go on to bid five no-trumps, which asks partner to state how many Kings he has: six clubs for none, six diamonds for one, six hearts for two, six spades for three, six no trumps for four. For example:

West	East
♠A K Q 8 5	♠10 9 7 4
♥Q J 6 2	♥A K 7 4 3
♦K J	♦9 7
♣K 8	♣A 3

Bidding	Bidding
1♠	2♥
3♥	4♠
4 NT	5♥
6♠	Pass

With West supporting his strong hearts, East tells West that he has support for his spades by a jump rebid, suggesting to West other values (i.e. his ♣A). West, with his strong hand, investigates the Ace situation with his bid of four no-trumps. Had East's response shown only one Ace, West would have stopped at five spades. He judged that spades was the better suit to be in because of his two minor-suit Kings. He was correct. Had the trump suit been hearts, a lead of a diamond from South might have killed the contract immediately.

Contesting the bidding When an opponent has bid entering the bidding should be a question of care, particularly if it is necessary to enter the bidding at the two level. Some suggest that a bid should be made only if, should it become the contract and partner is found with a poor hand, it would not be likely to be beaten by three tricks if not vulnerable and two if vulnerable. However, when an auction becomes contested by both sides, common sense is often the best guide.

A useful device is an artificial bid called the *take-out double*. The idea is that a double, as a first bid by a partnership, is not intended for 'business' but for 'take-out' i.e. the doubler has not got strength in the suit bid and is not expecting penalties. What he is doing is asking his partner to name his strongest suit. A take-out double is usually made with a hand with at least 13 or 14 points, and is particularly useful when a player has values in all the suits not bid by the opponents. For example:

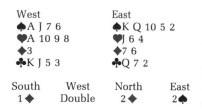

West	East
♠A J 7 6	♠K Q 10 5 2
♥A 10 9 8	♥J 6 4
♦3	♦7 6
♣K J 5 3	♣Q 7 2

South	West	North	East
1♦	Double	2♦	2♠

The *fit* in spades having been found, East/West might well go on to bid and make four spades.

When a pre-emptive bid has been made it is a possibility that the side yet to bid has the balance of power. So a player should not be too wary about competing (after all, the purpose of the pre-emptive bid was partly to try to stop him).

On the assumption that his side is probably strong in one of the other suits, one method to counter the pre-empt is to bid three diamonds over a pre-empt of three clubs, and three no-trumps over a pre-empt of three diamonds, hearts or spades. The bid is an invitation to partner to name his best suit. For example:

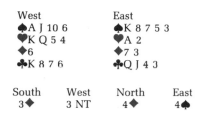

West		East	
♠A J 10 6		♠K 8 7 5 3	
♥K Q 5 4		♥A 2	
♦6		♦7 3	
♣K 8 7 6		♣Q J 4 3	

South	West	North	East
3♦	3 NT	4♦	4♠

If North/South do not carry the bidding further East/West are in a contract of four spades, which they should make with no difficulty at all.

What might happen in this case, however, is that North, in particular, will be aware that his side is much the weaker, and that a contract of four spades is very likely unbeatable, and he might bid five diamonds and even go up to six diamonds to force his opponents to buy the contract at a higher level. He knows that going down in five diamonds is unlikely to cost his side as many points as would a game of four spades made by his opponents. This is called a *sacrifice* bid.

The 'unusual two no-trumps' is another useful device by which a side can contest an auction that looks otherwise bleak for them. It is used by a player with strength in both minor suits and asks his partner to name his longer. For example:

West		East	
♠4 3 2		♠10	
♥5		♥Q 8 3	
♦A Q J 7 5		♦K 10 8 6 4 2	
♣K 8 6 5		♣Q J 7	

South	West	North	East
1♥	Pass	1♠	Pass
2♥	2 NT		

Whatever North bids, East will bid his diamonds, and West will if necessary bid a slam in diamonds to sacrifice against the easy game that North/South have in a major suit.

A final artificial device to be used by a side which is going to defend against a slam is the Lightner double. It is bid not for penalties but to indicate to partner that an 'unusual' lead is required, i.e. a lead in a suit bid by opponents. For example:

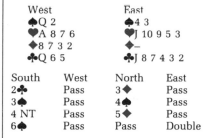

West		East	
♠Q 2		♠4 3	
♥A 8 7 6		♥J 10 9 5 3	
♦8 7 3 2		♦—	
♣Q 6 5		♣J 8 7 4 3 2	

South	West	North	East
2♣	Pass	3♦	Pass
3♠	Pass	4♠	Pass
4 NT	Pass	5♦	Pass
6♠	Pass	Pass	Double

In this auction, North could not bid two diamonds, which was a denial of 6 points, so he bid three diamonds to tell South that in fact he had a strong diamond suit. South's three spades indicated his suit at the lowest level, giving North time to say more if he wished. When North supported South in spades, South explored the slam situation with Blackwood, and finding North with one Ace, settled for the small slam. East, wanting a diamond led, could have doubled North's bid of five diamonds to indicate this, but realising that his partner possibly had useful cards in his opponent's suits, did not wish to deter South from bidding the slam. His double of six spades was a Lightner double inviting an unusual lead, which West interpreted as a diamond, allowing East to trump. All East has to do now is lead back a heart to defeat the slam. If he leads a club, his good work is undone.

It is stressed that none of the above suggestions about how to bid in certain situations is obligatory nor even necessarily the best. Many systems have been invented to convey information between partners, some of them so complicated that hardly any bid is natural, and an outsider would not be able to understand what was going on at all.

Ethics of bidding Players using artificial bids must announce them to their opponents and if necessary explain how they work before the game. However elaborate a system, a bid should convey the same information to an opponent as it does to a partner. If, during a game, a bid is made which appears to be conventional and is not understood by the opposing side, that side have the right to ask the partner of the bidder what was the significance of the bid, and only that player may answer.

Conventional bids mentioned in this article are all well known and are understood by their names by experienced players, and to say one uses, for example, Blackwood or Stayman is all that is necessary. There are, of course, many other popular conventions.

The ones mentioned are those that are often used in magazine and newspaper Bridge articles on the assumption that the reader knows their meaning.

Strategy in play

When a contract has been reached and play begins, there are two sides: the declarer and the defenders. The declarer has control of both hands on his side, so tactics so far as he is concerned relate to making the most tricks from the 26 cards at his disposal.

A top-class player will know the probabilities of how cards are distributed in the defenders' hands. For instance, if the defenders hold four cards in a suit, it is almost an even chance that one player holds three and the other one. That they are distributed two each is about a 40 per cent chance, and there is one chance in ten that one player holds all four. If defenders hold five trumps, it is comforting to know that on just over two-thirds of occasions, they will split 3–2, and three rounds of trumps will clear them.

Much of declarer's play is deciding from which hand to lead, and which card to lead, in certain holdings. The correct play to maximize chances has been worked out for many holdings, and they can be found listed in Bridge books. A few examples here will give the idea:

West	Dummy
♠A J 10	♠4 3 2

The best chance to make two tricks is to lead low from dummy and play ♠10. If it loses to North's

King or Queen, re-enter dummy to lead and play ♠J. Of course if South plays King or Queen on either trick, beat it with ♠A. This will win two tricks on all occasions except when North holds ♠K Q. Here is another example:

West   Dummy
♠A 3 2   ♠Q J 5 4

Lead the Ace, then low from West, playing Jack if North does not play King. If ♠J wins, return to hand and lead low, playing ♠Q if North does not play the King. This wins three tricks whenever North has the King, or South has the King and no others. The reader can work out what happens if the Queen is led from dummy, or if a low card is led first from West.

A final, more complex example:

West   Dummy
♠A K 10 4 2   ♠9 7 3

West needs to win four tricks in the suit. He first wins with Ace. If both players follow suit, he leads ♠7 from dummy, and covers what South plays. If South plays ♠8 he covers it with ♠10. The fact that South has played two spades means that if North can now produce the ♠Q or ♠J to win the trick, the suit must have been split to begin with 3–2, and West must thus draw the outstanding spade with his King, and make four tricks. Playing the ♠10 over South's ♠8 ensures him four tricks in the case of South having started with Q J 8 x (in Bridge articles the x means any small card).

These plays are known as *percentage* plays.

These ideas are based on what is called the *finesse*. This is the simplest example (East is dummy):

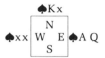

West leads and must make two tricks. If North plays low, West plays Queen from dummy; if North plays the King, West wins with Ace and the Queen is master. This is *finessing* the Queen.

Any such combination which must win two tricks if led up to is called a *tenace*. For example:

With only three tricks to play, and South requiring two of them for his contract, he will make them if West has to lead up to South's tenace. South leads his diamond, West wins, and South will make both spade tricks whatever West leads. Engineering such situations is not difficult for experienced declarers.

A final device of the declarer's which is frequently discussed in Bridge articles is the *squeeze*. It is a play which forces a defender to discard from a holding which without the discard would be sufficient to beat the contract. For example:

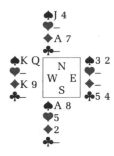

♠J 4
♥—
♦A 7
♣—

♠K Q
♥—
♦K 9
♣—

♠3 2
♥—
♦—
♣5 4

♠A 8
♥5
♦2
♣—

South, playing in a heart contract, needs to make all four tricks. West has the spades and the diamonds guarded, but when South leads the ♥5, West is squeezed. He must discard either a spade or a diamond. If he discards ♦9, South will discard ♠4 from dummy, make his ♠A, then lead ♦2 to dummy's ♦A, and dummy's ♦7 wins the last trick. If, on the other hand, West discards ♠K, South will discard ♦7 from dummy, take his ♠A and lead either his ♠8 or ♦2 towards dummy, which in either case will take the last two tricks.

The defenders' play is based on helping each other, much like in the bidding. The old precepts of Whist, such as 'third hand plays high', 'cover an honour with an honour', 'return partner's suit' must be tempered with the fact that the dummy allows each player to know where 26 of the cards lie immediately, and this might affect the old 'rules'. For example:

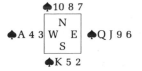

♠10 8 7

♠A 4 3

♠Q J 9 6

♠K 5 2

If East leads the Queen from his sequence it would be wrong for South to cover it with the King. West will win with his Ace, finesse against North's 10, and win four tricks in the suit. If South plays low, on the other hand, allowing Queen to win, North/South are assured a trick with the King or 10. If East next leads Jack, South now covers, because Jack is not from a sequence, West plays Ace perforce, leaving North's 10 as master. Defenders in general will lead from the top card of a sequence (except they will lead King from A K) but play the lowest card of a sequence when following to another lead.

Some systems of communication have become well known and proved. One is the *high–low* signal, also called an *echo* or *peter*. When a player plays or discards a high card in a suit, and subsequently a lower card, he is asking his partner to lead the suit. In a trump contract, an echo is an indication that only two cards are held in that suit and that a third round could be trumped. For example:

♠10 8 6 5
♥8 5
♦Q 7 3
♣A K J 4

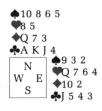

♠9 3 2
♥Q 7 6 4
♦10 2
♣J 5 4 3

South is in a contract of four spades. West leads the ♦K, which means he holds Ace as well. East plays the ♦10, a high card which encourages West to follow with the ♦A. East now plays the ♦2, completing the echo. West now knows (unless he holds six diamonds himself) that the lead of a third diamond will not be won by North's Queen, but by a trump from East.

It was said in the previous paragraph that East's play of the ♦10 was 'encouraging', and the play of what seems an unnecessarily high card in a suit is regarded as a signal to continue the suit. It might be the start of an echo. Similarly, a discard which seems unnecessarily high is an indication that a lead in the suit discarded is required. For example:

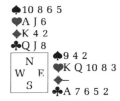

♠10 8 6 5
♥A J 6
♦K 4 2
♣Q J 8

♠9 4 2
♥K Q 10 8 3
♦—
♣A 7 6 5 2

If East/West are defending against three no-trumps and West leads a diamond, East could well discard ♥8, indicating to West that if West again gets the lead, a heart would be useful for East.

Similarly, of course, a low card might be considered discouraging. Had West led a spade in the above example, East would have played 2, indicating that he had no interest in that suit.

The rule of eleven is a useful tool for defenders against a no-trump contract. The defender making the first lead in such a contract should lead his longest suit, or a suit he knows partner is strong in (because he bid it) and in which he has support. When leading his own suit he should lead the highest in a sequence, or the King if he holds A K and an entry in another suit. Otherwise he should lead the fourth highest in his longest suit. By taking the denomination of this card from 11 (the rule of eleven) his partner can tell how many cards higher are held by the other three players. As he can see his own hand and dummy's, he knows how many cards declarer has higher than the card led. For example:

♠J 8 6

♠Q 10 7

West leads the ♠5 as the opening lead against three no-trumps by South. As five taken from 11 is six, East knows that there are six spades higher than the 5 between dummy, himself and declarer. As he can see all six, he knows declarer holds no spade higher than the 4. He can play a card sufficient to beat whatever dummy plays and knows that it will win the trick.

Example hand

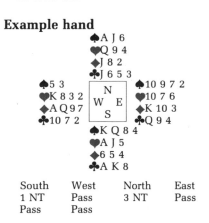

♠A J 6
♥Q 9 4
♦J 8 2
♣J 6 5 3

♠5 3
♥K 8 3 2
♦A Q 9 7
♣10 7 2

♠10 9 7 2
♥10 7 6
♦K 10 3
♣Q 9 4

♠K Q 8 4
♥A J 5
♦6 5 4
♣A K 8

South	West	North	East
1 NT	Pass	3 NT	Pass
Pass	Pass		

South had a balanced (except for

diamonds) 17 points and opened one no trump. North, with a balanced 9 points went straight to three no-trumps. With another spade or heart he might have used Stayman.

West led his ♦7. East could see immediately that South had no diamond higher than 6, and held only three at most. Declarer (South) played the 2 from dummy, hoping that East might play Queen or above. But East, knowing the position, played 10. He then led ♦K to allow West to see he could now overtake and win all four diamond tricks. After four rounds East/West needed only one more trick to beat the contract. West then led the fourth lowest in his other long suit, hearts, and hoped sooner or later to make the King. The play proceeded:

	West	North	East	South
1.	♦7	♦2	♦10	♦4
2.	♦A	♦8	♦K	♦5
3.	♦Q	♦J	♦3	♦6
4.	♦9	♣3	♠2	♥5
5.	♥2	♥4	♥10	♥J
6.	♠3	♠J	♠7	♠4
7.	♠5	♠6	♠9	♠K
8.	♥3	♠A	♠10	♠8
9.	♣2	♣J	♣Q	♣A
10.	♣7	♣5	♥6	♣Q
11.	♣10	♣6	♣4	♣K
12.	♥8	♥9	♥7	♥A
13.	♥K	♥Q	♣9	♣8

So East/West defeated the contract on the last trick, not by winning the ♥K as they expected, but because East covered the ♣J with the ♣Q on trick 9. Try as South might from then to conjure up an extra trick, he had to go one down. Had he held the ♣9 instead of the ♣8, all would have been well.

East/West scored 50 points *above* the line, and West dealt the second hand.

CALCULATION

Calculation is a one-pack **patience** or **solitaire** with a high skill factor. It is also called Broken Intervals.

Any Ace, 2, 3 and 4 are placed in a row as foundation cards (suits have no significance in Calculation). The object is to pile all the cards on these foundations.

Cards are built on the foundation cards as follows: on the Ace, singly; on the 2 at intervals of two; on the 3 at intervals of three; and on the 4 at intervals of four. Four completed foundation piles would thus contain these cards:

on the Ace: 2, 3, 4, 5, 6, 7, 8, 9, 10, J, Q, K
on the 2: 4, 6, 8, 10, Q, A, 3, 5, 7, 9, J, K
on the 3: 6, 9, Q, 2, 5, 8, J, A, 4, 7, 10, K
on the 4: 8, Q, 3, 7, J, 2, 6, 10, A, 5, 9, K

Notice all four piles end with a King.

The play
The cards in the pack are turned over from the hand one at a time. They can be played to a founda-tion, or to any of four waste piles below each foundation. These waste piles can be arranged so that each card can be seen.

The top card of each waste pile is available for play to a founda-tion at any time. The secret is to try to play onto the waste piles in descending sequences so that when a card becomes available to the foundations others will follow.

Example hand
The illustration shows a game in progress. Should readers wish to follow how it reached the state it is in, the following cards were turned from hand and played as described: Q to waste A, 8 to foundation D, Q from waste to foundation D, 6 to foundation C, 9 to foundation C, K to waste A (as Kings are the last cards on each

---

Calculation in progress as described in the text.

foundation it is well to reserve a waste pile especially for them, as a King will block all other cards below it in a waste pile until near the end), 8 to waste B, 4 to foundation B, J to waste C, 5 to waste B (hoping for a Q, 2 to go on foundation C which will allow 5, 8 to follow), 3 to foundation D, 7 to foundation D, J from waste to foundation D, Ace to waste C, 10 to waste C, K to waste A, 4 to waste D, 10 to waste C, 6 to foundation B, 2 to foundation A, 3 to foundation A, 4 to foundation A, 5 to foundation A, 8 to foundation B, 10 to foundation B, 4 to waste B, 9 to waste D, 3 to waste D, Ace to waste D, 5 to waste C, and so on.

Foundations B and C are both being held up by a Queen. Should one appear next it should be played to foundation B, allowing the Ace, 3 and 5 from the waste pile to be played to the foundation. The 4 on waste pile B will not be required for a while so can be discarded upon until a Queen appears.

California Jack

California Jack is based on All Fours (q.v.), but as it uses the whole pack it is considered a longer and more skilful game.

Players
The game is for two players.

Cards
The full pack of 52 cards is used. Cards rank from the Ace (high) to 2 (low).

Preliminaries
Each player draws a card to decide dealer (higher deals).

Dealing
Before each deal the non-dealer cuts the pack and shows the bottom card of the packet in his hand. This card fixes the trump suit for the next deal. The cards are then shuffled (dealer has the right to shuffle last), and cut by non-dealer.

The dealer then deals six cards, one at a time, to each player. The rest of the pack is placed face up in the centre to form the stock. The pack must be squared up so that only the top card can be seen.

The play
The game is a trick-taking one in which the object is to obtain specified scoring cards.

Non-dealer leads to the first trick, and subsequently the player who takes a trick leads to the next. The winner of each trick takes the top card of the stock, while the loser takes the next card. Each player's hand therefore remains at six cards. It follows that players will some-times wish to win the trick to take the top card, but if it is worthless they might try to lose it in the hope that the next card is better. This is why care should be taken not to expose any card in the stock below the top one.

Tricks are taken in the normal manner, by beating the lead in its own suit, or by playing a trump. Players must follow suit if they can, otherwise they may trump or discard. When the stock is exhausted, the players play out the last six tricks.

Players collect the tricks they win and at the end of the trick-taking phase count the points won according to the following:

high is scored by the winner of the Ace of trumps (1 point);
low is scored by the winner of the 2 of trumps (1 point);
Jack is scored by the winner of the Jack of trumps (1 point);
game is scored by the player who wins the majority of points on the basis of the Ace counting 4, King 3, Queen 2, Jack 1 and 10 ten (1 point). Game is not scored if the players tie.

There are therefore 4 points available on every deal, and they are scored in the order stated. The winner is the first to score 10 points (some players prefer first to 7 points), even though his opponent might be able to overtake him on the same deal.

Strategy
Skill relies on remembering the cards drawn and played. A player

who can remember perfectly will know well before the end of the trick-taking phase most of the cards in his opponent's hand and which ones remain in the stock, and can plan his play accordingly. Since losing a trick can be as vital as winning one, it is as well to keep losing cards in the hand as well as winning cards.

Variants

Shasta Sam is played in exactly the same manner as California Jack except that the stock is face down. This detracts from the skill element in the game, since a player cannot know whether it is better to win a trick or not.

All Fives This is a variant of California Jack rather than All Fours. It is for two players and the trick-taking phase is played in the same manner. The difference to California Jack lies in the scoring.

The winner of a game of All Fives is the first to reach 61 points, and it is convenient to score on a cribbage board (see under Cribbage).

Players score points *during* the trick-taking phase, scoring for the following trumps taken in tricks:

Ace:	4
King:	3
Queen:	2
Jack:	1
10:	10
5:	5

At the end of the trick-taking phase there is an extra point for *game*, based on the count as in California Jack, with an extra 5 points counting for the five of trumps.

There is therefore a total of 26 points at stake in each deal.

Calypso

This game was invented by an Englishman, R. W. Willis, in 1953. He was living in Trinidad, and called his new game after the type of West Indian topical song which was made familiar to all Englishmen in 1956 after West Indies had beaten England at cricket for the first time in England. It combines elements of Bridge and Canasta and deserves to be better known, as it is a neat, skilful and entertaining game which always lasts four deals.

Players
The basic game is for four players, playing in two partnerships. The game can be adapted for solo play and for three players, as outlined later.

Cards
Four identical packs are used. All 208 cards are shuffled together. The cards rank from Ace (high) to 2 (low).

Preliminaries
Each player draws a card. The two highest cards drawn indicate one partnership (if necessary players who tie draw again to determine precedence between them). The player who draws the highest card has choice of seat and deals first, his partner sitting opposite him. He also chooses his own trump suit. It is a feature of the game that each player has his own trump suit. Spades and hearts play against diamonds and clubs. It follows that if dealer chooses diamonds his partner's trump suit is clubs, and the opposing pair have spades and hearts. For uniformity, spades always sits to the right of diamonds and left of clubs. The choice of trump suit conveys no advantage – all suits are equal. Personal trump suits are established before the first deal, and each player retains his own trump suit throughout the game.

Dealing
The dealer has the right of the last shuffle, the player on his right cuts, and the dealer deals 13 cards to each hand, one at a time, clockwise. The remainder of the pack is set aside, as it is not needed until the next deal.

The play
The object of the game is to win tricks and form calypsos. A calypso is a complete suit sequence from Ace to 2.

The player to dealer's left leads to the first trick. Thereafter the winner of a trick leads to the next. Each player must follow suit to the card led if possible. If he cannot follow he may trump with a card of his own trump suit, or he may discard.

A player may lead a card of his own trump suit, or he may lead a plain suit. If he leads a card of his own trump suit he wins the trick if all other players follow suit, irrespective of the rank of the cards, because his own card is a trump.

However, a player leading his own trump suit can lose the trick if another player who is void in that suit trumps with his own personal trump suit. This trump need not be higher in rank than the card led. For instance, if a player leads the 8 of his own trump suit, he loses the trick if another player trumps with a 5 of his.

If a player leads a plain suit, i.e. a suit which is not his personal trump suit, and all follow suit, the trick is won by the highest ranked card. In other words, if a player's trump suit is hearts, say, and hearts are led, that player must follow suit and is not considered to have trumped, and only wins the trick if the card he played is the highest ranked in the trick.

Tricks can be overtrumped, but in this case the overtrump must be of a higher rank than the original trump. Where two cards are played of equal rank, each of which might win the trick, the trick is won by the player whose card was played first. The following examples of tricks show these possibilities. North led in each case.

North (♣)	East (♠)	South (♦)	West (♥)
1. ♣8	♠6	♠5	♠7
2. ♣8	♠A	♠5	♠7
3. ♣8	♠A	♦3	♠7
4. ♣8	♠A	♦3	♥5
5. ♣8	♠A	♦3	♦4
6. ♣8	♣10	♣4	♣J
7. ♣8	♠J	♦J	♠10
8. ♣8	♠J	♦K	♥K

In trick 1, North wins the trick, although East has played his trump suit. He is considered to have followed suit, not to have trumped.

In trick 2, East wins the trick because his card is highest in the suit led (not because it is his trump suit).

In trick 3, South wins the trick because he trumped.

In trick 4, West wins the trick because although South trumped, West overtrumped.

In trick 5, South wins the trick because he trumped. West in this case has discarded.

In trick 6, North wins the trick because he led a trump and no other player trumped in.

In trick 7, East wins the trick. His card and South's are equal highest in the suit led, but East played his first.

In trick 8, South wins the trick. Although West has also trumped with a King, South trumped with a King first. West would need the ♥A to overtrump.

A player can make calypsos only in his own trump suit, but any cards he takes in his partner's suit he may pass to him. For example, a player whose suit is clubs wins the following trick: ♦4, ♦K, ♣2, ♥10. The ♣2 he keeps face up before him on the table, the ♦K 4 are passed to his partner to keep likewise, as cards towards a calypso for him, and ♥10 he puts face down into his own discard pile.

A player can build calypsos only one at a time, and cannot keep cards towards a second calypso until the first is completed. For example, if a player has ♣A K 8 7 6 4 2 showing towards a calypso, and takes a trick containing ♣A 6 6 3 he can add only the ♣3 to the building of his calypso, and must put the Ace and two 6s into his discard pile. However, if, in this example, he had needed only the ♣3 to complete his calypso, he could complete his calypso with it and place the ♣A, 6 face up before him towards a second calypso, discarding only the second ♣6.

After the first deal calypsos, uncompleted calypsos and discards remain in place, the 156 cards not used are taken up by the original dealer, cut by him, and passed to the player on his left, who becomes dealer and deals 13 cards to each player. The game continues in the same way. The 104 cards not required are again placed aside, to be used for the third and fourth deals. The game ends when each player has dealt once. The scores are then calculated.

Scoring At the conclusion of the four deals, each player scores points as follows:

For his first calypso: 500
For his second calypso: 750
For any subsequent calypso: 1,000
For each card in an
  incomplete calypso: 20
For each card in his discard
  pile: 10

These scores are obtained by individual players, and then partners add their scores together. For example, if each partner scores one calypso, each scores 500, total

---

The deal for the hand of Calypso as described in the text.

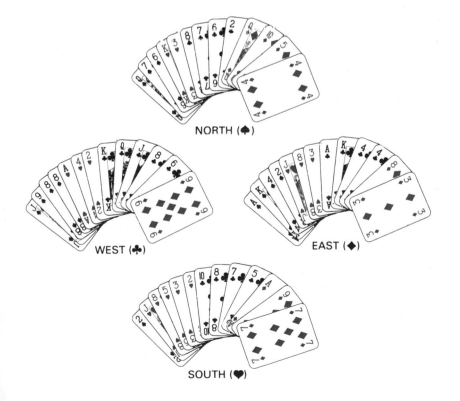

NORTH (♠)

WEST (♣)

EAST (♦)

SOUTH (♥)

1,000 – they do not count 500 for the first and 750 for the second.

Example hand

Four hands were dealt by North as in the illustration. Each player's trump suit is indicated. East decided that he might use his ♠A K to collect some spades, depriving North of cards he would want for calypsos. The play went as follows:

North (♠)	East (♦)	South (♥)	West (♣)
1. ♠6	♠A	♠2	♠8
2. ♠7	♠K	♥2	♠8

It worked for only one round. South was able to trump on the second round and win spades for his partner. He puts the ♥2 face up before him and passes the ♠K 8 7 to his partner to do likewise. All the cards in the first trick, taken by East, went on his discard pile. South now decides to lead his own trump suit, to collect hearts from the other players.

3. ♥K	♥3	<u>♥3</u>	♥2

South wins because his heart is a trump. His partner contributes the ♥K, but notice that West and East played ♥2 and ♥3. As South already has these cards, he is forced to discard them, as he is not allowed to begin a second calypso until he has completed the first. So South adds the ♥K 3 to his face-up cards, discarding the ♥2 and the second ♥3.

4. ♥3	♥8	<u>♥5</u>	♥4

North cannot help his partner and must contribute the ♥3,

which South must discard. Three of the ♥3s have now been played, so South can complete only two calypsos at best. He decides to lead his trumps for one more round and then switch, as his trump suit is unlikely to go round four times.

5. ♣2	♥J	<u>♥8</u>	♥A

North discards. There is no point trumping what is likely to be his partner's trick. South now decides to try to collect some diamond tricks to prevent East getting them.

6. ♦4	♦3	<u>♦A</u>	♦9
7. ♦5	♦8	<u>♦7</u>	♣6

West now trumps, takes the trick, and passes the three diamonds to his partner, keeping the ♣6 face up himself. He does not lead spades, as he knows South will trump, so he decides to make his big clubs.

8. ♣6	♣4	♣5	<u>♣K</u>

North plays the ♣6 which will not help West.

9. ♣7	♣A	♣7	<u>♣Q</u>

West must discard one of the two ♣7s taken. East was able to play the ♣A because West keeps the lead, his ♣Q being a trump.

10. ♣8	♣4	♣8	<u>♣J</u>

West now judges that his last club is almost certain to be trumped, and wants it in reserve, so he is forced to lead a spade.

11. <u>♠Q</u>	♠2	♣10	♠9

South, in fact, has no need to use

a trump, as North has won the trick anyway, so he throws the ♣10, a valuable card to West.

12. ♦Q   ♠4   ♦9   ♣8

West trumps and wins two diamonds for his partner.

13. ♦10   ♣K   ♥   ♠J

South's final trump he makes for himself, but has to discard it.

At the end of the first deal therefore, the cards face up in front of each player are as in the illustration. West has nine cards towards a calypso, South eight, North six and East five. East now deals the second hand, and play continues.

Strategy

The example hand demonstrates the tactic of leading low trumps, which is almost standard and worked well for South. However, this easy tactic can go astray if your trumps are themselves trumped by an opponent with a void in your suit. East's tactic of attacking an opponent's suit with his Ace, King is another which works well, but on this occasion East was unlucky in that South was able to trump.

The cards each player has on the table towards a calypso at the end of the first hand of the example game described in the text.

NORTH

EAST

SOUTH

WEST

Players should keep watch on the cards laid down in building calypsos, and should contribute to opponent's tricks cards which they cannot use, i.e. cards which duplicate those already showing. Of course the reverse principle applies in playing to partner's tricks.

One lead which is seldom advisable is the lead of partner's suit. Partner is the only player at the table unable to trump it.

Solo Calypso Calypso can be played without partners. The player who draws the highest card chooses his suit and seat, the player with the second highest his suit (which will determine his seat) and so on. The game is played in the same way, but a player obviously keeps from tricks only those cards in his own suit. It is less interesting than the partnership game. A player who cannot help himself can still affect the game by helping the player farthest behind rather than the player ahead, but the game is less clear cut.

Calypso for Three Players Calypso can be played by three players. Only three packs are necessary, and one suit is removed from each (usually spades, but it does not matter which). The method of play is the same. Each player plays for himself, and the game ends when each has dealt once, i.e. when the stock is exhausted.

CANASTA

A recent game, invented in Uruguay after the Second World War, Canasta rapidly spread through South America to the United States and thence to Britain, and for a period in the late 1940s and early 1950s threatened to become in all these places more popular than Bridge. The craze died, but Canasta remains a popular game. The word Canasta is Spanish for a basket, but the game Canasta is derived from the Rummy family.

Players

Canasta is best for four, though any number from two to six may play. If five play, one drops out in rotation. With two or three players each plays for himself; with four, five or six the players play in two partnerships. With four in partnership, partners sit opposite each other, with six each player sits between two opponents. The rules for four-handed Canasta are given first.

Cards

Two standard packs are used, plus four Jokers, making 108 cards in all (it was the popularity of Canasta that led playing card manufacturers to include two Jokers instead of one in each pack – at one time these were known as Canasta packs). All Jokers and all Deuces (2s) are *wild* cards, i.e. their holders can use them to represent any card they like.

Preliminaries

Players draw to determine partners and who is to be first player. The highest card determines first player, *not* first dealer, and if partners are required the highest two or three play against the lowest. For purposes of the draw only, the suits rank: spades (high), hearts, diamonds, clubs, and the cards from Ace (high) to 2 (low). A joker drawn must be discarded and another card drawn.

The player sitting to the right of the first player deals first, thereafter the deal passes to the left with each hand. The dealer shuffles last, and the player to his right cuts.

Dealing

Eleven cards are dealt to each player one at a time clockwise. The remainder of the pack is placed face down in the centre to form the *stock*. The top card is turned over and placed beside it. This is the upcard, and it begins a discard pile. If it is a red *trey* (3) or a wild card, another card must be turned over and placed upon it, and if necessary another, until the top card is not a red trey or wild. The discard pile is then said to be *frozen* (as explained in the description of the play).

Red trey

The red treys are bonus cards that can count for or against the side holding them. They do not form a part of the normal hand, and on his turn to play each player, if dealt one, must lay it face up on the table before him and draw a card from the stock to replenish his hand. On subsequent turns a red trey drawn from the stock is similarly laid on the table and a replacement drawn. However, if a red trey is acquired from the discard pile, although it must be laid on the table as usual, it is not replaced from the stock.

The play

The object of the play is to form *melds* (sets) of three or more cards of the same rank. A meld must in-

clude at least two natural (i.e. not wild cards) and no more than three wild cards. The game differs from Rummy in that sequences are of no value; a meld concerns only cards of equal rank. Black treys can be melded only on a player's last turn, i.e. he must go out in order to meld them. Melds cannot be composed of wild cards only.

A player may meld only on his turn.

A player may add one or more cards to his side's melds on his turn, including wild cards, with the proviso that a meld contains no more than three wild cards. There is one exception: wild cards can be added without restriction to a completed canasta.

From the top: examples of melds of 50, 90 and 120, a natural canasta and a mixed canasta.

A *canasta* is a meld consisting of seven or more cards. It might be laid down at one turn, or it may begin as a smaller meld to which further cards are added. Seven natural cards in a canasta make it a *natural canasta*. A canasta which includes wild cards is a *mixed canasta*. A wild card added to a natural canasta makes it a mixed canasta. Canastas carry bonuses (see *Scoring*).

Melds are made by a player on his turn only. The first person to play is the player to the left of dealer, and thereafter the turn passes to the left.

A turn consists of a draw, a meld (which a player might or might not make) and a discard. To draw, a player takes the top card of the stock or the top card of the discard pile. Having drawn the top card from stock, he may meld or not as required, and then discard. He can take the top card of the discard pile only if he can use it in a meld, and satisfy certain scoring requirements which follow. A player who takes the top card of the discard pile must show he has these requirements to meld, and having made a suitable meld, he takes the entire discard pile into his hand. Having made all the melds he wishes, he then discards. A discard ends the player's turn.

Melding The first meld made by a side in a deal is its *initial meld*. The initial meld must have a *minimum count* which depends upon that side's total of points at the beginning of the deal. The count of a meld is determined by the cards it contains, as follows:

each Joker counts	50
each Deuce	20
each Ace	20
each K Q J 10 9 8	10
each 7 6 5 4 black 3	5

The minimum count of a side's initial meld is as follows:

Side's total score	Minimum count
Minus	0
0 to 1,495	50
1,500 to 2,995	90
3,000 or more	120

To achieve his side's required minimum count, a player may make more than one meld on his turn (indeed he might need to). Once a side has melded, it can make further melds without the need to satisfy a count.

The discard pile The discard pile is frozen to a side until it has made its initial meld. It is frozen to both sides if it contains a red trey (as the upcard) or a wild card (either as the upcard or as a discard).

When the discard pile is frozen to him a player may draw the top card only to meld it with two natural cards from his hand.

When the discard pile is not frozen a player may draw the top card to meld with only one natural card plus a wild card, or he may draw it to add to a meld of his side.

When he takes the discard a player must show his entitlement to it by laying down the two or more cards from his hand that he wishes to meld with it, and placing the top discard with them. If making an initial meld, he must also make further melds from his hand to achieve his minimum count. Only when he has satisfied those requirements does he take the whole of the rest of the discard pile into his hand (this is obligatory). He may now make all the melds he likes from the cards originally in his hand and/or originally in the discard pile, and finally discard. Play then passes to the next player.

The discard pile cannot be taken when a wild card or a black trey is uppermost.

Going out A player *goes out* when he gets rid of all the cards in his hand by melding them. He may not do so unless his side has at least one canasta. In going out a player can make a final discard or not, as he wishes.

Going out concealed A player may go out with a *concealed hand* if he melds all his cards in one turn, not having melded previously. He must have the requirement of a complete canasta, but is not obliged to fulfil a minimum count. In going out concealed he may not add to his partner's melds.

Permission Before making any melds on his turn a player may ask his partner if he may go out. His partner's reply of 'Yes' or 'No' binds him to that decision. If the answer is 'Yes' and he discovers he cannot go out, the other side scores 100 points.

When a player goes out play ends and the deal is scored. If the last card of the stock is drawn before any player goes out, play continues while each player in turn takes and melds the card discarded by his right-hand opponent. When the stock is exhausted a player is obliged to take the previous discard if he can add it to an existing meld. Discarding so that the next player must keep the game going is called *forcing*. When a player does not take the discard play ends.

Should the last card of the stock be a red trey, the player drawing it cannot meld or discard: play ends.

Scoring

1. A side that goes out scores:

a) the point values of the cards in its melds
b) for each red trey, 100 (if having all four, 800)
c) for each natural canasta, 500
d) for each mixed canasta, 300
e) for going out, 100
f) for going out with concealed hand, another 100

From this total is deducted the point values of the cards in the hand of the player whose partner went out.

2. The opponents of the side that went out calculate their score in the same way, except that if the side did not meld, the value of its red treys is deducted. The point values of cards held in both partners' hands are also deducted. It follows that a side can end a deal with a minus score.

When the game ends with neither side going out, as described above, the scores of both sides are calculated as under (2) above.

Game is of 5,000 points. All deals are played out, even if one side has clearly passed 5,000. If both pass 5,000 on the same deal, the higher total wins. Settlement is on the difference between the two totals.

The score for each side should be kept for each deal together with a running total. It is a side's cumulative total at the end of each deal which determines its minimum count for an initial meld, as specified above, for the next deal.

Strategy

The chief aim is to make canastas, and a player should be trying to take a large discard pile and begin as many melds as possible. It is wise, however, not to leave oneself at the mercy of opponents by leaving too few cards in the hand. If a discard pile looks as if it might be vital, and it is frozen, one would want to have as many pairs as possible in the hand to be able to take it.

One should not make safe discards, like black treys, which have the effect of freezing the pack for one's left-hand opponent, too readily. It is better to retain these for as long as possible to be certain of a safe discard when it is vital.

The side that wins the first discard pile is on the offensive and should try to prevent the opponents getting a pile. It might even pay to discard from long holdings if they appear safe. A side which loses the first discard pile, on the other hand, might find its best policy is to attempt to go out quickly and try to catch their opponents with unmelded cards.

Canasta for two players

The only differences in the rules for two-handed ·Canasta (apart from those relating to partners) are as follows:

a) Each player is dealt 15 cards.
b) When a player draws from stock, he draws two cards, but he discards only one.
c) To go out, a player needs two canastas.

Canasta for three players

In three-handed Canasta each player plays for himself and is dealt 13 cards. Otherwise the rules are for the game described, except of course those that relate to partners.

Samba

Samba is a form of Canasta which can be played by the same number of players as the parent game. The differences from the parent game of Canasta are as follows:

Cards Three packs are used, with six Jokers, making 162 cards.
Dealing Each player receives 15 cards.
Draw When drawing from stock, a player takes two cards but discards only one.
Sequences Sequences can be melded. Three or more cards of the same suit and in sequence (Ace high, 4 low) constitute a valid meld. Cards have the same value as before in assessing the count for an initial meld. Sequences can be added to, as other melds. A sequence of seven is a *samba*, which cannot be added to and so is turned face down. A samba cannot include a wild card. For the purposes of going out a samba ranks as a canasta, and its worth in the final score is 1,500.
Wild cards No meld may contain more than two wild cards.
Adding to a canasta It is not permitted to add wild cards to a

canasta, only natural cards. The discard pile cannot be taken by adding its top card to a canasta.

Duplicate melds A side may make two or more melds of cards of the same rank, and these can be combined by either partner on his turn.

Taking the discard pile The discard pile may be taken only by melding its top card with a natural pair from hand, or, when it is not frozen, by adding its top card to a meld on the table. It cannot be taken by using the top card to make a sequence meld, which must be entirely from hand.

Red treys If one side has all six red treys they count 1,000 in the final score. Red treys count as plus scores only for a side having two canastas (a samba rates as a canasta for this purpose, as it does for going out).

Going out A side must have two canastas (see previous sentence) to go out. The score for going out is 200, with no extra for a concealed hand.

Game Game is to 10,000.

Initial meld The minimum count for an initial meld remains at 120 until a side has scored 7,000 points. If a side starts a deal with 7,000 points or more, its minimum count is 150.

CASINO

Casino is an old game from Italy and bears similarities to the game of Scopa, played there with a 40-card pack. The name is based on the word for a gambling hall, although in English it has often appeared mistakenly as 'Cassino'. Although regarded by the initiated as a children's game, it is a good game which offers considerable scope for skill.

Players
Casino is a game for two players. It can be played by three, or by four in two partnerships, as described later.

Cards
The full standard pack of 52 cards is used. Ace counts as one, court or face cards have no numerical value, and 2s to 10s count their pip value.

Preliminaries
The players cut and higher deals (Ace low, King high). The dealer has the right to the last shuffle. Non-dealer cuts the cards before the deal. The dealer deals until the pack is exhausted.

Dealing
On the first deal, dealer gives two cards face down to his opponent, two cards face up to the centre of the table and two cards face down to himself. This he repeats, so that the play begins with four cards face up in the centre of the table and each player holding four cards

in his hand. The rest of the pack is laid aside for the moment.

These hands are played out, upon which the same dealer deals four cards to each player, two at a time as before, but this time none to the centre. These hands are played, and the process is repeated until the pack is exhausted. There are therefore six deals to the pack, and the dealer must announce 'Last' before the last one.

The game can be played so that those six deals conclude it, or it may be continued until a certain number of points are scored. In the latter case, the non-dealer becomes dealer for the second six deals. It is essential that each time the pack is exhausted the cards are thoroughly shuffled, because the game depends on certain combinations of cards.

The play
The object is to capture cards from the layout, and in so doing score points. Each player, beginning with non-dealer, plays a card in turn until both players have exhausted their four cards.

On his turn a player has the choice of four plays:
Pairing A card from the hand can be matched with a card or cards of the same rank on the table, enabling the player to take them and place them face down before him. For example, if there is a 7 or 7s on the table, a player may use a 7 in his hand to capture them, placing cards from hand and table before him. This is the only way court

cards can be captured, e.g. a Queen from hand can capture a Queen or Queens from the table.

Combining A card from hand can be used to capture two or more cards from the table if its pip total equals the sum of the pip totals of the captured cards. For example, a 6 can capture two 3s, a 4 and a 2, a 5 and an Ace, a 3, 2, and Ace, etc. As with pairing a player can pick up more than one combination with the same card, e.g. an 8 can pick up 4, 4 and 6, 2, or it could pick up an 8 (pairing) and 4, 4.

Building A player may play a card from hand to the layout to make up a total that he can take on his next turn. For example, a player holding a 7 and a 2 in his hand, may play the 2 to a 5 in the layout, saying 'Building 7s' and take the two cards on his next turn with his 7. A player must hold the card enabling him to take the build – he cannot build the 2 to the 5 unless he holds a 7.

However, he need not capture the build on his next turn. He may prefer to capture another card first, or if his opponent makes a build which he himself can capture he may capture that, leaving his own build for the following turn.

He might also prefer to create a multiple build. For instance, having built 7 as described above, he might be able to build another 7 by placing, say, an Ace from hand onto a 6 on the table. He will then be able to take both builds with his 7 on his following turn.

A player can also make a multiple build on a single card. For example, a player holding two 5s, with another in the layout, might add one of his 5s to that in the lay-

out and announce 'Building 5s', taking both on his next turn with his remaining 5. Similarly, if holding two 5s and with a 3 and a 2 in the layout, he can combine the 3 and 2 and add his first 5, saying 'Building 5s' and collect the lot next turn.

A player can also increase a build. For example if a player plays a 5 to a 4, announcing 'Building 9s' and he also has in his hand an Ace and a 10, he can on his next turn increase the build to 10 by playing his Ace, taking the whole build the following turn with his 10. No build can be further built beyond 10, of course, since 10 is the highest value card, and a player must hold the card which will allow him to take the build on his next turn.

A build is not the property only of the player making it. A player building a 2 on a 6, for example, announcing 'Building 8s' might find that his opponent has an 8 and takes the build before him. Similarly, his opponent might increase the build. In the present case, for example, if the opponent held a 2 and a 10, he can play the 2 to the layout announcing 'Building 10s', taking the build on his next turn. The player who made the first build to 8, now finds that his 8 is useless; increasing an opponent's build is clearly a good play.

However, it is not permitted to increase a multiple build. For example, if a 5 is paired with a 2, and a 4 with a 3 by a player building 7s, it is not possible to increase the build on one of these pairs by adding another card. Note that if a player adds a 2 to another 2 and announces 'Building 2s', this is a multiple build and cannot be increased. If, on the other hand the player adding a 2 to another had announced 'Building 4s', this is a simple build and can be increased by any card of 6 or lower (always with the proviso that the builder holds a card to take it).

A build can be increased only by a card from hand, not from the table. Therefore, a player making a build knows that his opponent has one turn to capture it or increase it, before he can take it himself.

To repeat: a player making or increasing a build that is not taken or increased by his opponent must have a card to capture that build. While the build remains in the layout, and the card remains unplayed, he is not allowed the fourth option of play, which is to trail.

Trailing If a player on his turn cannot pair, combine, build or increase a build, as described, he must trail, that is add a card from his hand face up to the table layout. He can trail even if he is able to pair, combine or build, unless he has a build already in the layout, as mentioned above.

Trailing is the way that the layout is replenished. If all the cards in the layout are taken (called a *sweep*) then the next player has no choice but to trail. It follows that the number of cards in the layout, after the initial deal of four, changes with each play.

Scoring
The object of the play is to capture the majority of the cards, with particular attention to scoring cards. The points to be scored are as follows:

cards (for capturing the majority of the 52 cards): 3
spades (for capturing the majority of the 13 spades): 1
big casino (for capturing the ◆10): 2
little casino (for capturing the ♠2): 1
Aces (for capturing an Ace): 1 point each

There are thus a total of 11 points to be won in this fashion, although cards is not scored if each player takes 26 each.

A further point is scored by each sweep recorded. A player scores a sweep each time he makes a capture which clears the layout of cards. A sweep is recorded by turning one of the cards taken face up instead of face down, so that at the end of the play each face-up card represents a point for sweep.

When the last card is played any cards remaining on the table in the layout belong to the last person who made a capture. They count in the calculation for cards and spades, but this does not count as a sweep.

A game can be played as one deal, in which case the player with the majority of points wins, or it can be played to 21 points. If the latter is chosen, 'counting out' might be allowed. By this convention a player can claim the game as soon as he has scored 21 points, e.g. if he begins the deal with 18 and takes big casino and an Ace. If counting out is not allowed the points at the end of a deal are added to each player's score in the order set out above, from cards down to sweeps, a player winning as soon as he totals 21.

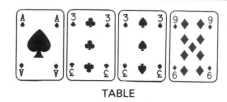

TABLE

DEALER   NON-DEALER

The deal at the beginning of the hand of Casino described in the text.

Irregularity

Most irregularities in this game can be seen immediately and corrected at the table, e.g. that of a player attempting to capture illegally. But if it transpires that a player made a build without having a card to capture it then he loses the game.

Strategy

A good memory is required, as playing well depends on memorizing the cards played, so that the ranks of those to come are known. A good player will also keep count of the cards and spades won by him and his opponent.

It is best at the beginning to try to take as many cards as possible with each card in the hand, while at the same time trying for spades. However, two non-spades are worth one spade, at least until you are confident that you, or your opponent, have the majority for cards, when you can concentrate on spades.

An Ace or a casino held in the hand which cannot be paired or built, should be kept for the final trail, particularly by non-dealer, who thus gives dealer only one chance to capture it before he himself has four further cards with which to capture it.

Example hand

The two hands and the layout are dealt as in the illustration. Non-dealer makes the first play.

1. Non-dealer takes the ♣3, ♠A 3 with his ♣7, an excellent start.
2. Dealer trails ♦ Q.
3. Non-dealer trails ♦ 6.
4. Dealer trails ♣5.
5. Non-dealer takes ♦ 6 with ♥ 6.
6. Dealer trails ♠K.
7. Non-dealer trails ♥ 8.
8. Dealer trails ♠J.

Dealer deals a further four cards to each hand. The situation now is as in the next illustration.

TABLE

DEALER

NON-DEALER

9. Non-dealer plays ♥A to ♥8 and adds the ♦9 from the table, announcing 'Building 9s'.

10. The ♦9 in the layout which duplicated the build of 9 for non-dealer, saved him from an unlucky play. Had the ♥A been added to the ♥8 in a simple build, dealer could have added his ♦A to announce 'Building 10', capturing on his next turn four cards including an Ace and big casino. As it is, he must take the ♦Q with his ♠Q, intending to build his ♣4, ♦A on the ♣5 later.

11. Non-dealer plays his ♣9 to take his multiple build.

12. Dealer plays ♣4 to ♣5, announcing 'Building 9', confident that non-dealer does not hold another 9.

13. Non-dealer captures ♠J with ♥J.

14. Dealer plays ♦A to the ♣5 4, announcing 'Building 10'.

15. Non-dealer captures ♠K with ♥K.

16. Dealer captures his build of 10 with ♦10. This removes all the cards from the layout, so dealer achieves a sweep and turns face up

The position after the first cards have been played and another set dealt.

one of the cards he takes to signify this.

Dealer now deals four cards to each hand again, and non-dealer's first play must be to trail, as there are no cards in the layout, and so on.

In this game so far, dealer has taken six cards to non-dealer's 14, so non-dealer is doing well for the 3 points for cards. Dealer has one spade to non-dealer's four, so non-dealer is well ahead here, too. Dealer has scored 2 points for big casino. Dealer has 1 point for Aces and non-dealer 2. Dealer has 1 point so far for a sweep. Non-dealer has the overall advantage, but dealer has scored 4 points already.

Variants

Because a sweep is rather fortuitous, some players do not allow a point for a sweep.

Three-handed Casino This is not a good game, because the dealer and the eldest hand have an advantage over the player in the middle. Each player receives four cards as before, with four cards in the initial layout. Eldest hand plays first and dealer last. Should there be a tie on cards or spades, no points are scored. The game is usually played to 11 points, but a fairer game might be for each player to deal once.

Partnership Casino Four players can play in two partnerships, partners sitting opposite each other. Partners' captures are combined. The play is as for the two-handed game, and each player must observe the rules, e.g. a player seeing his partner build 9, cannot himself build a 9 for his partner to take, without holding a 9 himself.

Each deal can be game in itself, or a game might be to 21 points, as in the two-handed game.

Royal Casino This is often said to be a better game than the parent game. It is more complicated and requires even more concentration. The only difference to the parent game is that court cards, instead of not having a value, are given the following: Jack 11, Queen 12 and King 13. Thus they can be used for building and capturing builds, e.g. 7, 4, 2 might be captured with a King. In addition, Ace may be counted as one or 14 at the discretion of the player. Scoring is as for the parent game.

Spade Casino This brings a variation to the scoring which can be applied to all the above games. Instead of there being one point for spades, each spade is worth one point itself, except for Ace, Jack and 2 (little casino), each of which is worth two points. Thus the total points to be won in a deal increases to 24, plus sweeps, and it is convenient to play the game to 61 points, which allows it to be scored on a crib board.

Draw Casino This brings a variation to the dealing which is applicable to all above versions. After the first deal and layout the remaining cards are placed face down in the centre to form a stock. Thereafter each player, when he plays a card, draws a replacement from the stock pile, so that each player's hand remains constant at four cards. When the stock is exhausted each player plays his last four cards as usual.

CINCH

Cinch is a game in the All Fours family with the added attraction of bidding. It began to be very popular around Denver and Chicago towards the end of the nineteenth century, and was taken up in many places in America. It is also called Double Pedro and High Five. It is a game of skill which lost a lot of its popularity with the growth of Bridge, but remains an excellent game for players not wishing to plunge into the intricacies of Bridge conventions.

Players

Cinch is a game for four players, playing as two partnerships. It is possible to play with from two to six, as described later, but the game is not so good as with four.

Cards

The full pack of 52 cards is used. The cards rank from Ace (high) to 2 (low), with one exception. There is a trump suit, and the 5 of the suit of the same colour as the trump suit is also a trump, ranking between the 5 and 4 of the trump suit. Thus if hearts are trumps, the trump suit in order of rank is

♥A K Q J 10 9 8 7 6 5 ♦5 ♥4 3 2

The 5 of the trump suit is called the *right pedro*, the 5 of the same colour is called the *left pedro*. Cards in the trump suit have a value to the player winning them in tricks as follows: right pedro 5 points, left pedro 5 points, Ace (high) 1 point, 2 (low) 1 point, Jack (Jack) 1 point, 10 (game) 1 point. Thus 14 points are at stake on each deal.

Preliminaries

Players draw a card each, and the two highest play against the two lowest, highest having choice of seat and also becoming dealer. Any players drawing cards of equal rank draw again to determine precedence. The dealer may shuffle last, and the player to his right cuts the pack before the deal.

Dealing

The dealer deals nine cards to each player, beginning with the player on his left, in bundles of three.

Bidding

Beginning with eldest hand (to left of dealer), each player makes a bid, or passes. A bid is made by a player naming a number of points that he is contracting to make in play, with partner's help, and naming his own trump suit. Each bid must be higher than the previous one. The minimum bid is one, and the maximum bid is, of course, 14, the maximum points available. There is only one round of bidding. After the bidding the highest bidder names the trump suit. He is not allowed to consult with his partner, nor must signals be made. Should the first three players pass, the dealer names the trump suit without the obligation of making a contract.

Discarding

The trick-taking part of the game will commence with each player holding six cards. The next stage is therefore a discarding stage, but it also offers each player the opportunity of drawing new cards. Beginning with eldest hand, each player discards as many cards as he wishes, face up, and asks the dealer to give him the number of cards necessary to bring his hand up to six cards. These are dealt from the top of the pack. A player must make at least three discards, in which case he draws no new cards. No player may discard a trump, unless he is dealt seven or more trumps, when he has no choice but to discard at least one.

When it is the dealer's turn to discard the procedure is different. He may *rob the pack*. By this means he is entitled to look through the remainder of the pack and take any cards he wishes into his hand. If between his hand and the remainder of the pack there are more than six trumps, so that he cannot take all into his hand, he must show the remainder so that all players know which trump or trumps is outstanding.

The play

The object is to take tricks containing the scoring cards, so that the contract is either made (the object of the contracting side), or not (the object of the opponents).

The player who decided the trump suit (the *maker*) leads to the first trick. Subsequently the winner of each trick leads to the next. If a trump is led, a player must follow suit if he can. If a plain suit is led, a player cannot discard if he holds a card of that suit, but he may trump even if he is able to follow suit.

Scoring

When all six tricks have been played out each side counts the number of points won. If the making side has made its contract, i.e. at least the number of points bid, the side with the higher total wins the difference of the totals. For example, a side contracting to make 11 points and making 12 will score the difference between 12 and the opponents' two, i.e. 10. It is possible for the making side not to win the points. For example a side contracting to make 6 and making exactly 6 does not score: opponents make 2.

If the contracting side does not make its contract the other side scores their total in points plus the amount of the bid. For example, if a side contracts to make 11 and makes 9, the opposing side scores 5 for the points it made plus 11, the amount of the bid, i.e. 16.

If all players pass and dealer makes trumps without a contract, then each side scores the points it makes in the play. The winning side is the first to reach a total of 51 points.

Strategy

A side making its contract and taking all 14 points is credited with 14 to its score, the maximum for a making side. A side defeating a contract, on the other hand, scores at least 15. So it is bad policy to overbid – it hands points to the opposition.

Since all the cards with points values are trumps, it follows that no points can be won with plain-suit cards. Cinch is virtually a one-suit game, plain suits being useful only for getting off lead. The lead is not an advantage except to the side having master trumps. Therefore, low cards in side suits can be more useful than high. Playing fourth to a trick is the best position. Since only tricks containing scoring cards are worth winning, it is more valuable to hold high trumps than long trumps.

In practice, players often discard all their non-trumps in the hope of picking up the high trumps in the draw. The play frequently is concentrated on capturing the pedros. It is dangerous to allow a player in fourth position to a trick to be in a position to win it with a 5 of trumps, since that contributes 5 points to his side, so a player in third position will often trump higher than

the 5 to prevent this happening. This is called *cinching* a trick.

In the bidding phase, as each player is allowed only one bid, the first bidder in each partnership should attempt to give information to his partner. Systems of bidding have been invented, of which the following have become conventional:

with a 5, bid five to show it;
With A x x or A x x x, bid six;
with Ace and King, even without other cards in the suit, bid seven;
with A K J x x or better, bid eleven;
with A K Q x, bid eleven or twelve.

Example hand
Four hands are dealt by South as in

The deal for the hand of Cinch described in the text.

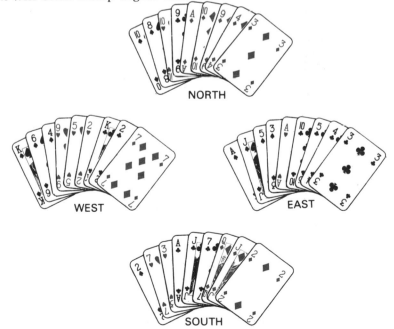

NORTH

WEST

EAST

SOUTH

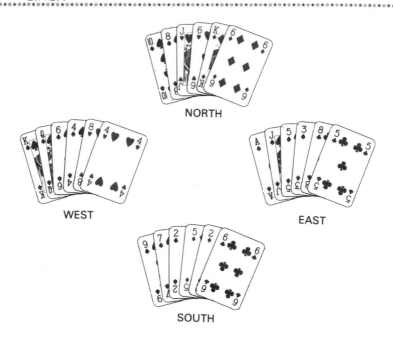

NORTH

WEST

EAST

SOUTH

The hands after discarding and drawing.

the first illustration. West has the first bid, and since he holds a 5 bids five. North holds A x x x x in diamonds and makes a bid of six. East holds an excellent hand in spades, with Ace, Jack and both pedros. He knows his partner's 5 is no use, but wishes to play this hand in spades, so bids eleven. There is no point in bidding ten, since he would need to take both pedros to score ten points, and he is sure to make ♠A, so if he makes ten he must make eleven.

South decides he cannot advance on eleven.

East announces spades as trumps.

West, North and East discard all their non-trumps, drawing three, six and one card respectively.

West draws: ♠Q ♥ 8 4
North draws:♥ J 6♦ K 6
East draws: ♣8

South takes four cards, robbing the pack of ♠9 7♦ 5 ♣6.

The hands are now as in the second illustration.

East leads the ♣8, and West plays ♠6 as an insurance against North holding a pedro. He knows that he and his partner hold at least nine of the 14 trumps, and would not mind if North took a point with ♠10 or ♠J. North would have to lead, and with his ♠K Q West knows his side controls the next two or three tricks. North holds his ♠10, hoping for something better than 1 point for *game*. On winning the first trick West decides to give his partner the good news by leading ♠K. The play proceeds:

	East	South	West	North
1.	♣8	♣6	♠6	♦K
2.	♠5	♠7	♠K̲	♠8
3.	♣5	♠9	♠Q̲	♣10

East-West have already collected 11 points, and nothing can stop them making all the rest.

4. ♠A̲   ♠2   ♠4   ♥J

East has the only trumps left and makes them.

East–West, having made their contract, score the difference in points between the two sides, 14 points.

It is not good strategy to lead out big trumps like West did without being certain that you can clear out the opposition trumps. If the opposition hold a pedro and can follow without conceding it, the tactic will fail.

Variants
In some schools the dealer must discard before robbing the pack. This increases the chances that there will be a trump not in play, and if so, the dealer must expose it so that all players are aware of it. *Cut-throat Cinch* Cinch can be played by from two to six, each player playing for himself. With two or three players the dealer does not rob the pack, he discards and draws as the other players.

The scoring with two players is as for the two sides in partnership cinch. With three to six players, when a contract is made, the side with most tricks (either the maker or each of the other players) scores the difference between the two totals. If a player fails to make his contract each of his opponents

scores the amount of the bid plus the number of tricks made by himself individually. With five or six players, each player is dealt six cards only, and therefore receives in the draw the same number of cards as he discards.

Auction Cinch This is the most interesting version of the game for five or six players. (It is also known as *Razzle Dazzle*). Each player plays for himself. Six cards are dealt to each player, in bundles of three, and each player bids as in Cinch. When the highest bidder names the trump suit all players in turn discard all their non-trumps and draw the same number of cards to bring their hands back to six each. The high bidder, or maker, then names a trump not in his own hand (usually the highest trump he is missing) and the holder of that card acknowledges it, and he and the maker become partners against the rest. They do not change seats, and may in fact be sitting next to each other. The scoring is as in Cinch. If the contract is made each of the players on the side with most points scores the difference in points won by his side and the opponents (it might be the contracting side or the others who score). If the contract fails then each player in the non-contracting side scores the number of the contract plus the number of points he himself made individually.

A variant of Auction Cinch requires that the holder of the card named by the maker does not acknowledge it. Otherwise the game is the same – he still plays in partnership with the maker, but until he plays the card named, only he knows who he is. This version brings some tension and surprise to the play.

Cinch with a widow This game for four players is the basic game with a variation on the drawing procedure. Each of the four players is dealt 13 cards: the usual nine plus a widow of four, which is dealt after the first bundle of three and which remains face down in front of him. After the usual bidding each player picks up his widow and adds it to his hand. The maker then names the trump suit, each player discards seven cards to bring his hand to six, and play proceeds as before. If a player is forced to discard a trump he must show it to all players.

Cinch with a widow for six players is a game in which players play in three teams of two, each player sitting opposite his partner. Eight cards are dealt to each player, the last four being placed face down in the centre to form a widow. The highest bidder picks up the widow, names the trump suit, and then discards six cards to bring his hand to six. All other players discard two cards. Play proceeds as usual. When a contract is made each team on the side with most points makes the difference in points. When a contract fails the two non-contracting teams each make the value of the contract plus the number of points made individually.

CLOCK

This very simple **patience** or **solitaire** does not find its way into many books of card games but is included here because it can be understood and enjoyed by any child old enough to play cards at all.

The play

Only one pack is required. It is shuffled and laid out in the form of a clock face. Twelve packets of four cards are dealt face down in a circle to represent the twelve numbers on a clock face. The last four cards are placed face down in the centre of the clock face.

_____

A game of Clock in progress.

Play begins with the top card of the central pack being turned over, and placed face up behind the pile at its appropriate place on the dial. Jacks and Queens naturally go at 11 and 12 o'clock, Aces at 1 o'clock, and Kings to the centre.

The game is won if all cards are turned over before the fourth King appears. The appearance of the fourth King, except as the last card, loses the game, as there is no other card left in the centre pack with which to continue.

A game in progress is illustrated. The 3s and 6s are already exposed. The next card to be played is the ♦7, which is packed on the ♠7, the top card exposed from the 7 pile, and played to its place, and so on.

Comet

Comet is believed to have been invented around 1759, when Halley's Comet reappeared as predicted by Edmund Halley 50 years earlier, and 'comet' became a fashionable tag for all sorts of inventions. A variant, called Commit probably through illiteracy, is described later.

Players

The parent game is for two, but it can be played equally well by three, four or five, as described under *Variants*.

Cards

Two identical packs are required. All the Aces are rejected and all the red cards are separated into one pack and the black cards into another. Then a red 9 and a black 9 are interchanged. Thus two 48-card packs are formed, each with a 9 of the 'wrong' colour, and the two packs are used alternately, deal by deal. The 9 of the opposite colour is called the *comet*, and its function is similar to that of a wild card. The cards are ranked from King (high) to 2 (low), and suits are irrelevant.

Preliminaries

Players cut for deal, and the lower is dealer, who shuffles. Non-dealer cuts.

Dealing

Eighteen cards are dealt to each player, three at a time, and the remaining 12 are set aside face down – they take no further part.

The play

Non-dealer plays any card he wishes to the centre of the table and continues to play so long as he can add cards in ascending sequence, announcing the cards as he lays them and announcing the number at which he stops. For example, he may lead 7, 8, 9 announcing the numbers and then saying 'without 10' or 'no 10'. The turn then passes to the dealer, who must continue the sequence by playing (to follow the example) 10, followed by Jack, etc, until he in turn cannot go, at which the turn passes back and so on.

If a player on his turn cannot continue the sequence he says 'pass' and the player who effected the *stop* begins a fresh sequence by playing another card or cards of his choice. A King is always a stop.

Both players' cards are played to the one central pile, face up, and neither player may look at the cards already played.

If a player holds four cards of the same rank, or three 9s, with or without the comet, he can play them simultaneously if he wishes. For example, he may announce: '4, 5, four 6s, 7, without 8', leaving the next player to continue, if he can, with an 8.

The comet can be played as a card of any rank the holder wishes and acts as a stop. But it can only be played in turn, i.e. it cannot be played to stop an opponent continuing a sequence. The comet also has additional value in scoring.

A player must play a card if possible, whether the previous card has been played by himself or opponent, except he may reserve the comet if that is the only card he can play.

The object of the game is to get rid of all the cards in the hand.

Scoring

The winner scores the total number of pips left in his opponent's hand when he goes out, the court cards counting 10 points each. If a player goes out while his opponent holds the comet he doubles his score. If a player goes out by playing the comet as his last card, he scores double, and if he goes out by playing the comet as a 9 he scores quadruple.

Strategy

One should try to get rid of duplicated cards first, but the most important thing is to remember which cards are stops for the opponent and to try to play cards up to them. Naturally, if the opponent is close to going out, it is advisable to get rid of as many cards as possible, particularly high-scoring ones, by playing off sequences.

Variants

Comet for three to five players With three players, each receives 12 cards in bundles of three, with 12 in the dead hand; with four players, each receives ten in bundles of two with eight dead; and with five each receives nine in bundles of three, with three dead.

The player to left of dealer plays first, and when a sequence comes to a stop the player to the left of the last player has the option of con-tinuing, if he passes the next and so on. If everybody passes to the last player he begins a new sequence.

Commit This is a variant for from three to seven players played with the standard 52-card pack from which the ♦8 is removed. Aces are left in, the cards ranking from King (high) to Ace (low). The ♦9 is the comet. It is usually played as a gambling game.

Cards are dealt one at a time. With three players, each receives 15 cards, six remaining face down as dead cards. With four to seven players, the cards are dealt as far as possible to give each player an equal hand, the remainder being dead.

Before the deal, each player puts an agreed stake, representing one unit, to the centre.

Play proceeds as for Comet, except that suits are now relevant, and only one card can legally continue each sequence, e.g. the ♣4 must be followed by the ♣5. Kings and the ♦7 are natural stops and other stops are created by the dead cards.

The holder of comet may play it whenever he might otherwise have had to say 'without'. When he plays the comet he can continue to play either by following to the card the comet represented, or by following with the ♦10, the natural card to follow the ♦9.

For example, the holder of the comet has followed the ♥3 by playing ♥4. If he wishes he can now play the comet (representing ♥5) and continue with either ♥6 or ♦10. If he has neither of these cards and says 'without', the player to his left may play either, and so on. As soon as one or other of the two cards is played the sequence continues from there.

A player who plays the comet receives two chips, or units of stake money, from each of the other players and a player who plays a King receives one chip. The player who goes out first receives all the chips in the pool, plus one from any player caught holding a King and two from any player holding the comet.

Coon can

Coon Can derives its name from a Spanish game which probably dates back to the seventeenth century called Conquian (con quien = with whom). It became popular in Mexico and spread to the United States, where it is also known as Double Rum because of its similarity to Rummy and because it is played with two packs.

Players

Any number up to eight may play, each playing for himself. It is best for five to eight players, four or fewer probably prefering Rummy (q.v.).

Cards

Two full packs including Jokers are required (i.e. 106 cards), with cards ranking from King (high) to Ace (low). The Jokers are wild cards.

Preliminaries

Cards are cut to decide dealer, and the lowest deals. The dealer shuffles last and the player on his right cuts.

Dealing

Ten cards are dealt one at a time to each player. The remaining cards (the stock) are placed face down in the centre of the table and the top card is turned face upwards and placed alongside it to begin a discard pile.

The play

Each player, beginning with the player to the left of the dealer, plays in turn. He must take into his hand either the top card of the stock or the top card of the discard pile, and discard a card from his hand face up to the discard pile. Between drawing a card and discarding one he may meld, and/or add to melds already on the table, whether his own or opponents'.

A meld is a set of matching cards, either three or four of the same rank or three or more of the same suit in sequence.

The object is to get rid of all ten cards in one's hand by melding.

A Joker can be used in a meld to represent any card. A Joker which is melded to form one end of a sequence may be moved to the other end by a player who, on his turn, can replace the Joker with the card it represents. For example, if a melded sequence is ♦4 5 6 Joker, a player holding the ♦7 can play it in place of the Joker, moving the Joker to represent the ♦3. A Joker can be moved only once, and when moved is placed sideways in the sequence to show that it cannot be moved again. A Joker in the middle of a sequence, for example, ♠9 10 Joker Queen, cannot be moved, neither can a Joker used in a set of cards of equal rank.

If the stock is exhausted before the game has been won, and the next player does not wish to take the card on the discard pile, he may turn over the discard pile to form a new stock, drawing the top card. But if the stock is exhausted a second time play is ended, and all players, instead of paying the winner, pay into a pool according to the cards they hold, the pool going to the winner of the next hand.

Players pay the winner (or the pool) one unit for every pip on the unmelded cards in their hands, Jokers counting 15, Aces 11 and court cards 10.

Variant

Some players play so that any player who replaces a Joker at the end of a sequence, instead of moving the Joker to the other end of the sequence, may take it into his hand for use by himself.

CRIBBAGE

Cribbage (often called just Crib) is believed to be an invention of Sir John Suckling (1609–42), an English poet. It is an adaptation of an older game called Noddy. Scoring is kept on a Cribbage board, which is also called a Noddy board. The game is unique in its scoring, and is considered one of the best of all for two players. It is still played in its original form, in which each player was dealt five cards. Nowadays it is much more common to play with six cards in the hand, so this version is described as the main game, the five-card version being described at the end as a *variant*.

Players
Cribbage is an excellent game for two players. It has been adapted satisfactorily for three players and for four players in partnerships of two, as explained later.

Cards
The full pack of 52 cards is used, cards ranking from King (high) to Ace (low). Cribbage is a counting game in which King, Queen, Jack, 10 are valued as ten, Ace as one and other cards as their pip count.

A Cribbage board (illustrated) is usually used for keeping score (it can be done with pencil and paper). The Cribbage board contains two groups of 60 holes, one for each player, with usually at one end a central hole available to either player. Each player scores on his own side of the board by means of two pegs. After his first

score, he scores by advancing the second peg the relevant number of holes ahead of the first, so that the two pegs leap-frog each other round the board. Game is either of 61 or 121 points, so that the player who moves his pegs either once or twice round his side of the board and claims the last hole is the winner. Scoring is thus called *pegging*.

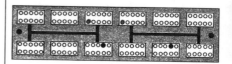

A Cribbage or Noddy board, traditional for scoring at Cribbage and sometimes used for other games.

Preliminaries
Cards are cut, and the player with the lower card deals. He shuffles and non-dealer cuts.

Dealing
Dealer deals six cards to each player, one at a time, face down, beginning with non-dealer. The deal alternates on each hand, as the dealer has a distinct advantage.

The play
Each player examines his cards and *lays away* two cards face down. The four cards form the *crib* (often called the *box*) and are placed aside in a pile until later. They create, in effect, a third hand which in its turn will belong to the dealer.

After laying-off, non-dealer cuts the pack and dealer turns over the top card of the lower half and places it face up on top of the re-united pack. This card is known as the *start*. If it is a Jack, dealer immediately pegs 2 points (*two for his heels*).

Non-dealer now lays his first card (players do not combine their cards but lay them in front of them as play progresses, because each player needs his hand again later), and announces its value (court cards count as ten, as stated earlier). The dealer then plays a card, announcing the cumulative count, and the players continue to play alternately up to but not exceeding a count of 31. If a player adds a card that brings the total exactly to 31 he pegs 2 (*thirty-one for two*).

If a player is unable to play a card without exceeding 31 he says 'Go' or 'No'. His opponent then continues laying cards until he too cannot play another without exceeding 31. The last player to play a card pegs 1 for *last* (unless, of course, he brings the total to exactly 31, when he pegs 2).

The opponent of the player who played the last card now lays another card, beginning a new count which starts at zero. It is customary to turn over the cards already played, so that the new count can be clearly seen. The player who plays the last card of all pegs 1 (it follows that the dealer is certain to peg at least 1).

During the play, certain combinations also allow a player to peg, as follows:

Fifteen A player who lays a card to bring the count to 15 pegs two (announced as 'Fifteen two').

Pair and pair-royal A player who lays a card of the same rank as the previous card pegs 2 (*two for a pair*). A player who lays a third card of the same rank pegs 6 for a pair-royal, and he who lays the fourth pegs 12 for double pair royal. Although all court cards have a value of ten, only cards of the exact rank form a pair, e.g. Jack and Jack are a pair, King and Queen are not.

Run or sequence A player who plays a card which, with the two or more played immediately beforehand makes a sequence, pegs 1 for each card in the sequence. Suits do not matter in the sequence, nor does the order of the cards. Thus 3, 5, 4 played in that order constitute a run and the player who laid the 4 announces 'Twelve, and three for the run'. If the next player lays 2 or 6 he pegs four for the run. If he lays another 3, he can still score three for the run 5, 4, 3 (and incidentally two for fifteen). He would announce 'fifteen two, and three for the run is five').

These combinations are all scored, even if only one player is laying i.e. when the other cannot go, or is out of cards. No combination can carry over from one count of 31 to another however. A run cannot contain two cards of the same rank, e.g. 3, 4, 5, 5 is not a run. However, 4, 3, 5, 4 is two runs, the player who laid the 5 scoring three for a run and the player who followed with the second 4 also scoring three for a run.

After the play as described, each player gathers up his hand and scores further for the *show*.

Non-dealer shows and pegs first, dealer second, and then dealer turns over the crib which is his, and scores for that in the same way.

For the show, the start is combined with each hand (there is no need to move the start from its place on the pack). Each hand in effect is of five cards. Combinations are scored as follows:

Fifteen For each combination of two or more cards which total fifteen a player pegs 2;
Pair For each pair a player pegs 2;
Run For each run of three or more cards a player pegs the number of cards in the run;
Flush For four cards in the hand in the same suit, a player pegs 4 (one for each card). If the starter is also in the same suit he scores 5. A flush is scored in the crib only if all five cards are of the same suit.
His nob A player who holds the Jack of the same suit as the start pegs *one for his nob*.

Every separate combination scores separately, i.e. a card can be used more than once in different combinations. For example, the illustration shows two hands and the start. Hand A contains six combinations making 15 (each of the three court cards combined with

♠5, and each of them combined with ♥ 5). It also contains one pair (♠5 and ♥ 5) and the ♥ J scores one for his nob.

Hand B contains two combinations making 15 (♠8 with each of ♣7 and ♦ 7), two runs of four (5, 6, 7, 8 twice) and one pair.

It is customary for players to score hands by announcing 15s first, runs next, then pairs and last flushes. In the usual style among Cribbage players, player A would announce: 'Fifteen two, fifteen four, fifteen six, fifteen eight, fifteen ten, fifteen twelve, three for the run fifteen and two for the pair makes seventeen'. Player B would announce: 'Fifteen two, fifteen four, eight for the runs makes twelve and two for the pair makes fourteen'.
Muggins A player counts his hand aloud and displays it on the table, so it is up to his opponent to check and correct him if he claims too many. If a player claims fewer points than he is entitled to, his opponent may say 'Muggins' and score the missing points himself. This is not general, and players in new groups should ascertain if 'Muggins' is being played.

Scoring

The usual game is 121 points, i.e. twice round the Cribbage board and into the central hole. Scores are in order, i.e. his heels, the pegging

---

The two hands and the start discussed in the text.

 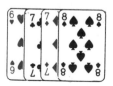

A   START   B

in the play, the non-dealer's hand, the dealer's hand, the crib hand. Thus if a player *goes out* during the pegging in play, the hands are not shown, or if non-dealer goes out with the points scored in the show of his hand, that ends the game, even though dealer might have points in his hand and crib which would give him more than the winner.

If a player wins before his opponent gets more than half-way round the board, i.e. does not reach 61, then the loser is *lurched*, and the winner scores two games. Some players like to play a short game, which is 61 up.

Strategy

Non-dealer should try to contribute to the crib non-matching cards, i.e. those not possible to make into a run or into multiple combinations of 15: King, 9 for example. On the other hand dealer should try to help his crib with cards like 8 7 or 3 2.

In the play, a safe start for non-dealer is a card of 4 or lower – it cannot be added to to make fifteen. If holding 3 2 either is a good lead, since if dealer lays a ten count the other will make fifteen. If holding a hand like 7 6 6 5 a 6 is a good lead. Any card from opponent between 4 and 8 will provide an opportunity to score. The opponent, of course, if he cannot lay 9 for a fifteen, will play a card away from the 6, e.g. a ten-count card would be safe.

Always watch the score, particularly near the end, when sacrificing a good hand to baulk opponent scoring might be the best play.

Example hand

Suppose non-dealer holds ♥K, ♠K, ♦Q, ♥8, ♦3 ♣2. His best choice is to lay off the ♦Q, ♥8 to crib, these being safe cards and leaving him with at least six points in his hand for the show.

Dealer holds ♥J, ♣8, ♥7, ♦6, ♠5, ♣4. He has two possible choices: ♣8, ♥7 would help his crib and leave him with seven

The deal for the example hand described in the text.

NON-DEALER

DEALER

CRIB

START

points; ♥J, ♠5 would also help, but leaves the ♣4 in his hand not contributing, so he chooses the former. The more 'active' cards in a hand, the better chance there is of additional scores with the start.

The start is then turned up. It is the ♥3. Thus the two hands, the start and the crib are as shown in the illustration.

The play proceeds as follows.

Non-dealer leads ♦3. Dealer decides to lay ♣4, announcing 'seven', since if non-dealer makes a run, he can add to it. Non-dealer lays ♣2, announcing 'nine, three for the run', and pegging three. Dealer could now play ♦6 for fifteen, but decides on ♠5, announcing 'fourteen, and four for the run'. He knows that non-dealer is quite likely to hold an Ace, in which case he could now peg seven (five for the run and two for fifteen) but as dealer holds the ♦6, he, too, could continue the run. As it happens, non-dealer does not hold an Ace, so lays ♥K, announcing 'twenty-four'. Dealer must now play ♦6, announcing 'thirty'. Non-dealer says 'no', dealer also says 'no', since neither can lay a card without the count exceeding 31, so dealer pegs one for last. They turn their cards over, non-dealer leads ♠K, announcing 'ten', and dealer ♥J, announcing 'twenty' and pegging another 1 for last.

Dealer pegged 6 in the play, to non-dealer's 3.

Non-dealer now pegs for his hand: 'Fifteen two, fifteen four, fifteen six, fifteen eight, two for a pair ten, two for a pair twelve'.

Dealer pegs for his hand: 'Fifteen two, fifteen four, four for a run, eight, one for his nob, nine'.

Dealer then pegs for his crib: 'Fifteen two, fifteen four, two for a pair is six'.

So after the first hand, dealer has pegged 21, non-dealer 15. Non-dealer now becomes dealer, collecting the cards and shuffling thoroughly. His opponent cuts and the game continues.

Variants

Five-card Cribbage For those wishing to play the traditional game, the differences from the above are as follows.

Each hand is dealt five cards only. Two are laid away to the crib, as before, so that the players' hands are of three cards, while the crib is of four.

The game is of 61 points (scoring is slower with the smaller hands). Because the first dealer has a bigger advantage than in the six-card game, non-dealer begins with a start of 3 points.

A flush, of course, counts only 3 in hand, 4 with the start, but it still scores 5 in the crib, since a flush can only be scored in crib if all five cards are of the same suit.

In five-card Cribbage, the crib is more valuable than the hands, having an extra card, so the strategy is even more concentrated on baulking the crib for non-dealer and helping it for dealer.

Three-handed Cribbage Crib can be played by three players, each playing for himself. The deal passes to the left, as does the turn to play. Each player is dealt five cards and dealer deals one card to the table to start the crib. Each player lays away one card to the crib, so the crib and all hands end as four cards each. The eldest hand (to left of dealer) cuts for the start.

When a player calls 'go', the next player to the left lays, and so on. The last player to lay scores the point for last, and the player to his left begins the new round.

The game is 61 up. Triangular Cribbage boards, and boards with an arm which pivots, have been produced for three-handed play but are rare, and it will probably be necessary to score with pencil and paper. At the show the hands are scored in the order eldest hand first, then the player on his left, then dealer, then crib.

Four-handed   Cribbage   Each player draws a card, and the lowest two play against the highest two. The drawer of the lowest card deals first. Partners sit opposite each other.

Five cards are dealt to each player. Each hand lays away one card to crib, so all hands are of four cards when play starts. Eldest hand cuts for the start, and leads. When a player calls 'go', the turn passes to the next player and so on. The last player to play pegs the point, and the player on his left begins the new round. The scores made by partners are pooled, so the usual Cribbage board is adequate for scoring. At the show the hands are scored in rotation, eldest hand first, crib last. There can be no discussion or collusion between partners. Game is 121 points.

Cribbage   Patience   Various **patience** or **solitaire** games based on Cribbage have been published. The author prefers this simple one of his own.

The cards are shuffled and dealt, one card at a time, into two hands of six cards, face down. The first hand is examined and two cards laid away to the crib. The second hand is then examined and two cards laid away from that. The top card of the pack is then turned over as the start, and the hands scored as they would be in the show at Cribbage.

The 13 cards used are then cast aside and two new hands dealt. Four rounds can thus be played, using all the cards in the pack. To win the player must score 100 points, and an astute player will win about 40 per cent of the trials. Extra satisfaction will be obtained by a player who scores 121 points.

CROSSWORD

This single-pack **patience** or **solitaire**, invented by the late George F. Hervey, resembles a crossword puzzle.

The 12 court cards (Kings, Queens, Jacks) are removed from the pack and laid aside for separate use. The rest of the pack of 40 cards is shuffled and held in the hand.

The play

The top card is turned over and placed anywhere on the table. The second card is placed so that it is next to the first, either above, below, at the left, at the right or 'touching' at any corner. Subsequent cards played must also be next to a card already played.

The object is to form a square of cards, seven cards by seven, so that the pips of the cards in the rows (the 'across' words) and the pips of the cards in the columns (the 'down' words) all add up to even numbers. The court cards previously set aside do not count – their pip value is nil – and they are

---

A game of Crossword in progress.

used as required to serve as stops in the way that the black squares divide the words in crossword puzzles.

If all the court cards have been used by the time there is one square of the crossword to be filled, there will be four cards left in the player's hand, and he is entitled to look at them and choose which he wants to fit into the last square.

The illustration shows a game in progress.

Demon

Probably the best known of all **patience** or **solitaire** games, Demon is known in the United States as Canfield, after the famous gambler and casino owner Richard A. Canfield, who would 'sell' the pack at $1 per card and pay out $5 for each card in the foundation row at the end of the game, thus making a profit if fewer than 11 cards ended in the foundation row. The game is also known as Fascination and Thirteen.

The play

The standard pack of 52 cards is used. After shuffling, 13 cards are dealt face down to a pile known as the *heel*. The top card is then turned face up. Four cards are dealt face up to the right of this pile to form the tableau. The next card is dealt face up above the first card of the tableau to become the first foundation card. In the United States it is customary to deal the first foundation card before the tableau, but it makes no difference

to the game. The rank of the first foundation card decides the rank of all foundation cards and the other three cards of that rank are played, as available, above the other tableau cards to form a foundation row.

The object is to build all cards onto the foundations in suits and in ascending order up to Kings and then Aces onwards.

Cards are built onto the tableau piles in descending order of rank and in opposite colours, e.g. ♦ 6 may be built on ♣7. A tableau pile may be played onto another as a whole unit, e.g. a tableau pile built on the ♦ 10 can be transferred to another tableau pile which has a black Jack as its top card.

The top card in a tableau pile is available for play to a foundation. If a space in the tableau becomes empty it is filled immediately by the top card of the heel, when the next card in the heel is turned face up.

The cards in the hand are turned up in packets of three at a time, and are played to the table to form the talon. The top card of the talon is available for play to the founda-

---

The tableau of Demon as dealt for the example described in the text.

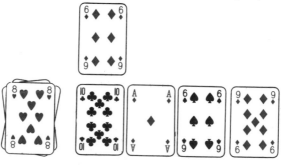

The game of Demon in progress (as described in the text).

Example hand

The heel, tableau and first foundation are dealt as in the illustration on the opposite page. Play proceeds as follows.

Immediately the ♠6 is played to the foundation row, all 6s being foundations. The ♥8 is played to the space created, and the next card in the heel exposed – the ♠8.

The ♦9 is played to the ♣10, creating a space filled by the ♠8, the next card of the heel being exposed – it is the ♠7. The ♠8 can be played onto the ♦9 in the tableau, creating another space, filled by the ♠7. This is played to the spade foundation, and the new top card of the heel fills the space. This is the ♦Q. The next

tions or to the tableau. It is not mandatory to play a card from the talon – a player might wish to wait for another round. When all the cards in the hand have been played to the talon (the last packet might be of one or two cards only) and all building completed, the talon is turned over and taken into hand again and the process repeated. The hand/talon is never shuffled.

If the heel becomes exhausted, then spaces in the tableau may be filled by the top card in the talon, but not necessarily immediately –a player might wish for a more suitable card to become available.

Play continues until the game is won or until the whole hand has been played to the talon without it being possible to play any cards to the layout.

top card of the heel, when exposed, proves to be the ♥2. All possible moves have now been made, so the top three cards of the hand are turned over to start the talon. The up card is the ♣K. The layout now looks as in the second illustration.

The ♣K is now played on the ♦A, exposing the ♦4. The ♦Q can now be moved to ♣K, and the new space in the table filled by the ♥2. The ♦4 cannot be played, and no further moves are possible, so the next three cards are turned from hand onto talon, and so on. This particular game has started very well, and has good prospects.

Variants

There are numerous variants to this most popular game. One which is fairly common borrows an aspect from other games in that the Aces are the foundations.

In this form the heel consists of 11 cards only, and it is customary to deal it face down. Four cards are dealt to the tableau, but none to the foundations.

The game is played in the same way. Aces are played to the foundation row as they become available, and are built on in suits up to the King.

EASY GO

Easy Go is a very simple, fast, gambling game depending on pure chance. It is suitable for any number up to eight players, the more the better.

The standard pack of 52 cards is used.

One player is banker and dealer, and the bank passes round the table clockwise. There is no advantage to the banker.

The play

After the banker shuffles and the player on his right cuts, the banker deals five cards, one at a time, to each player, except himself, face up. He then faces the next card to himself, and any player who holds the card of the same rank and colour pays 2 units into a pool. A player holding a card of the same rank but a different colour pays 1 unit into the pool. A player holding two or more cards of the same rank must pay into the pool for each. The banker then deals a second card to himself, and the players pay into the pool three units for the card of the same colour and two units for the opposite colour. On the third card the rates are 5 units for the same colour, 4 for the opposite; on the fourth 9 units and 8 units; on the fifth 17 units and 16 units.

All players have now put into a pool according to their obligations. Now the dealer deals himself another five cards. After each card the players are paid from the pool at the same rate as they put in. After this, anything remaining in the pool is taken by the banker. Should there not be enough in the pool to pay the players he must, of course, make good the pool.

Example hand

Five cards are dealt to six players, A to F, as in the illustration.

Banker then turns over his first card, the ♥ 7. Players A and F contribute 1 unit each and Player E 2 units. On the next card, ♣3, Player B contributes two units and Player E 5 units (three for ♠3 and two for ♦ 3). And so on.

After the first round players have contributed thus: A 18 units, B 2 units, C nil, D 20 units, E 7 units, F 9 units.

On the second round of banker's cards, notice that F, with his two 2s, receives 17 units when the ♦ 2 is turned up, nine for ♥ 2 and eight for ♠ 2. Also that Player D collects twice on his ♦ 9, five and 16 units.

During the second round, players draw from the pool thus: A draws 3 units, B 10 units, C 1 unit, D 23 units, E 2 units, F 17 units.

Players B, C, D and F win respectively 8, 1, 3 and 8 units. Players A and E lose respectively 15 and 5 units. The banker ends level, a coincidence which does not happen often.

PLAYERS

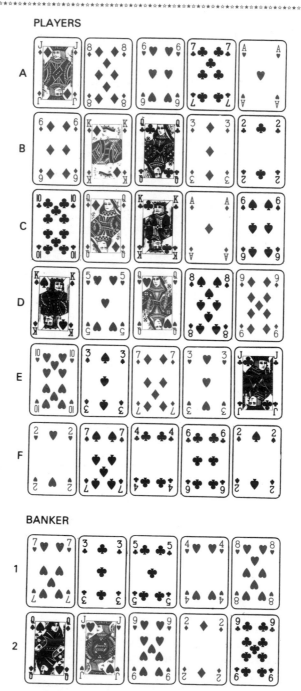

BANKER

The deal for the hand of Easy Go described in the text.

ÉCARTÉ

Écarté is a French gambling game, once of great popularity.

Players
Écarté is for two players.

Cards
Écarté is played with a pack of 32 cards, i.e. the standard pack from which the 6s, 5s, 4s, 3s and 2s are removed. The cards rank King (high), Queen, Jack, Ace, 10, 9, 8, 7.

Preliminaries
Each player draws a card to decide dealer – the higher card deals. The dealer shuffles and the non-dealer cuts.

Dealing
The dealer deals five cards to each player, either in bundles of three and two or of two and three – whichever he chooses remains the order for the rest of the game. The 11th card is turned face up on the table to denote the trump suit. If it is a King, dealer immediately scores 1 point. The remainder of the pack is placed face down beside it to form the stock.

Playing or proposing
The players examine their hands, and non-dealer states either 'I play' or 'I propose'. If he plays, the hands dealt are immediately played out. If he proposes, the dealer has the option of refusing the proposal, which he does by saying either 'I refuse' or 'I play', or of accepting the proposal, which he does by saying 'I accept'. If he refuses, the hands are played out. If he accepts, the players may change any number of cards they wish, beginning with non-dealer. Non-dealer must change at least one card by discarding face down into a dead pile and drawing from stock the equivalent number. Dealer may change any number but is not compelled to change.

After the two draws, the non-dealer may again play or propose, and if he proposes the dealer may again refuse or accept. This continues until either non-dealer says 'I play' or dealer says 'I refuse' or 'I play'. If eventually there are not enough cards in the stock to allow a player to take as many as he wishes, he must take those that remain and discard accordingly. When play starts, each player holds five cards.

The play
Non-dealer makes the opening lead. If either player holds the King of trumps, and he announces it before he plays to the first trick, he scores a point for it. It is not obligatory to announce it.

It is customary for the player leading to a trick to announce the suit of the card played. His opponent must follow suit if able to, and must win the trick if able to, either by playing a higher card in the suit led or by trumping if he is void.

The winner of a trick leads to the next.

The object of the play is to make the majority of the tricks. This is called making the *trick*. If a player can make all five tricks, it is called making the *vole*.

If the hands originally dealt are played then the player who decided to play scores 1 point for trick or 2 points if he makes vole. If he fails to make trick, his opponent scores 2 points (there is no extra for vole).

If a proposal has been accepted, however, then the scoring is the same whoever decides to play: the player who makes trick scores 1 point, or if he makes vole 2 points. There are a maximum of 3 points

at stake on a deal, therefore, 1 for King of trumps and 2 for vole, and a minimum of 1 point, for trick without the King of trumps. Game is to 5 points, and a player with 4 and holding the King of trumps will expose it immediately since he cannot lose.

Strategy
There is little judgement in the play in Écarté, since it is obligatory to win a trick if possible. However, there is skill of a kind involved, which lies in the decisions about playing, proposing and accepting. This is based on a knowledge and application of the probabilities involved in these choices.

Examples of jeux de règle *hands, with* diamonds *as trumps.*

To play on the hands dealt, a player should have odds of better than 2–1 in his favour, since he scores only 1 for trick if he succeeds and concedes 2 if he fails. The minimum hands which offer these chances of success are known as *jeux de règles*. Examples are:

a) *a hand with four or five trumps*;
b) *a hand with three trumps and two other cards of the same suit*;
c) *a hand with two trumps, and King 7 in one suit and 9 in another*;
d) *a hand with one trump, and four cards headed by a King in another suit; or with three cards headed by King, Queen; or with three cards headed by King in one side suit and King in another; or with two cards in each of two side suits headed by King, Ace and King, 7; with two cards in each of two side suits headed by Queen, Jack and Queen, Ace; or with cards in three side suits with the doubleton headed by King or Queen, Jack, and with a King as one of the singletons*.
e) *a hand with no trumps but with each outside suit headed by a King or Queen, Jack*.

The *jeux de régles* should always be played when held by the non-dealer, who has the advantage of leading.

When discarding, only trumps and Kings should be retained. With three trumps and/or Kings it is usually best to play, unless the master trump is held when an attempt might be made to score vole (holding the master trump is an assurance that vole cannot be conceded). When a player discards only one or two cards his opponent should guess that vole is his object, and should choose to play himself, conceding only one.

EUCHRE

A trick-taking game played with the short pack, Euchre belongs in the same family as several other games, like Écarté (q.v.) and Spoil Five (q.v.). Euchre is the version which became very popular in the United States.

Players
Euchre is for four players, playing in two partnerships. Variants for two and three players are described later.

Cards
The short pack of 32 cards is used, i.e. a standard pack from which the 6s, 5s, 4s, 3s and 2s have been removed. Cards rank from Ace (high) to 7 (low), except in the trump suit. In the trump suit, the Jack (called the *right bower*) is the highest trump, and the Jack of the same colour (the *left bower*) is the second ranked trump. The trump suit thus has nine cards. The suit of the same colour (called the *next* suit) has seven cards, and the two other suits (called *cross* suits) contain eight cards each.

It is customary to use two packs, dealt alternately, dealer's partner shuffling the second pack while the other is dealt.

Preliminaries
Cards are drawn by each player. The lowest card has choice of seat and is first dealer, the next lowest is his partner and sits opposite him. The dealer shuffles last and the pack is cut by the player on his right.

Dealing
The dealer deals each player five cards, beginning on his left, in two bundles of three and two, or two and three, whichever he prefers. The undealt pack is placed face down and dealer turns up the top card, which proposes the trump suit. The deal passes to the left after each hand.

Making
The proposed trump suit can be accepted or rejected by each player in turn. If it is accepted by any of them the turn-up becomes part of the dealer's hand. To accommodate it, the dealer discards a card from his hand by placing it face down crossways below the pack. It is customary for him not to pick up the turn-up, but to leave it where it is until he plays it.

The first chance of accepting the trump suit falls to eldest hand, who can accept it by saying 'I order it up' (he is ordering dealer to take it into his hand). To reject it he says 'I pass'. The turn passes round the table. Dealer's partner accepts it by saying 'I assist'. All players say 'I pass' to reject it.

The dealer accepts by merely placing his discard under the pack. To reject the trump suit, he puts the turn-up face up crossways below the pack.

If all players reject the trump suit eldest hand may now name any of the other three suits as trump suit, or he may pass. The other players in turn have the same opportunity until one names a trump suit. If a player makes trumps the same colour as the turn-up he is said to be 'making it next', otherwise he is said to be 'crossing it'.

If all players pass on this round the deal is abandoned, and the next player deals.

Playing alone

The player who decides trumps, either in the first round or by naming another suit in the second round, is known as the *maker*. The maker has the right to play alone (there is a bonus for this). He must announce this by declaring 'I play alone' before a card is led. The partner of the lone player then lays his cards face down on the table, and he and his cards do not take part in the play, although all points scored are for the partnership.

The play

If the maker plays alone, the opening lead is made by the player on his left. Otherwise the opening lead is made by eldest hand.

Players must follow suit to the card led. If unable to follow suit, a player may play any card. There is no obligation to trump or to win the trick if possible. Each trick is won by the highest trump or the highest card in the suit led, and the winner of a trick leads to the next.

The object is to win the majority of the tricks. If the making side fails to win at least three tricks, it is *euchred*. A side making all five tricks wins the *march*.

If the maker plays with his partner the side scores 1 point for making three or four tricks. For making all five (march) they score 2 points. If the maker plays alone, the side still scores 1 point for three or four tricks, but 4 points for march.

If the making side is euchred the opponents score 2 points.

Game is of 5 points, and it is usual for each side to keep a record of its own score by using a 3 and a 4 from the rejected cards as shown in the illustration.

Some players prefer a longer game of 7 or 10 points.

Strategy

There is little opportunity for skill in the play itself, as the usual pattern is for the player with top trumps to lead them, and there is little chance for finesse with only five tricks.

The main opportunity for judgement comes in the decisions regarding making trump and playing alone. On average there will be just over $1\frac{1}{4}$ trumps in each

---

Method of keeping score at Euchre with two cards showing one, two, three and four points.

hand, so ordering up the trump is likely to give dealer at least two trumps, possibly three. So the non-dealing side will not order up trumps without three fairly sure tricks. Even then, if one of these tricks is left bower and he has other cards in the next suit, he might wait to make that suit trumps, as he will not then have to concede a trump (the turn-up) to dealer. If in the meantime dealer's side makes trumps, he has a good chance to euchre them.

Dealer's partner, if holding a hand like two trumps and a side Ace, might announce 'I assist', knowing that his partner will take the turn-up and they should hold the balance of power. On the other hand, if the turn-up is high, like a bower, he might decide to pass, hoping that dealer might take it up and be able to play alone and make march.

A side with four points is said to be *at the bridge*. If eldest hand's side is at the bridge, with opponents on two points or less, then eldest hand can be more adventurous, knowing that if he ordered up the trump and is euchred his side still do not lose the game. If in this situation the call gets round to dealer, he will probably take the trump, to deprive the opposition of the chance to make trumps and score the point they need.

Variants

Two-handeded Euchre This is played with the 8s and 7s removed from the pack, reducing it to only 24 cards. It is played in the same way as the parent game, except that, of course, there are no extra points for playing alone, since each player plays alone throughout.

Three-handed Euchre This variant is played like four-handed Euchre, except that the player making trumps plays against the other two, who are in temporary partnership. The play is like a maker playing alone in four-handed Euchre.

The scoring must be amended, however. A maker winning three or four tricks scores 1 point; if he wins the march he scores 3 points; if he is euchred his opponents score 2 points each. Players keep their own scores and game is to 5 points.

Call-Ace Euchre This game can be played by four, five or six players. Each player plays for himself, although temporary partnerships are formed.

The trump is made in the usual way, and maker has the option of playing alone or playing with a partner. To play with a partner, he announces 'I call on the Ace of . . .', naming a suit. The holder of this card does not reveal himself, so only he knows which side all the other players are on. The partnerships become known to all only when the nominated Ace is played.

It is possible that the Ace named is in the pack, of course, in which case the maker is playing alone.

A maker playing alone scores 1 point for making three or four tricks. If he plays with a partner each player scores 1 point. For march, a lone player scores 1 point for each player in the game, including himself. Players in partnership winning the march score 2 points each if there are four players, 3 points each if there are five or six players. If a lone player or partnership is euchred each opponent scores 2 points. Players keep their own scores.

FAN TAN

Fan Tan developed from a game called Play or Pay. A further development led to the game called Parliament, which is the game played today and which is described, but the name of Fan Tan proved more popular, and the game is known widely under that name. It is often played as a gambling game. Children enjoy it for its own sake and call it Sevens.

Players

Any number of players from three to eight may play.

Cards

The full pack of 52 cards is used. The cards rank from King (high) to Ace (low).

Preliminaries

Players sit at random and any player deals the cards one at a time face up to each player beginning with the player on his left. The player to be dealt the first Jack becomes dealer. The dealer shuffles last and the pack is cut by the player to his right. Before play begins each player puts a stake of one unit into a pool.

Dealing

The dealer deals the whole pack one at a time, beginning with the player to his left. Some players will get one card more than others. This is sometimes ignored, as the deal circulates to the left with each hand, and all players have the extra card in turn, but some players prefer that those with a card short put an extra unit into the pool.

The play

The play passes from eldest hand clockwise. Eldest hand must play a 7 to the table. If he cannot the turn passes to the next player and so on until a 7 is laid. Once a 7 is laid, then a player on his turn can lay the 8 or the 6 of the same suit on the 7. In this way the suits get built up in rows, in one direction from 7 to King and in the other from 7 to Ace. The 7s are always playable. Only one card is played at a turn.

A player must go on his turn if able. It is not permitted to halt the development of a row by passing instead of playing an eligible card. On the other hand, a player with a choice of cards to play will obviously play the one which suits him – that is the essence of the game.

If a player cannot play a card to the table he contributes one unit to the pool and the turn passes to the next player.

The first player to get rid of all his cards wins. Each of the other players must add one unit to the pool for each card he holds in his hand, and the winner takes the whole pool.

The game can be played without stakes – the first player to go out is the winner.

Strategy

A player should attempt to build up those suits in which he holds several cards, and stop those

The game in progress referred to in the text.

The illustration shows a game in progress.

The player holding the hand must obviously hold up his ♣7 as long as he can, as it is blocking other players but not him. He should hold up his ♦ J for the same reason. His ♥5 will not help anybody else at once, and will allow him to play ♥4 later, but there is no rush to play these cards – nobody can hold him up in that direction. He has excellent chances of winning if he can get the spades moving down to his Ace and up to his Queen, and his best play is therefore the ♠4.

which are of little use to him. Should he hold a King or Ace he should try to develop the relevant suit in the relevant direction, since he clearly cannot win unless all the intermediate cards are played up to his Ace or King.

A 7 should be kept for as long as possible to force others to miss a turn, unless a player has several other cards in the suit, and in particular Ace or King, when he will want the suit developed.

FARO

The most popular gambling game of all in the United States in the late nineteenth century, Faro has lost pride of place in the casinos to Craps, a dice game, and is now not much played. The game was originally spelt Pharoah, and might have got its name from the fact that a picture of a Pharaoh was commonly used on the backs of seventeenth-century French playing cards.

To play the game in casinos, a staking table is necessary, as illustrated. A green cloth contains representations of the 13 ranks of the cards, usually spades, although the choice of suit is of no significance. A counting frame is also used, as illustrated, on which

a casekeeper keeps track of the cards played.

The play
The full pack of 52 cards is used, and they are dealt by a dealer, a casino employee, from a dealing box.

Players can bet on any rank of card, either to win or lose. Stakes are placed on the chosen card on the staking table. If the bet is that the card will lose, a small copper token is placed on the stake.

Players can bet on combinations of cards to win or lose by the

The staking table as used in a casino to play Faro.

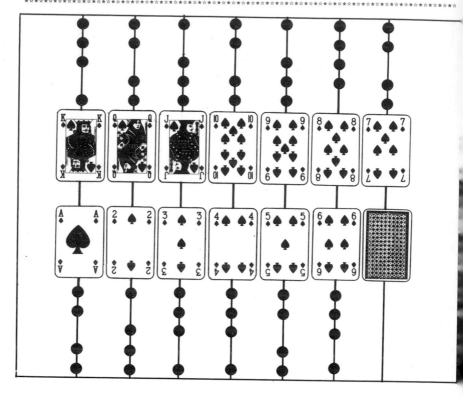

The counting frame for Faro.

---

placing of their stake. A stake between the 2 and 3, for instance, is a bet that one of those ranks will win (or lose), between the 2 and Queen that one of those will win (or lose), a stake in the centre of the square formed by 2, 3, J, Q a bet on these four ranks.

When bets are placed the cards are shuffled, cut, and placed in the dealing box, with the rank of the top card showing. This top card is known as the *soda*. It has no effect on the betting. It is taken from the box and placed to one side. The second card is now taken from the box – this card is a loser, and begins a losing pile. The next card exposed in the box is a winner.

That completes a turn, and all those who bet on the winning rank to win or the losing rank to lose are paid at 1 to 1 (or evens). Those who backed the contrary lose their stakes. Those who included the winning or losing ranks in a group are paid or lose according to their bets. If a player backs a combination which both wins and loses (for example, he backs ranks 2 and 3 to win, and 2 loses and 3 wins) the bet is a stand-off.

Unsettled bets remain on the layout, and players have the opportunity to make additional bets before the next turn.

Behind the 24th winning card in the box there will be three further cards. Their ranks are known because the casekeeper has been keeping account of the cards played. Bets on individual cards are now cancelled, and players may bet on the order of the last three cards. If all are of different rank odds of 4 to 1 are paid for specifying the correct order. This is called *calling the turn*. If there is a pair in the last three cards it is called a *cat-hop*, and the house pays 1–1 (evens) to a player who can name the order.

House edge
In the case of calling the turn, the house edge is 16⅔ per cent (since the real odds of naming the order is 5 to 1) and in the cat-hop it is 33⅓ per cent (since the real odds are 2 to 1). Otherwise the house edge comes from *splits*. When two cards of the same rank appear together as losing and winning cards, the house takes half the stakes bet on that rank, returning half to the players. It is estimated that the house edge on these bets is about 1½ per cent.

Variant
Stuss This is a less complex version of Faro for casual play at home. The dealer holds the cards in his hand face down. There is no need

to keep a record of cards played because calling the turn and cat-hop are not played. A suit from another pack of cards laid out on the table on which players can place their stakes is an advantage. It is usual to back cards to win only, not to lose, and cards are not backed in combination. The dealer shuffles, another player cuts, and the dealer has a final cut. There is no need for a soda.

The dealer, who is the banker, turns over the top card and places it to his right. It is a loser and he collects stakes on that rank. He then turns over the second card and places it to his left. This is a winner, and dealer pays out on it. Players can then make additional bets if they like. The last four cards are not played. There is an advantage to the dealer, arising from the fact that the losing card is dealt first. Notice that in the case of a split, dealer has already collected *all* the stakes on that rank as a loser before he turns over the card of the same rank as a winner. Naturally that rank has no stakes on it. The dealer's advantage is therefore twice that in a casino: about 3 per cent.

Therefore all players should have the bank for an equal number of deals.

FIVE HUNDRED

This is not a variation of Euchre, although it has some similarities and was invented in the early twentieth century to appeal to the Euchre-playing public. It succeeded, and in the United States for a while became the most popular card game for playing at home. It retains its appeal, although some other games have overtaken it.

Players

The game is best for three players, but two to five may play (see later). With four, they play in partnership.

Cards

For three players, as described here, the short pack is used, i.e. the pack stripped of the 6s, 5s, 4s, 3s and 2s. However, the Joker is added to make a pack of 33 cards. With more players, as described later, the pack is enlarged. Cards are ranked in the trump suit as follows: Joker (high), Jack (*right bower*), Jack of the same colour as the trump suit (*left bower*), A, K, Q, 10, 9, 8, 7 (low).

The cards in the plain suits rank from Ace (high) to 7 (low) in normal precedence, except that the suit of the same colour as the trump suit will not contain a Jack (which has become a trump).

Thus the trump suit contains ten cards, the suit of the same colour seven cards, and the other two suits eight cards.

The suits rank: hearts (high), diamonds, clubs, spades.

Preliminaries

Players draw for the first deal. The lowest deals (in the draw Ace counts low and Joker lowest of all). The dealer shuffles last and the player on his right cuts.

Dealing

The dealer deals three cards to each hand, beginning on his left, then three to the centre to form a *widow*, then four to each hand followed by three, so that each player holds ten cards, the remaining three being the widow.

Bidding

When each player has examined his cards the bidding starts with the player to dealer's left. He may bid or pass. Thereafter each player may bid or pass until two players pass in succession, whereupon the final bid becomes the contract and the player who made it plays the hand against the other two players in partnership.

A bid is an offer to make a certain number of tricks with a suit named by the bidder as trumps, or he may specify 'no-trumps'. Each bid must be higher than the previous bid.

The values of the bids are:

	Six	Seven	Eight	Nine	Ten
Spades	40	140	240	340	440
Clubs	60	160	260	360	460
Diamonds	80	180	280	380	480
Hearts	100	200	300	400	500
No-trumps	120	220	320	420	520

If each player passes without making a bid, the deal is

abandoned and passes to the next player clockwise.

The play

The player whose bid is the highest takes up the widow and discards three cards face down to keep his hand to ten cards. He then leads to the first trick. Other players must follow suit if able, and if not they may trump or discard. The trick is won by the highest trump, or if there are no trumps played, by the highest card in the suit led. The winner of the trick leads to the next.

In a no-trump contract the Joker becomes a trump suit on its own. The usual rules apply – it can be played only if its holder is void of the suit led. When the Joker is led in a no-trump contract, the leader specifies the suit to which the other players must follow – the Joker in effect represents the highest card in that suit.

The object of the play, so far as the bidder is concerned, is to make the contract, i.e. the number of tricks he promised. The object of his opponents is to defeat (set) the contract. The two opponents keep their individual tricks separate.

Scoring

If the bidder makes his contract he scores its value in the table set out under 'Bidding'. Any overtricks he makes are not added to the total, with one exception: a player whose bid was worth less then 250, scores 250 if he makes all ten tricks. In other words a player taking ten tricks scores either 250 or the value of the bid, whichever is higher.

If the bidder is set back, i.e. he fails to make his contract, the value of the bid is deducted from his score. A player may thus have a minus score, signified by drawing a circle round the score, which is said to be in the hole.

Each opponent of the bidder scores 10 points for each trick

The deal for Five Hundred for the example hand described in the text.

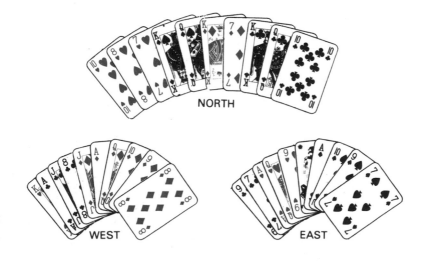

made by himself, whether the contract is made or set.

The game is to 500, as the name implies. Should two or more players pass 500 on the same deal, the bidder wins the game. Should the two non-bidders only pass 500, the winner is the first to take the trick with which he reached 500.

To prevent a player in the hole bidding optimistically and shutting out the others, an optional rule is to set a limit to the hole – either at 500 or 1000. When a player is in the hole to the maximum amount, the opponent with the higher score is the winner.

Example hand

The hands are dealt as in the illustration. The first bidder is West, who bids six diamonds. He thinks he might make at least four trumps and ♣A, and that should he find in the widow another diamond, or a guard for his ♥K, he should make six tricks. North passes. East is an adventurous player. He does not like the prospect of defending against six diamonds, but would have to bid seven spades to overcall. Should the widow be kind he might make the contract, but prudence advises him to pass.

West thus has the contract and takes up the widow. He finds ♠J 8 and ♥J. The ♥J gives him left bower and guarantees his contract. He takes it into his hand but discards the two spades with the ♥K. He thinks the third club might be more valuable than the bare ♥K, which is almost certain to lose to ♥A. The adjusted hands are in the second illustration. East's Joker now becomes in effect a diamond, i.e. the top trump.

With such a strong trump suit and two voids, West leads his trumps immediately.

The play proceeds:

The hands after the bidding and West has taken up the widow and discarded.

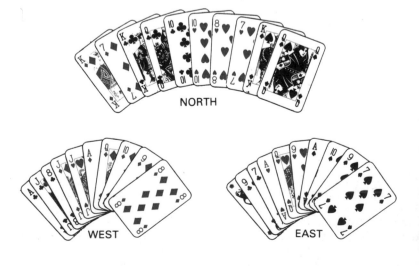

NORTH

WEST

EAST

	West	North	East
1.	♦J	♦7	Joker
2.	♦8	♣Q	♠A
3.	♥J	♦K	♠7
4.	♠A	♥7	♠9
5.	♥Q	♥8	♣7
6.	♣A	♣10	♣9
7.	♣J	♣K	♥9
8.	♦9	♠K	♠10
9.	♦10	♥10	♥Q
10.	♣8	♣Q	♥A

West made seven tricks and his contract. He thus scored 80 points, while North scored 20 and East 10. Had West bid seven diamonds, he would have made 180 points.

It is interesting to note that had East risked a bid of seven spades, the widow would have been extremely helpful. He would have taken all three cards into his hand, discarding ♣9 7 and ♥9. He would have drawn all adverse trumps in two rounds, and West's bare ♥K would have fallen under the ♥A, so that East would have taken all ten tricks to score 250.

Strategy
The main skill lies in assessing the correct bid. In the deal each player's longest suit will be at least four cards, so this is the minimum trump holding for a bid, and only then if the top trumps are held and are supported by side Aces. When five trumps are held the chances are 5 to 4 in favour of another being in the widow; with six trumps and more the odds are against.

Given at least four trumps, a rough guide to a bid valuation is to count all trumps of Ace or better as one point, all trumps in excess of three as 1 point each, and masters in other suits as a point each, e.g. A K counts as 2, etc. At a stretch a guarded King might count as 1

point. In the example hand above, by this method West's hand was worth the six diamonds he bid, while East's hand was worth no more than five, so although, as it happened, East could have bid ten spades successfully, even seven spades would have been a rash bid.

In the play the bidder, unless his strength is in side-suit winners, should almost always draw trumps immediately, and lead a long side suit to establish it.

Variants
The main variant is in an extra bid of nullo. This is an offer to win no tricks at all in no-trumps. Its value is 250, ranking it between eight spades and eight clubs. A player holding the Joker and defending against nullo can play it only when void of the suit led. When the bidder makes nullo, his opponents do not score at all. When he fails he is debited 250, and the opponents score 10 points each for each trick the bidder makes. Thus, the hand is played out even when the bidder is set by being forced to take an early trick.

Another variant lies in the bidding, where some players prefer a free auction, i.e. bidding continues until the highest bidder is found. In the original game, each player was allowed one bid only, where clearly a player bidding must make his optimum bid straightaway, as he will not get another chance. Some players compromise between the two systems of one bid only or a free auction, by allowing players to remain in the auction only until they pass, i.e. a player who passes is not allowed to bid in a subsequent round.

A variant which saves the need to abandon hands is one preferred by some players: when all players pass, the hand is played as a no-trump hand, each player against each other, with eldest hand leading to the first trick. Each player scores 10 points for each trick made.

Five Hundred for two players The cards are dealt as for the three-handed game described, the third hand being dead and placed aside. The winning bidder takes the widow and the play proceeds as in the parent game. With ten unknown cards not being used in the game, the skill factor is reduced and bidding can become a matter of chance.

Five Hundred for four players With four players, the pack is enlarged to 43 cards by including the 6s, 5s and the two red 4s. Each player has ten cards as before, with a three-card widow. Two pairs play against each other, each player sitting opposite his partner. The player to dealer's left makes the first bid, and bidding proceeds as described above, the highest bidder taking the widow and discarding. Highest bidder leads. Play is two against two, and one score is kept for each partnership. *Variation:* Some players prefer not to use the Joker, in which case the widow is of two cards only.

Five Hundred for five players The full pack of 52 cards plus Joker is used. Each player is dealt ten cards each with three going to the widow. Each player plays for himself and bids for himself, but on the understanding that should he win the contract he can call upon another player to be his partner in the play. There are two ways to determine which, and players should agree on the method to be used before play starts.

a) A player who successfully bids six or seven may name any other player he likes to be his partner. He will usually choose a player who has also bid, and who therefore might have a good hand. A player who bids eight or more can choose two partners, so that three are in partnership to make the contract, and two are in partnership to set it.

b) The successful bidder may name the holder of a specific card to be his partner. This will usually be his highest missing trump or an Ace in a vital side suit. The holder of the card does not announce it, and is therefore a 'blind' partner until he plays the card named.

Each partner in a successful contract scores its value, and is debited with it if set. Opponents score 10 points for each trick taken individually.

GERMAN WHIST

German Whist is a form of Whist (q.v.) for two players. It is a simple game but offers scope for judgement and is particularly rewarding for a player with a good memory.

Players

German Whist is a game for two players.

Cards

The full pack of 52 cards is used, cards ranking from Ace (high) to 2 (low).

Preliminaries

Players cut for deal, and the higher card decides dealer. Dealer shuffles and non-dealer cuts. The deal passes after each hand.

Dealing

The dealer deals 13 cards to each player one at a time, beginning with his opponent. He places the stock on the table between the players and turns over the top card, placing it beside the stock. This card denotes trumps for the deal.

The play

Non-dealer leads to the first trick; at all times the second player must follow suit if able, otherwise he may trump or discard. There is no obligation to win a trick.

The object is to win the most tricks.

The winner of the first trick keeps it by him and takes the up-turned card into his hand, and the loser takes the top card of the stock (he does not show it to his opponent). The next card in the stock is then turned over, and the second trick is played, the winner taking the new turn-up, the loser the top card in the stock, and so on. The

---

The German Whist hand discussed in the text.

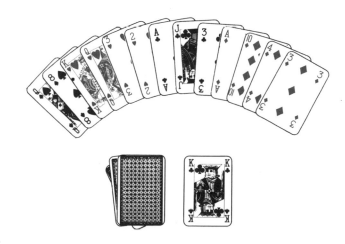

winner of each trick leads to the next.

After 13 tricks the stock is exhausted, and the second 13 tricks are played out from hand. At the end the winner scores the difference in the numbers of tricks won. The game is to any agreed total of points, the usual being 50.

Strategy

The game is one of balance. A player must judge when to win a trick or try to win a trick with a high card and when to lose a trick when the upturned card is a poor one, in the hope of taking a better one off the top of the stock. He must always remember that the card he takes might be no better than the one he rejected, and also that even if it is a good card, he has given away a trick for it.

It pays to try to command as many suits as possible. In the illustration, diamonds are trumps. The turn-up is the ♣K, a useful card to hold. The player holding the hand illustrated should not, however, lead his ♣A, which would win the trick, because that would leave his hand exactly as it was. He should lead ♥K. If it wins the hand is improved. If it loses to opponent's ♥A, then he still holds the master card in hearts and clubs with ♥Q and ♣A.

A player with a good memory will know the cards held by his opponent when the last 13 tricks are to be played (or some of them!) and can plan his play accordingly.

GIN RUMMY

Gin Rummy is a form of Knock Rummy (q.v.); both games are in the Rummy family (q.v.). The invention of Gin Rummy is credited to E. T. Baker, who devised it in a card-playing club in New York in 1909, calling it Gin, maintaining the alcoholic link with the parent game, which was then called Rum. The game achieved its present great popularity in the 1940s when it was taken up by film stars in Hollywood at a time when the crazes of the film colony received wide publicity.

Players

Gin Rummy is for two players, but there are ways in which three or four may play (see later).

Cards

The full pack of 52 cards is used. Cards rank from King (high) to Ace (low). Two packs used alternately are convenient, non-dealer shuffling one while dealer deals the other.

Preliminaries

Each player draws a card, and the higher has choice of dealing or asking his opponent to deal. Dealer may give the pack its final shuffle, and non-dealer cuts. After the first deal the dealer is the winner of the previous hand.

Dealing

Ten cards are dealt, one at a time alternately to each player, beginning with non-dealer. The remainder of the pack is placed face down between the players and forms the stock. The top card is turned over and placed face up beside the stock to become the first upcard.

The play

The players pick up their cards and arrange them in their hands. Non-dealer may take the first upcard into his hand or refuse it. If he refuses it the dealer has the same right. If either player takes the upcard into his hand, he replaces it with a discard from his hand, thus retaining ten cards.

If both players refuse the upcard non-dealer takes the top card of the stock into his hand and discards one by placing it face up on the old upcard. This card now becomes the upcard and begins a discard pile. The card discarded may be the same one taken into the hand from stock.

Thereafter each player in turn has the option of taking either the upcard or the top card from the stock into his hand, discarding a new upcard onto the discard pile. Unless agreed to beforehand, players may not look back through the discard pile to see which cards are no longer available.

The object of the play is to form the hand into sets of three or more cards. A set may be of two kinds: three or four cards of the same rank or three or more cards in sequence in the same suit. Ace is in sequence with 2, 3 not King, Queen.

Cards not included in a set are unmatched cards. After drawing (and only after drawing) a player may go out (called *knocking*) if the unmatched cards in his hand (not counting the discard) count 10 points or less. For this purpose, court cards (King, Queen, Jack) count 10 points, Ace 1 point and other cards their pip value. To knock, the player lays down his ten cards, arranged in sets with the unmatched cards to one side, and discards his eleventh card.

The count of the unmatched cards represent a score against the player. If all ten cards are matched and the count against the player is nought, he is said to *go gin*.

If the fiftieth card is drawn from stock and the drawer discards without knocking, leaving only two cards remaining in the stock, the opposing player may pick up this discard and knock, but he may not take a card from stock. If he does not knock the deal is abandoned with no score for either side, and the player who dealt the hand deals again.

Laying off
When a player knocks his opponent then lays down the matched cards in his own hand, and unless the knocker has gone gin may lay off any of his unmatched cards on the sets of the knocker, i.e. adding cards which match to the knocker's sets, thereby reducing the count against him (see illustration).

The player with the hand on the left has knocked with a count of 5. His opponent can lay off his ♥8 only, on the set of 8s. His count is 15, and the knocker therefore scores 10.

Scoring

If the knocker has the lower count in unmatched cards he scores the difference in the two counts. If, however, the opponent's count is equal to or lower than the knocker's, he is said to have undercut the knocker. He then scores the difference, if any, between the two counts plus a bonus of 25 points. If the two counts are equal, the opponent does not score for the difference, but scores the bonus of 25.

When the knocker goes gin he cannot be undercut as his opponent cannot lay off his unmatched cards. He scores the count of his opponent's unmatched cards, plus a bonus of 25 points.

The score is entered on a score sheet in two columns, one for each player. The first player to score 100 points wins the game.

To calculate the winning margin, bonuses are now added to the scores. Each player gets a bonus of 25 points for each hand (called a box or line) won. The winner gets

In this example the player on the left has knocked with a count of 8, but is unlucky as his opponent can lay off ♥J Q on his sequence and his count is only 4. He undercuts the knocker and scores a bonus of 25 plus the difference in the scores, i.e. 29 in all.

an additional bonus of 100 points for game. The difference between the two totals now represents the winning margin, with one further consideration. If the loser did not score a single point, the winner's total is doubled. Such a game is called a *shutout* or *schneider*, and the loser is said to be schneidered, skunked or blitzed.

There is a more complicated system of scoring which became popular in Hollywood and which is known as Hollywood Scoring, and this is explained under *Variants*.

Strategy

A player must use judgement in deciding how long to hold high cards presenting a good chance of a set but representing a high count against him should the opponent knock. For three or four draws it might pay to hold them, as high cards are likely to be discarded early by the opponent. After this high cards become dangerous, as many Gin hands are won after six or fewer draws, with perhaps as many as three or four unmatched cards. A pair of unmatched court cards will then be expensive.

It follows that low cards, if drawn, should be retained, both to offer a chance of knocking and to reduce the count if the opponent knocks.

A player in a position to knock must weigh the chances of being undercut. In the first few draws it usually pays to knock as soon as possible, but after, say, eight draws, it may be assumed that the opponent has sets, and knocking with a high count might lead to being undercut. The decision whether or not to knock will lie in assessing how many upcards the opponent has taken into his hand and how many draws from stock he has retained. It is wise, therefore, to take all draws from stock into hand, even if the card drawn is immediately discarded – the opponent cannot tell whether the draw has improved the hand or not.

It seldom pays to wait for the opportunity to go gin if able to knock.

Variants

A variant which gave Gin great popularity in the 1940s is the system of scoring known as Hollywood Scoring. The score-sheet is ruled up into columns as illustrated. It is as if three games were being played simultaneously. Every deal and its score is

Hollywood Scoring. A game in progress. Jack has won game 1, is leading in game 2, but is behind in game 3.

	GAME 1		GAME 2		GAME 3	
	Jack	Jill	Jack	Jill	Jack	Jill
Box 1	18	6	16	5	10	28
Box 2	34	11	26	33	35	48
Box 3	44	39	51	53	51	54
Box 4	71	59	67	59	71	76
Box 5	87		87	81	74	
Box 6	107		90			
Box 7						

known as a *box*. When a player first scores, his points are entered in the first column only, under Game 1. The second time he scores, his points are added to those in the first column and also entered in the second column. The third and subsequent times that he scores, the points are entered in all three columns.

When a player's score reaches 100 in any column that column is closed. If a player reaches 100 under Game 1 before his opponent has scored then the opponent's first score is entered under Game 2, and his next under Games 2 and 3. In other words, once Game 1 is closed no scores can be entered in it for either player. Play continues until all three Games are completed.

The winner of a column or Game scores 100 points for winning plus 20 points for each box he has won in excess of his opponent. If his opponent has won more boxes then 20 points for each extra box is deducted from the winner's 100 points.

If a player fails to score in any column or Game he is *blitzed*, and the total score of the winner of that Game is doubled. Each player's points from the three Games are totalled – the lower total is subtracted from the higher to give the winning margin.

Oklahoma Gin is a variant in which the upcard for each deal fixes the number of points with which a player can knock. For example if the upcard is ♦7, the knocker cannot have more than 7 points in unmelded cards. Court cards (K, Q, J) count as 10. In some circles an Ace as an upcard

requires a player to go gin to go out. Another optional rule is that when the upcard is a spade, points scored in that deal are doubled. Game is usually to 150 points.

Round-the-Corner Gin is a variant in which Ace can rank high or low, and sequences are continuous (i.e. go *round the corner*). For example, a sequence might be Q, K, A, 2. An unmatched Ace is worth 15 points. In some circles, the opponent is allowed to lay off on knocker's hand even if he has gone gin and, moreover, if he too can reduce his count to zero neither player scores on that deal. Game is usually to 125.

Gin Rummy for three players Gin Rummy is essentially a game for two, but three may play with one player standing out at each deal. The players cut, and the lowest stands out on the first deal, while the next lowest is the dealer. The two players play out a deal, whereupon the loser stands out and his place is taken by the player who previously stood out. The winner of each hand stays in and becomes dealer for the next. Each player keeps a score of the hands he wins. When a player reaches 100, he is the winner. He adds 100 to his score, all players add 20 per box won to their score, and each player settles with each other player. A player standing out is not allowed to advise either of the other players.

Gin Rummy for four or more Any even number of players may play in teams. For instance six players would play in two teams of three. Each player in Team A plays an opponent from Team B. At the end of the three hands both teams' points are totalled, and the team with the higher total wins the difference for that round. Each player then plays a different oppo- nent, and so on. Game can be to an agreed number of points, or for an agreed number of rounds, e.g. until each player has played each oppo- nent three times.

GO FISH

This is one of the simplest of children's games for any number of players between two and six. It is suitable for children aged between six and ten years old.

The play

A dealer deals cards one at a time to each player in a clockwise direction. If there are two players each has seven cards, if three or more, each has five cards. The remainder of the pack is placed face down in the centre of the table to form the stock. Beginning with the player on dealer's left, each player in turn may ask any other player to hand over any cards he holds of a certain rank. The request is in the form of: 'John, give me your Kings'. The player asked must hand over all the cards he holds of that rank. A player must not ask for cards, however, unless he himself holds at least one card in that rank.

Should the player asked not hold any cards in that rank he says 'Go fish', and the asker must then take the top card of the stock. A player successfully obtaining a card he requested, either by being given it by the player asked or by drawing it from the stock (in which case he shows it) is entitled to another turn, and indeed keeps the turn until he is unsuccessful when it passes to the player on his left.

The object is to obtain sets of four cards. As soon as a player has four cards of the same rank he lays them in front of him on the table. A player who is not holding any cards when his turn arrives is allowed to take the top card of the stock, but must wait until his next turn before asking for a card from another player.

The winner is the player with the most sets at the end, when all the cards should be laid on the table.

Warning: a small child playing for the first time can be disappointed when, after successfully asking for a 9, say, to add to the pair in his hand, immediately finds himself asked to hand them over by the player holding the fourth.

GOLF

A **patience** or **solitaire** game, Golf can also be played as a 'competitive patience or solitaire', if that is not a contradiction! Like the real game, it can be played by one person only, trying to beat 'par', by two in match-play or medal-play, or for real addicts by any number in medal-play. When played by one player the full 52-card pack is used.

The play

Seven cards are dealt face up in a row, with four more rows built upon them and overlapping as in the illustration. This is the tableau consisting of 35 cards, otherwise known as the *links*.

The remaining 17 cards are held in the hand and are dealt one at a time face up to form a talon, or waste heap.

Any card exposed in the bottom row of the links is available to play onto the talon in either ascending

or descending order. Suits are immaterial. However, sequences are not 'round the corner': only a 2 can be played on an Ace, not a King. And a King automatically stops a sequence.

For example, suppose the links was as in the illustration, and the first card turned over from hand was the ♠9. Onto it is packed the ♦10, ♦J, ♦Q, ♣J, ♥10, ♣9, ♦8, ♠7, ♣6, ♥5, ♣4, ♠5, ♠6. No further moves are possible, so the next card is turned to the talon and so on. When all 17 cards from hand have been turned and all moves made, there are likely to be a few cards left in the links. The number of them represents the score for the 'hole'.

It might be that all the cards are removed from the links before the 17th card is dealt from hand, in which case the cards left in the hand are 'credited' to the player and deducted from his score at the end of the 'round' of 18 holes. The object of a player playing on his own is to beat the 'par' for 18 holes of 72 'strokes'.

The deal for the example hand of Golf described in the text.

The score-card will not resemble that of a real round of golf — there might be holes where a 'minus' score is recorded, and others where a dozen strokes are taken, but the final score should be fairly authentic.

Competitive Golf Two players can play against each other by each having a pack of cards and playing each hole simultaneously. Scoring can either be by 'match-play', by which each hole is won, lost or halved, so that at each stage of the round a player is, for instance, 'one up' or 'two down', etc, or by 'medal-play', where the score for each hole is recorded for each player and he with the lower total wins. This latter method can be used if three or more want to play competitively, of course.

HASENPFEFFER

This a game somewhere between Euchre and Five Hundred, and is said to have been invented by the Pennsylvania Dutch. It is a good game for four players, less serious and quicker than Bridge, but presenting an opportunity for skill.

Players
Four players are required, playing in two partnerships, partners sitting opposite each other.

Cards
From the standard pack are removed the 8s, 7s, 6s, 5s, 4s, 3s and 2s, but the Joker is added to make a pack of 25 cards.

The Joker is the highest trump, and in the trump suit the cards rank: Joker, Jack (*right bower*), Jack of the same colour as the trump suit (*left bower*), A, K, Q, 10, 9. In the plain suits the rank is normal: A (high), K, Q, J, 10, 9. Thus the trump suit has eight cards, the suit of the same colour five cards, and the two suits of the opposite colour six cards.

Preliminaries
Each player draws a card. The two with the lowest play as partners, and the lowest is dealer. Players who tie redraw if necessary. The dealer has the last shuffle, and the player on his right cuts.

Dealing
Beginning with the player on his left, the dealer deals six cards to each player, in bundles of three.

The last card is placed face down in the centre to form a *widow*.

Bidding
Beginning with the eldest hand, each player has one opportunity to bid or to pass. A bid is a promise by a player that his side will make a specified number of tricks if permitted to name the trump suit. He does not name the trump suit in the bid. Each bid must be higher than a previous bid. When all players have had the opportunity to bid the high bidder names the trump suit. He then takes the widow into his hand and discards one card face down. If all players pass, then the player holding the Joker must acknowledge it and bid 'three'. Should it happen that the Joker is the widow the deal is abandoned, and passes to the next player.

The play
The high bidder makes the opening lead. Players must follow suit to the card led, and if unable to, may trump or discard. The highest trump wins the trick, or if none is played the highest card in the suit led. The winner of the trick leads to the next. The object of the contracting side is to make as many tricks as promised, while their opponents' object is to *set them back* by preventing them from making their contract.

Scoring
If the contracting side makes its contract it scores 1 point for each

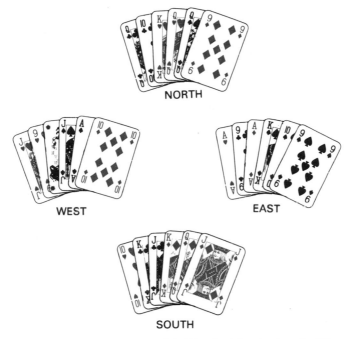

NORTH

WEST

EAST

SOUTH

The deal for the hand of Hasenpfeffer described in the text.

trick made. If it fails, the amount of the bid is deducted from its score. The opposing side scores 1 point for each trick it makes, whether the contract is made or not. Game is 10 points.

Example hand

Four hands are dealt as in the illustration. South dealt, and West bids four. With spades as trumps, he is certain to make two tricks, is likely to make a third with ♠A, and hopes to make one from the widow or partner. If he had bid three only, it is possible that he might have four bid over him, as it is likely that one at least of his opponents will have strong clubs. North passes. East has an excellent hand to support partner no matter what suit partner chooses as trumps, but of course cannot bid five because he would then have to name trumps, and is not strong enough himself in any one suit. South must also pass. West names spades as trumps, picks up the widow, which is the ♣A, and discards ♦10. He leads trumps. Play proceeds:

	West	North	East	South
1.	Joker	♠Q	♠9	♣J
2.	♠J	♦9	♠10	♥10
3.	♣A	♣10	♣9	♣K
4.	♥9	♥K	♥A	♦J
5.	♥J	♥Q	♦A	♦Q
6.	♠A	♣Q	♠K	♦K

West found partner and widow so helpful that he won all six tricks and his side leads six to nothing after one deal.

Strategy

With eight trumps there will be an average of two per hand. A rough method of evaluating a hand is to count one trick for each master trump, half a trick for a third trump and one each for a fourth, fifth or sixth, and one trick for each outside Ace. It is better to be brave than ultra-cautious in the bidding, as widow and partner can usually be counted upon to add another trick. In the play a high bidder whose strength is in four top trumps, say, will probably lead them to denude the opposition, but keeping one back to regain the lead, especially if he is hoping to make one of an outside doubleton. However, if he is relying on partner for a trick, he must try to give him the opportunity to win one, so might need to give him the chance of trumping a loser before he removes the trumps.

HEARTS

Hearts is a trick-taking game but employs the principle of losing tricks instead of winning them. Many games use this principle as part of the game (e.g. Solo Whist), but in Hearts it is the whole game. There are many variants and they follow the main description, with the exception of Black Maria and Omnibus Hearts which are sufficiently different and popular to justify descriptions as separate games.

Players

Hearts can be played by from three to six players, with four perhaps the best number. There is also a variant for two players, described later.

Cards

The pack of 52 is used if there are four players. For three players one small card must be removed, e.g. ♣2. For five players two cards must be removed, e.g. ♣2, ♦2. For six players four cards must be removed, e.g. ♣3, ♦2, ♠2. Cards rank from Ace (high) to 2 (low). There are no trumps.

Preliminaries

Cards are cut for first deal, lowest dealing. Thereafter, the deal passes in rotation to the left. The dealer shuffles and the player to his right cuts.

The deal for the hand of Hearts described in the text.

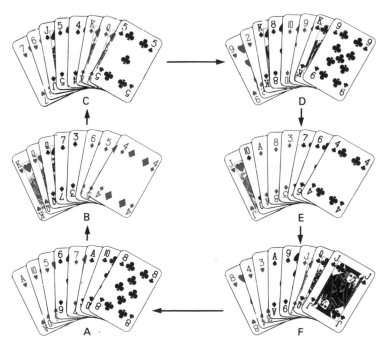

Dealing

The pack is dealt one card at a time to each hand, beginning with the eldest hand (i.e. that to left of dealer), and continuing clockwise.

The play

Eldest hand makes the opening lead. Players then play in turn clockwise. Players must follow suit to the opening lead if able to, if not they may discard any card they wish. When all players have played the trick is taken by the player who played the highest card of the suit led.

The winner of a trick leads to the next trick, and play continues thus until all cards are played and tricks won.

The sole object of the play is to avoid taking tricks which contain hearts, which are penalty cards.

Example hand

There are six players, and the hands are as in the illustration.

It is A's lead, and he decided to lead one of his singletons, and chooses the ♦7:

	A	B	C	D	E	F
1.	♦7	♦6	♦K	♦9	♦A	♦J

E decided it was good policy to risk playing his Ace with only F to follow, and having gained the lead he decided to lead his singleton ♠10:

	A	B	C	D	E	F
2.	♠6	♠Q	♠J	♠K	♠10	♠A

F decided to step in quickly with his ♠A and risk collecting any hearts, recognizing that his club holding is dangerous and wishing to lead his 'safe' hearts to eliminate them before clubs can be led:

	A	B	C	D	E	F
3.	♥5	♥K	♥7	♥9	♥J	♥3

The interesting choice was that of A – he doesn't know it but he could have played his ♥10 quite safely. Now he is in a little trouble, but luckily for him, B's best lead is probably the ♦5:

	A	B	C	D	E	F
4.	♥A	♦5	♦Q	♦10	♦8	♣Q

F rightly decides his ♣Q is more dangerous than his heart holding, while A, with big hearts and clubs, decides to ditch his ♥A. C, feeling now unlikely to take any more hearts, leads his club:

	A	B	C	D	E	F
5.	♣10	♥Q	♣5	♣K	♣7	♣J

D decides to risk all on everybody having a club, intending to lead his ♥2 if he won the trick. F breathed a sigh of relief. A, not being certain of being able to lose the lead if he played his ♣A, decided on the ♣10, which, with ♣K Q J played, has the same value as ♣A. But he was only delaying the inevitable:

	A	B	C	D	E	F
6.	♥10	♦7	♥6	♥2	♣6	♥4

Had A played his ♥10 at trick 3 he would have been safe. Now there is only one heart left:

	A	B	C	D	E	F
7.	♣8	♦4	♠5	♣9	♣4	♥8

F will win the last trick, but there are no hearts left. The final tally of hearts for each player is:

A4;   B6;   C1;   D2;   E0;   F0

It is interesting to note that E and F won the first two rounds with Aces, and were the only two players to finish without taking a heart.

Scoring

Each heart taken by a player counts as one penalty point against him.

There are three main ways of scoring a game:

Cumulative scoring With this system, the number of hearts taken by each player is recorded in a running total column. It is best to agree beforehand on the length of the game, which should be a number of deals divisible by the number of players, so that each player deals an equal number of games. For example, with five players, 20 deals might be agreed as the length of a game, each player dealing four times.

The winner is the player with the lowest score. If the game is played for stakes settlement is as follows. At the end of the game the total points scored will always be divisible by the number of players, and making the division will give an average score.

For example, with 20 deals and five players the final scores might be:

A	B	C	D	E
74	52	63	37	34

The total of scores is 260 (i.e. 20 × 13), and the average score 52 (260 ÷ 5). Players with more than 52 points put the difference in stake (agreed beforehand) into a pool, from which players with less than 52 points take out the difference between their scores and 52.

Thus this game is settled as follows:

A	B	C	D	E
−22	Level	−11	+15	+18

Sweepstakes This is another way of settling with stakes. At the end of each deal players put into a pot one chip for each heart won. If one player took no hearts (called being clear) he takes the pot. If two players or more are clear they share the pot, any odd chips being left in the pot for the next deal. The exception is that if one player takes all the hearts the pot becomes a jackpot, and the whole of it is left in for the next deal. The pot similarly becomes a jackpot if all the players are *painted*, i.e. all have taken a heart and none are clear. With this method of scoring play can stop by arrangement at an agreed time.

Howell settlement This is a popular method of settlement that again allows settlement after each hand. Each player puts into the pot for each heart taken as many chips as there are other players. For example, if there are five players in the game a player will contribute four chips for every heart won, i.e. for five hearts, 20 chips. When all have contributed each player removes one chip for each heart he did not take, i.e. 13 minus his total.

For example, in a four-handed game:

	A	B	C	D
Hearts taken	6	4	3	0
Put in pot	18	12	9	0
Taken from pot	7	9	10	13
Win or loss	−11	−3	+1	+13

Variants

Domino Hearts Each player is dealt six cards only, the remainder forming a stock face down in the centre of the table. Play is as usual, except that a player unable to follow suit must draw from the stock until he can. When the stock is exhausted the game continues, but players may now discard. Players will have unequal numbers of cards, and each drops out when his cards are all played. If a player wins a trick with his last card then the active player nearest his left leads to the next trick. The last player adds his remaining cards to the cards he has won, and if the stock is not exhausted he adds those cards, too. Each heart taken counts 1 point, and game may end after an agreed number of deals, or when any player reaches an agreed number of points.

Joker Hearts In this variant the Joker is added to the pack. It ranks below ♥ J and above ♥ 10. It cannot be played if its holder has a card of the suit led. However, it also has the function of a kind of trump, and it takes any trick to which it is played, *unless* the trick contains one of the four higher hearts, ♥ A, K, Q or J. In this case, the highest heart takes the trick. It follows that the holder of the Joker can prevent himself from winning a trick with it only by playing it in a trick containing one of these four cards.

In some circles the Joker counts as one point against its taker, as the other hearts, making 14 points at stake in each deal, but in other circles it counts as five points, making 18 at stake in each deal.

Hearts for two players The full pack of 52 is used, but only 13 cards are dealt to each player, the remainder forming a face-down stock in the centre of the table. The non-dealer leads to the first trick, subsequently the winner of a trick draws the top card of the stock, the loser the next card. Each player thus continues to hold 13 cards until the stock is exhausted, whereupon the last 13 cards are played out as normal. The player with the fewer hearts in his tricks at the end is the winner by the difference in the two totals.

Heartsette This is a variant in which a widow is used. If five or six play the full pack is used, but if three or four play the ♠ 2 is removed. When there are three players each player is dealt 16 cards, when four each is dealt 12 cards, when five each is dealt ten cards and when six each is dealt eight cards. The remaining cards (three, three, two and four respectively) are placed face down in the centre to form a widow. The player to the left of dealer leads to the first trick. The player who wins the first trick takes up the widow, and discards the same number of cards face down from his hand. The game continues as for the parent game.

Hoggenheimer

Hoggenheimer is a gambling game for any number of players. It is sometimes called English roulette because it originated in England, and because the stakes are placed on the layout in a similar manner.

Cards

The standard pack is used from which are stripped the 6s, 5s, 4s, 3s, and 2s. A Joker is added to make 33 cards.

Preliminaries

The game requires a banker. Any player who wishes may be banker. Should more than one wish to be, cards are drawn and the highest (Ace high) is the banker for an agreed maximum period or until he wishes to give up the bank. At the odds quoted later there is no advantage to the bank.

The play

The banker has the last shuffle, and may ask any other player to cut the cards. The banker lays out 32 cards face down in four rows of eight, laying aside the last card.

The rows represent, from the top, spades, hearts, diamonds and clubs respectively, and the columns, from the left, Aces down to 7s.

Players place their bets by placing their stakes on a card or a combination of cards. They are betting that the card or combination will be turned face up by the end of the game. For example, a stake on the card at the top left of the layout is a bet that the ♠A will be upturned, a stake at the foot or top of a column that the whole column will be upturned, a stake between two cards that both cards will be upturned. This staking is similar to the way stakes are placed on a roulette table.

When all the bets are placed the banker turns over the odd card and places it in its place in the layout, taking up the card which is already there, exposing it and putting it in its respective place, and so on. He continues thus until the Joker is turned up, at which stage the game ends and the banker settles bets according to which cards are turned up. Should the Joker be the odd card at the beginning of the game, the banker naturally wins all bets.

The illustration shows a completed game. It contains an example of all of the possible bets. These bets, and the odds they pay, are as follows:

a) On a single card: in the illustration stake 1 is successful, stake 2 has failed. The odds paid are 1–1, or evens.

b) On any two adjacent cards, either in a row or column: stake 3 (on ♠J ♥J) and stake 4 (on ♣8 ♣7) are both successful. The odds paid are 2–1.

c) On any four cards, either in a square or column (called a *street* in roulette): stake 5 (on the four Queens) and stake 6 (on ♥10 9 ♦10 9) are both successful; stake 7 (on the four Aces) is unsuccessful. The odds paid are 4–1;

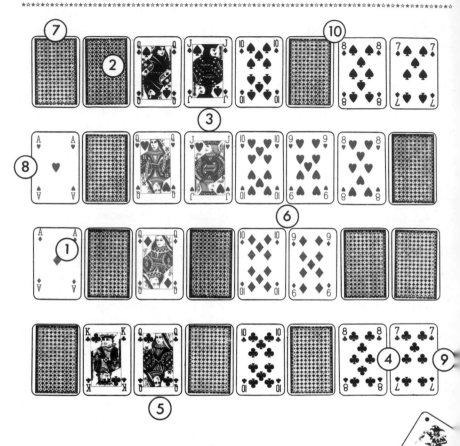

A completed game of Hoggenheimer. The bets, odds and settlement are described in the text.

d) on any eight cards, either in a row or in adjacent columns: stake 8 (on the row of hearts), stake 9 (on the row of clubs) and stake 10 (on all 8s and 9s) are all unsuccessful. The odds paid are 8–1.

KLABERJASS

Klaberjass is a game which in various forms has been played in Europe and the United States. It is often confused with an old Hungarian game called Kalabrias, but is not the same game. It is colloquially known as 'Klab', 'Klob', 'Clabber', etc, and was popular along Broadway in the 1930s, when Damon Runyon's 'guys and dolls' played it.

Players

Klaberjass is essentially a game for two players. It can be played by four in two partnerships, as described later.

Cards

The standard pack, from which are removed the 6s, 5s, 4s, 3s and 2s, is used. In the trump suit the cards rank J (high), 9, A, 10, K. Q, 8, 7. The Jack of trumps is called *jasz* (pronounced yahss), the 9 *menel* and the 7 *dix* (pronounced deece). In plain suits the cards rank: A (high), 10, K, Q, J, 9, 8, 7.

Preliminaries

Each player draws a card and the lower deals. Dealer shuffles last and his opponent cuts.

Dealing

Six cards are dealt to each player in bundles of three, beginning with non-dealer. The 13th card is turned up and placed in the centre with the remainder, the stock, placed face down on it so as to partly cover it. The turn-up proposes the trump suit.

Bidding

Non-dealer bids first, and has the choice of three declarations. He may *take it* (i.e. accept the proposed suit as trumps), *pass* (i.e. refuse the proposed suit as trumps) or *schmeiss* (i.e. offer to abandon the deal, the decision being that of the dealer).

If the non-dealer takes it he becomes the *maker* of trumps. If he says 'Schmeiss' the dealer may refuse the offer to abandon the deal by saying 'No' or 'Take it'. In this case the up-card becomes trumps and non-dealer (i.e. the schmeisser) becomes the maker. If the dealer accepts the schmeiss by saying 'Yes', the deal is abandoned.

If non-dealer passes, dealer has the same three options: he may take it, in which case the turn up becomes trumps with him as maker, he may pass, or he may schmeiss, in which case the non-dealer can refuse, and force dealer to be maker with the upcard as trumps, or accept, when the deal is abandoned.

After this round of bidding therefore, there are three possibilities: that the upcard is trumps, with one or other of the players the maker, that the deal is abandoned, or that both players have passed.

In the last case there is a second, and final round of bidding. Non-dealer's three options now are to name one of the other three suits as trumps, to schmeiss or to pass. Should he name the trump suit he becomes the maker with that suit as trumps. Should he schmeiss, the dealer again has the choice of refusing, in which case non-dealer must name his trump suit and become maker, or accepting, in which case the deal is abandoned. Should he pass, dealer can name his trump suit and become maker or abandon the deal.

After two rounds of bidding, therefore, the deal is either abandoned or there is a maker, who has either accepted the upcard or named his own trumps, whether it be by choice or because his schmeiss was refused.

Further deal

Once the trump suit is fixed, the dealer deals from the top of the stock three further cards, one at a time, to each player, beginning with his opponent. The bottom card of the stock is then exposed and placed face up on the top of the stock. It does not enter play, and is exposed only to give information to the players.

Sequences

With both players holding nine cards, they now declare *sequences*. A sequence is a group of three or more cards of adjacent rank within the same suit. For this purpose only the cards are ranked as normal: A (high), K, Q, J, 10, 9, 8, 7.

A sequence of three cards counts 20, of four or more 50. Only one player can score for sequence, and there are no ties. If non-dealer holds a sequence he announces its value, either 'Twenty' or 'Fifty'. If dealer lacks a sequence of equal or better value he says 'Good', and non-dealer scores the points for sequence. If dealer has a better

sequence he says 'Not good' and scores for sequence himself. If he has an equal sequence he says 'How high?' and non-dealer responds by naming the highest card in the sequence. Dealer again says 'Good', 'Not good' or 'Equal.' In the last case if either player's sequence is in the trump suit he says so, and scores for sequence. Otherwise, with both sequences equal, non-dealer scores for sequence.

The player who scores for sequence may also score for any additional sequence he holds (e.g. a sequence of four plus another of three would score 70 points). A player scoring for sequence must show his opponent all scoring sequences after play to the first trick. It is not compulsory to declare sequences. Either player may keep a sequence secret, but cannot, of course, score for it.

The play

If the upcard is accepted as the trump, a player holding the dix (7 of trumps) may exchange it for the upcard and so obtain a higher trump.

Non-dealer makes the opening lead, and subsequently the winner of a trick leads to the next. The second player to a trick must follow suit, and if unable to follow must trump if possible. On a trump lead the second player must play a higher trump if able. A trick is won by the higher trump or, if no trump is played, the higher card in the suit led.

If a player holds the King and Queen of trumps he may score 20 points for *bella*. This is scored during play if he announces 'Bella' on playing the second card of the two. He might not wish to announce it (see under *Scoring*).

The object of the play is to win tricks which include cards of counting value (see under *Scoring*) and the last trick, which counts 10.

Scoring
Cards won in tricks have the following point values:

jasz (Jack of trumps)	20
menel (9 of trumps)	14
any Ace	11
any 10	10
any King	4
any Queen	3
any other Jack	2

Each player totals his points won in tricks and adds them to any points won in sequences, bella and last trick. If the trump maker has the higher total, each player scores the points he won. If the totals are the same the maker does not score, but his opponent scores his points. If the non-maker's total is higher he scores the sum of both players' scores, and maker scores nothing. This is called going *bete*, and is the reason a maker would not announce 'Bella' if the points were to go to his opponent.

Game is to 500, and the usual practice is to play out the last hand if both players are about to go over 500 – the player with the higher final score wins. However, some players agree in advance that the first to pass 500 during play wins.

Example hand
Players are dealt the two six-card hands as shown in the illustration, with the ♥8 as upcard.

Non-dealer decided to pass, hoping that dealer would also pass, in which case he would name diamonds as trumps and hold jasz. Dealer, however, holding the Jack of the upcard and powerful clubs, decides to take it.

After the additional three cards the hands are as in the second illustration, and the ♣10 is exposed as the bottom card of the stock.

Non-dealer says 'No sequence', and dealer says 'Twenty'.

Dealer holds dix but does not bother to change it for the upcard which is of no better value.

The hands and upcard as dealt for the example hand of Klaberjass described in the text.

DEALER

NON-DEALER

DEALER

NON-DEALER

The hands after the additional cards are dealt and the bottom card of the stock (♣10) exposed.

Non-dealer leads his ♠A and wins the trick. Dealer shows his club sequence. Non-dealer does not now have a satisfactory lead so decides to lead a club to dealer's suit, putting the onus of leading onto dealer. The play proceeds:

	Dealer	Non-dealer
1.	♠K	♠A
2.	♣A	♣9
3.	♣K	♣8
4.	♣Q	♥10
5.	♦10	♦J
6.	♥J	♥K
7.	♦Q	♦8
8.	♦9	♠J
9.	♥7	♣10

Neither player scores for bella. Dealer scores 20 points for sequence, 10 for last and 20 for jasz, 11 for an Ace, 20 for 10s, 8 for Kings, 3 for a Queen, and 4 for Jacks, total 96 points. Non-dealer scores 28. As dealer was maker, each player scores his points.

Strategy

The main strategy lies in when to make trumps. It is largely a question of judgement born of experience. The main purpose is to establish a Jack, otherwise a middle-ranking card, as jasz, worth a certain 20 points. As a rough guide a player should consider making trumps if he can see about 40 points in his hand. This is based on the assumption that about 60 points will usually be enough to win the hand, around 110 points being average for a deal, and that the extra three cards should produce the other 20 points needed. In the example hand 124 points were scored. Dealer was justified in taking it because he could see 20 points for jasz, 11 for ♣A, a probable 20 for sequence and likely points from ♣K, Q and ♦10.

The Jack of trumps (jasz) and to a lesser extent the 9 (menel) are important in this assessment. In the example hand non-dealer would not take it even with 10 K in the trump suit, because of the danger of his opponent holding jasz or menel. With the bete convention, it is a big setback for the maker not to win the majority of points. Non-dealer's best policy was to hope he could promote his   J to jasz.

Schmeiss should be called if the hand is not strong enough to take, but where the upcard suit is nevertheless the best trump choice. It prevents the opponent from naming his choice of trumps, which would probably be much worse than the proposed suit.

There is little room for choice in the play. It is usually best to try to establish a long suit by leading it, to draw trumps if strong in side suits, and avoid leading from tenaces, but there is usually little scope to alter the outcome.

Klaberjass for four players Four can play in two partnerships. Cards are drawn, the two lowest playing against the two highest. The lowest deals and the partners sit opposite each other.

Eight cards are dealt to each player, so all cards are in play. The dealer turns over his last card to denote the proposed trump. There is no schmeiss. Beginning with eldest hand, each player may either take-it or pass. If all pass, there is a second round where each player in turn has the opportunity of naming the trump suit. If all four players pass in this round the deal is abandoned. The player who makes the trump suit becomes the maker. The players play as individuals so far as scoring for sequence or bella are concerned. At the end of the deal each partnership totals its score, and scoring is thereafter as for the parent game.

KLONDIKE

The Klondike and the Demon (q.v.) are probably the two most widely played **patience** or **solitaire** games. They sometimes get confused, and Klondike is frequently called Canfield, which is in fact another name for Demon.

The play

The full pack is used. The cards are shuffled and 28 are dealt as follows: the first card is dealt face up to the left of the tableau, and six cards are dealt face down in a row alongside it. A second face-up card is dealt overlapping the first face-down card, followed by five face-down cards in a row to its right, and so on. The result is a tableau as shown in the illustration.

The four Aces are the foundations, and as they become available they are built to a row above the tableau, in the spaces marked in the illustration. The object is to build on the foundations in suit sequences from Ace to King.

The cards available for playing to the foundations are the face-up cards at the foot of each column in the tableau. These cards can also be built on each other. A card can be built on a card of the next rank higher and the opposite colour, e.g. the ♣9 can be built upon the ♦10. All face-up cards in a tableau column may be built upon an appropriate card in another

---

The layout for the game of Klondike described in the text.

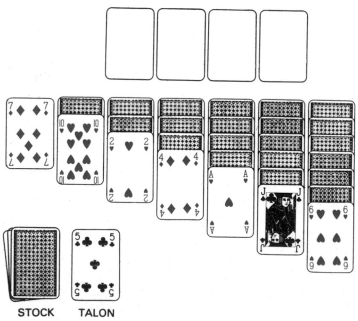

STOCK   TALON

column, but must be moved as a unit, e.g. to continue the example given earlier, the ♦10, ♣9 can be build on the ♠J.

When a card or cards are transferred, the face-down card at the foot of the column is exposed and becomes available for play. Should a column become empty, its space can be filled by a King, with or without an attached sequence, but only if the King is available to play.

The stock is taken into hand and turned over one card at a time onto a talon, or waste-pile. The top card of the talon is available to play either to a foundation or to the tableau.

It is not compulsory to build on a foundation, and a card that is built to a foundation cannot be moved back to the tableau. The stock is only turned over once. The game is won when all foundations are built to Kings.

In the layout in the illustration the ♥A can be played to a foundation, and the ♥2 packed upon it. The ♥10 is built upon the ♣J. The ♣5 in the talon is built on the ♥6, and the ♦4 built upon it. During these operations four face-down cards will have been exposed, and further moves may be possible. When all moves are exhausted the next card from the stock is turned over to the talon, and so on.

KNAVES

Knaves is an excellent trick-taking game which combines scores for winning tricks with penalties for winning certain cards. The penalty cards are Jacks, otherwise known in England as Knaves, from which the game gets its name.

The deal for the hand of Knaves described in the text.

Players
Knaves is a game for three players.

Cards
The full standard pack of 52 cards is used.

Preliminaries
Players draw for deal, the player drawing the highest card being dealer.

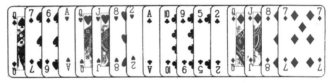

A

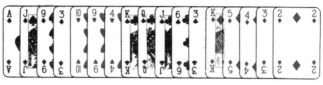

B

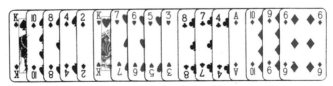

C

TRUMP

Dealing

Seventeen cards are dealt to each player one at a time, beginning with the player to dealer's left (eldest). The last card is turned face up in the centre to denote trumps. It takes no part in the game.

The play

Eldest leads to the first trick, thereafter a player who wins a trick leads to the next. Players must follow suit to the card led if able, otherwise they may trump or discard.

The object is to win tricks, each trick being worth 1 point, while at the same time avoiding taking tricks containing Jacks, which are penalty cards. A player taking the ♥J loses 4 points, the ♦J 3 points, the ♣J 2 points and the ♠J 1 point. There are thus 7 points on offer in each deal: 17 for tricks minus 10 for penalties (unless one of the Jacks is the turn-up for trumps).

Game is to 20 points. The game is interesting because some tricks are better won and some better lost, so all hands have their possibilities.

Example hand

Player A dealt the three hands in the illustration. The ♠5 was the turn-up. B has the first lead and regards his small diamonds as excellent cards to get off the lead. The play proceeds:

	A	B	C
1.	♦Q	♦2	♦9
2.	♣10	♣K	♣8
3.	♦8	♦3	♦10
4.	♣9	♣Q	♣7
5.	♦7	♦5	♦6
6.	♣5	♣6	♣4
7.	♦J	♦4	♦A
8.	♥A	♥10	♥7
9.	♠6	♠A	♣4
10	♥Q	♥9	♥6
11.	♠7	♠9	♠10
12.	♠Q	♠J	♠8
13.	♥8	♥4	♥K
14.	♥2	♣J	♥3
15.	♥J	♣3	♥5
16.	♣A	♠3	♠K
17.	♣2	♦K	♠2

B's diamonds were very useful for him to get off lead when winning early tricks. He established ♦K, but could not make a trick with it. Player C was forced to take the ♣J near the end, but avoided the ♥J and took the last two tricks.

A took six tricks, but lost five points by taking the ♥J and ♠J so ended with 1 point only. B took four tricks with no penalty points so ended with 4 points. C took seven tricks, but included the ♦J and ♣J, so ended with 2 points.

Strategy

With the conflicting objects of the game, low cards, particularly 2s, are very useful for getting off lead, and avoiding taking a trick containing a penalty card, while high cards are necessary, of course, to win tricks. Players should not be afraid to take tricks, as the game cannot be won without. Good leads early on are 10s and 9s – they are unlikely to win a trick but cannot take one containing a Jack. It is necessary to keep track of the cards played. At trick 15 in the example hand player C knew that his lead of ♥5 would saddle player A with the Jack, and that he, C, was therefore certain to win the last two tricks.

Towards the end of the game players adjust their tactics to suit the score, e.g. they will try to pass penalty cards to a player who is near to 20 points, or will try to lose tricks to a player well behind rather than to a close rival.

Loo

Around 1800 Loo was England's most popular card game. It was originally called Lanterloo, from the French word *lanterlu*, meaning 'fiddlesticks'. It is a gambling game, and as with most popular games there are several versions, the main variant being between three-card Loo and five-card Loo. Three-card Loo is described first.

Players

Any number may play up to 17, although the game is best for six or seven players.

Cards

The full standard pack of 52 is used, but if less than five play it is best to strip the pack of the 6s, 5s, 4s, 3s, and 2s, and use the 32-card pack. The cards rank Ace (high) to 2 (low), or, in the short pack, Ace (high) to 7 (low).

Preliminaries

Players may sit at random, and one deals a card face up to each player clockwise to his left, and the player dealt the first Jack deals in the game.

The pool

Before dealing the dealer puts an agreed stake into a pool. It must be divisible by three, so it can be regarded as a stake of 3 units.

Dealing

The dealer deals three cards, one at a time, to each player and to an extra hand called *miss*. He turns up the top card of the remainder of the pack to denote trumps.

The play

Each player in turn, beginning with eldest, has three choices: first, of playing with the cards dealt him; second of exchanging his cards for miss and playing with those; or third, of refusing to play, in which case he places his cards in the centre face down. Of course, once a player has chosen to take miss, subsequent players have two choices only: to play or refuse. Once a player on his turn has decided to play or not, he cannot subsequently change his mind.

The player who first decided to play (i.e. the player nearest dealer's left) leads to the first trick. Thereafter the winner of a trick leads to the next.

The rules of play are different from normal trick-taking games, and the following rules must be followed:

1. A player must follow suit, if able, and if void, must trump if able. In either case, he must *head* the trick, if able, i.e. beat all previous cards.
2. If a player on lead holds the Ace of Trumps (or the King if the Ace is the turn-up) he must lead it.
3. If a player on lead holds two or more trumps he must lead one of them, and if there are only two players in the game he must lead the higher or highest.

If a player fails to observe these rules the pool is divided among the others in the game and the offender pays the full amount back into the pool.

When the hand is finished, the winners of tricks share the pool (one-third of the pool for each trick won, which is why the pool must divide by three).

A player who played but did not win a trick is *looed*, and must put into the pool the amount it contained at the beginning of the deal. This is called *unlimited* stake loo. In practice it is best to agree upon a limit, because otherwise the pool multiplies astronomically – eight doubles of the original 3 units is 768 units. It is best to agree that a player looed must put into the pool 3 units.

The stakes put into the pool by looed players constitute the pool for the next deal. If no players are looed, then the new dealer puts in three units, as at the beginning of the game.

If all players refuse to play, the dealer takes the entire pool, and the next dealer has to put in 3 units for the next pool. If only one player chooses to play, then the dealer is obliged to play against him. He can protect himself against loss, however, if he wishes, by announcing that he will play for the pool. This means that should he fail to win a trick he is not looed. In return, he gives up the right to take from the pool any amount to which he would otherwise be entitled for winning tricks.

Variants

Five-card Loo The following differences apply in five-card Loo:

1. Each player is dealt five cards, and since the pool must be divided by five, the pool must consist of five units.
2. There is no miss.
3. A player may exchange any number of cards by discarding and drawing from stock. He must have decided to play before exchanging, however. A player cannot exchange and then decide whether or not to play.
4. The ♣J is the highest trump no matter what suit the upcard is. It is known as *pam*. Its holder must obey the rules regarding the necessity to trump and to take a trick, with one exception. If a player leading the trump Ace announces 'Pam be civil', then the holder of pam is barred from playing it on the trick.
5. Should a player hold five cards of one suit, or four plus pam, he has a *flush* and exposes it, automatically winning the pool. All other players are looed. Should two or more players hold flushes, a flush in the trump suit takes precedence over one in a plain suit, otherwise the highest card decides precedence, if equal the second highest and so on. If two or more flushes are exactly equal, the pool is divided.

Irish Loo This is the variant many players think best. Each player is dealt three cards. There is no miss and no pam, but a player who decides to play may exchange a card or cards by drawing from the stock. The main difference from the forms already mentioned lies in the convention that should clubs be trumps everybody must play. Since a number of players are certain to be looed, it is clear that this game cannot be played for unlimited stakes, or the game will get out of hand.

Strategy

The real decision lies in whether to play or refuse. The amount in the pool must be a factor, as must the number of previous players who have decided to play. Suppose in three-card Loo there are 12 units in the pool. A player taking a trick will win 4, but should he be looed he will lose 12, so he needs odds of 3 to 1 on that he will win a trick to make playing a reasonable proposition.

Note that even a twice guarded King of trumps is not a certain trick. If a player holds, say, K 6 5 in trumps, and the Jack is led on his right, he must by the rules play the King, which could well lose to the Ace. And when he plays his small trumps in the remaining rounds he could easily find both overtrumped. Against this there is a lot of luck connected with which cards are sleeping, and a player with the K 6 5 of trumps mentioned above could easily find himself winning two or even three tricks if the Ace is sleeping.

Miss Milligan

Miss Milligan is a double-pack **patience** or **solitaire** which is difficult to get out and recommended for those players seeking the satisfaction of achieving something after weeks or months of failure.

The play

The two packs are shuffled, and eight cards are dealt face up in a row. The pack can now be laid aside for a moment. Any Aces in this row are played to a foundation row above the tableau. The object is to build on them in suit-sequence up to Kings. Any other cards in this first row can be packed on any other in downward sequence of alternate colours.

In the illustration the ♥A is played to a foundation, the ♦J is packed on the ♠Q, the ♣4 is packed on the ♦5 and both these cards are packed on the ♣6. This ends the moves so far possible. It leaves four columns blank.

Now the pack is taken into hand again, and a further eight cards are dealt, one to each column, where necessary overlapping those cards already in the column. For readers wishing to follow this example, let us imagine that the eight cards are, from the left: ♦9 ♠A ♠10 ♥7 ♥2 ♥J ♣3 ♥5.

Now the ♠A is played to a foundation, the ♥2 is played to its Ace in the foundation, the ♠10 is packed on the ♥J, the ♦9 on the ♠10, the ♠8 on the ♦9, the ♥7 on the ♠8 and the sequence headed by the ♣6 on the ♥7. This leaves all the cards in the tableau in three columns only.

Another eight cards are now dealt. Let us imagine that they are: ♦6 ♣9 ♥3 ♦4 ♥5 ♠4 ♥K ♣7. the new tableau now looks like that in the second illustration.

Now, the ♥3 is played to the foundation. The ♦6 is packed on the ♣7. One of the spaces can now be filled by the ♥K. A space may be filled only by a King, with or without a sequence attached to it. This releases the ♣3 to be packed on the ♦4, and this in turn allows the sequence headed by the ♠Q to be packed on the ♥K. The ♠4 can be packed on the ♥5. That is all the moves possible at this stage, so a further row of eight cards is dealt. And so on.

Rules to remember are that no packing may be done until all the eight cards in a row have been dealt; similarly an Ace or any other card cannot be played to its foundation until all eight cards have been dealt. As mentioned, a

---

The layout at the start of the game of Miss Milligan described in the text.

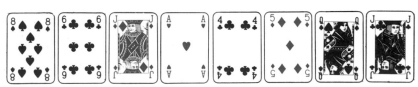

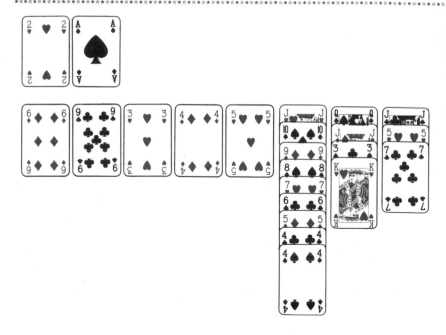

The game described in the text in progress.

space can be filled only by an exposed King.

It helps that not only can a single card at the bottom of a column be packed on another column, but that a sequence at the bottom of a column can also be packed on an appropriate card in another column.

One other help is given. When the stock has run out (there are 13 rows of eight cards in the two packs) the player can take into his hand any exposed card that is hindering him by blocking a packing or a series of packings. This is known as *waiving*. However, the player will not win the game unless, after he has made the transfers that the waiving allowed, he can replace the waived card in a legitimate place in a foundation or on an exposed card at the foot of a column.

If he can achieve this he can then waive another card and repeat the process. He is allowed to waive as many cards as he wishes, but only one at a time.

MONTE BANK

Monte Bank is a simple gambling game in which betting is on the turn-up of a card.

Players
Any number may play, one of whom is a banker.

Cards
The full pack from which the 8s, 9s and 10s have been removed is used, i.e. a pack of 40 cards.

The play
The banker shuffles and the player to his right cuts the cards. The banker then draws two cards from the bottom of the pack and places them side by side face up on the table. This is known as the bottom layout. He then places two cards from the top of the pack face up in a row above the other two to form the top layout.

Players place their bets upon whichever layout they choose. As with all casual gambling games, it is best to agree on minimum and maximum stakes beforehand. The banker then places the pack on the table face upwards, i.e. so that the bottom card is exposed. The arrangement is shown in the illustration. The bottom card is the gate.

If either layout includes a card

TOP LAYOUT

BOTTOM LAYOUT

GATE

The arrangement of a hand of Monte Bank. Backers of the top layout win, those of the bottom layout lose.

———

of the same suit as the gate, those who staked on that layout win. If the layout does not include a card of the suit of the gate, backers of that layout lose. Should a layout contain two cards of the same suit, backers of that layout are paid out at 3 to 1. Otherwise bets are settled at odds of 1 to 1.

When there is one card of each suit in the two layouts, there is no advantage to either side, but if there is a duplicate the banker has an advantage in his favour on all bets.

NAPOLEON

Napoleon, or Nap, has been popular in England for 200 years and has given the language a slang expressing, to 'go nap', meaning to take five of anything. It is a gambling game.

Players
From two to eight may play, with four being perhaps the best number.

Cards
The full pack of 52 is used, the cards ranking from Ace (high) to 2 (low).

Preliminaries
Players draw to decide first dealer, the lowest being dealer, and (for this purpose only) Ace counting low. After each deal the deal passes to the left.

Dealing
Five cards are dealt to each player, face down, one at a time, in a clockwise direction.

Bidding
After the deal each player, beginning with the player to dealer's left, has one chance to bid or pass. A bid is a contract to make a given number of tricks, bidder naming the trump suit (he does not reveal the suit until after the bidding). A bid of 'Five' (i.e. a contract to make all the tricks) is called *napoleon*, or usually *nap*. The lowest bid permitted is 'Two', unless all players round to dealer pass, in which case he is allowed to bid 'One'.

The play
The highest bidder (the *declarer*) leads to the first trick, and the card led denotes the trump suit. The usual rules of trick-taking games apply: players must follow suit to the card led if able, and if unable may trump or discard. A trick is won by the highest trump, or if no trumps are played by the highest card in the suit led.

The object of the game for declarer is to make his contract, i.e. the amount of tricks bid, and for his opponents to prevent him. Tricks made by declarer in excess of his contract are of no value to him.

Scoring
Settlement is usually made at the end of each deal, with declarer either receiving from or paying each player according to whether or not he made his contract. He is paid one unit for each trick of his contract, except for Napoleon, for which he receives 10 units if successful, and pays 5 units if unsuccessful.

Strategy
If there are less than six players there are more cards sleeping than in play, so evaluating a hand is an inexact undertaking. Each hand will include a suit of at least two cards, so a 'substantial' trump suit ought to include at least three cards. With three trumps it might be possible to make both Ace and another in a side suit, but unless the trumps include Ace and

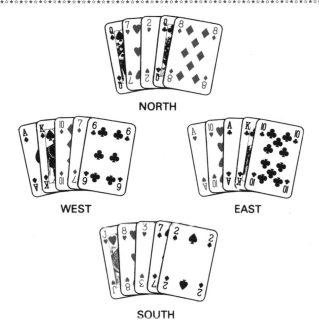

NORTH

WEST   **EAST**

SOUTH

another high one, it is quite likely one trump will be lost.

When a player goes nap his opponents should watch each other's discards when trumps are led, so that the high cards each keeps in a side suit might be of different suits. It is usually better to retain a King and a small card in a side suit rather than separate Kings.

Example hand

South dealt the hands as shown in the illustration. West has two certain tricks with his two top spades as trumps, but is very unlikely to make another, so bids 'Two'. North passes. East, unless another player has three clubs to the Queen or Jack, will make four tricks at least, and five unless another player has two hearts to the King, Queen or Jack and keeps them for the last two rounds.

The deal for the hand of Napoleon described in the text.

Because the reward for making nap is twice the penalty for failing, he decides to take a chance and calls 'Nap'.

The play proceeds:

	East	South	West	North
1.	♣A	♠2	♣6	♣Q
2.	♣K	♠7	♠A	♠Q
3.	♣10	♥3	♦7	♦8
4.	♥A	♥8	♦10	♥2
5.	♥10	♥J	♠K	♥7

At trick 2, West discarded ♠A as a clear indication (reinforced by his bid) to his temporary partners that he held the ♠K, so they could discard spades, which North promptly did. East was unlucky. It is interesting to note that had his fifth card been the ♦2, he would have been successful, suggesting that North would have done better to have kept ♦ 8 and to have discarded ♥ 2 on trick 3.

Variants
Some players allow a higher bid than napoleon, to cater for those instances where two or more players have excellent hands simultaneously. This is called *wellington*, and can only be bid if napoleon has already been bid. It contracts to make five tricks but at double the usual stakes for napoleon. If allowed, it is usual also to allow *blucher*, which can be bid only after wellington, and is a contract to make five tricks at triple stakes. In some schools the double or triple stakes for wellington and blucher are paid only when the contract fails.

A further bid sometimes allowed by agreement is *misère* or *misery*, an undertaking to lose all five tricks, without a trump suit (although some schools make the declarer's opening lead the trump suit as usual). The bid ranks above Three but below Four and is settled at 3 units per player.

Some schools allow a convention called *peep*. Any player on his turn may look at the top card of the undealt stock by paying an agreed stake to a pool. A player who pays for a peep, should he become declarer, may take the card from stock into his hand, discarding another. If he makes his contract he recovers the pool; otherwise it remains and is taken by the next successful contractor.

NEWMARKET

Newmarket is a modern version of an old game called Pope Joan (q.v.). It is a game of a family called Stops, by which name it is also known. There are many versions of the game which differ slightly from each other, and the names have become interchangeable. Thus the game is also called Boodle in Britain, and Michigan, Chicago or Saratoga in the United States. One popular version is described first, then another later under the name Michigan, but it is emphasized that the games are now so mixed that elements of one are often transposed to the other. It is a gambling game.

Players

Any number from three to eight may play.

Cards

The full pack of 52 cards is used, ranking from King (high) to Ace (low). However, four cards from an old pack are also required as boodle cards: a King, Queen, Jack and 10 of differing suits.

Preliminaries

The four boodle cards are laid out in a row in the centre of the table, with a saucer for a pool or kitty. The first dealer is decided by any agreed method, e.g. by a player dealing the cards round face up until the first Jack appears to denote dealer. The deal thereafter passes in turn to the left, since dealer has an advantage. Before the deal each player contributes one unit of stakes to the kitty, and an agreed number (often four) to boodle cards of his choice (he may place them one on each card, all on one card, or however he pleases). The illustration shows a layout ready for play.

Dealing

Cards are dealt one at a time to each player clockwise, the number each player receives being determined by the number of players as follows:

The boodle cards and kitty primed for a game of Newmarket.

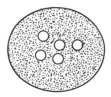

Players	Cards	Remainder (dead)
3	15	7
4	12	4
5	9	7
6	8	4
7	7	3
8	6	4

The dead cards are placed face down to one side and take no part in the deal.

The play
The player to dealer's left (eldest) begins by leading a card from whichever suit he prefers, but it must be the lowest he holds in that suit. He announces the rank and suit. He plays it before him, not to the centre. The player who holds the next higher card in that suit

then plays it and announces it and so on. The sequence continues until it is *stopped*, either by reaching the King or because an intermediate card is in the dead hand. The player who played the last card now begins a new sequence by playing a card from any suit of his choice, provided it is the lowest he holds in that suit. He may play the suit just stopped if he wishes.

When a player lays a card corresponding to one of the boodle cards, he collects the stakes on that card. The first player to get rid of all his cards takes the kitty. Should any stakes on a boodle card not be won, they remain on the card for the next deal.

The deal for the hand of Newmarket described in the text.

Example hand
The boodle cards are *primed* (i.e. stakes are placed) as in the first

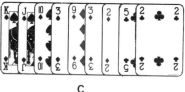

C

B

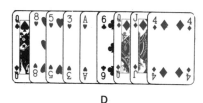

D

A

E

illustration, and five players, A, B, C, D, E have hands as shown in the second illustration. It is A's first lead, and he can immediately collect the stakes on the ♥J by beginning the play ♥10 J, and when the sequence stops here, because the ♥Q is dead, he plays the ♥K and begins a new sequence with ♠2. This runs up to his ♠7 and stops, so he now has clubs only left, and leads ♣4. This stops at ♣8, and player E begins the next sequence, and lays ♠A, which he knows is safe (♠2 has already been played). He should then play ♣J, as he knows his ♣K will stop the suit. Player A will now be down to one card, the ♣10. Player E tries his diamonds next. And so on. There are many possible outcomes to this deal, but player A will still be left at the end holding his ♣10. The best lead is frequently a matter of guesswork because of the dead hand.

Michigan

In Michigan Ace counts high, and the boodle cards are therefore A K Q J. Before the deal the dealer puts 2 units of stake on each boodle card, the other players 1 each. There is no pool, but the player who goes out collects 1 unit for each card the other players hold in their hands.

Cards are dealt one at a time so far as they go. There are no dead cards, but there is an extra hand, dealt between dealer and eldest, which is the *widow*. When dealer has examined his hand he can, if he wishes, discard it face down and take up the widow. He cannot look at the widow first, and once he has taken it he cannot revert to his original hand. In some schools a dealer satisfied with the hand he has been dealt must offer the widow to the highest bidder among the other players. He who buys it discards his dealt hand face down.

Play proceeds as in Newmarket, except that when a suit is stopped, the player who played last must change the suit, i.e. he cannot begin a new sequence in the suit just stopped. In some schools he must not only change suit, he must change the colour of the suit. In either case, should he not have a card he can legitimately play, he says so and the player on his left begins the new sequence (he is bound by the same rule of changing suit or colour).

General

As stated earlier, this family of games has become intermixed, and the main variants: the amount and method of staking, the use of a kitty, the use of a widow and the changing of a suit or a colour after a stop, are a matter of choice (as is the name by which the game is called). Players should agree beforehand which rules apply.

OKLAHOMA

Oklahoma is a melding (set-making) game of the Rummy and Canasta family, perhaps being halfway between these two games. Two packs are used. It is not the same game as a version of Gin Rummy called Oklahoma Gin.

Players

Oklahoma can be played by two to five players, but is generally considered best for three.

Cards

Two standard packs of 52 cards are used, plus a Joker. Cards rank from Ace (high) to 2 (low) but the Joker and all 2s are wild, and can represent any card that the holder chooses. Ace may be considered high in a sequence of A K Q, or low in a sequence 3 2 A but cannot be used 'round the corner' as in 2 A K.

Preliminaries

The players draw cards and the lowest deals first (Joker counts low). Thereafter the winner of a hand deals to the next.

Dealing

Thirteen cards are dealt to each player one at a time. The rest of the pack (the *stock*) is turned face down on the table and the top card turned over and placed alongside it, face up.

The play

The object is to form sequences of three or more cards in the same suit, or sets of three or more cards of the same rank, irrespective of suit. These are laid on the table in front of the player as he makes them.

The player to dealer's left (eldest) may take the upcard into his hand or refuse it. If he refuses it the next player may take it and so on. The card can only be taken if it is immediately melded (made into a set or sequence of three or more cards) and laid on the table before the player who took it. A player who takes the card discards one face up in its place.

If none of the players takes the exposed card, eldest on his next turn takes the top card from the stock into his hand and, whether he melds or not, he discards onto the upcard, which now becomes a discard pile. Play then proceeds with each player either taking the top card of the stock or the top card from the discard pile.

When a player takes the top card of the discard pile he must immediately meld it, either by adding it to a meld he already has on the table, or by forming a new one by adding two or more cards already in his hand. He must then take up the whole of the discard pile into his hand (i.e. taking the top card of the discard pile is equivalent to taking the whole discard pile into the hand). He may

---

Oklahoma in progress. West wishes to pick up from the discard pile a Jack, Ace, King, 8 or wild card to get out, discarding ♣Q. The other players have rapidly melded.

NORTH

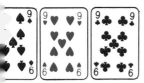

WEST

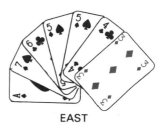

EAST

then make as many fresh melds as he pleases from the whole of his new hand before discarding a card to begin a new discard pile.

A melded sequence may be as long as 14 cards (a complete suit with an Ace at each end), but a set of cards of equal rank cannot exceed four cards.

When melding with a Joker or a 2, the player must announce the card that it represents. This means that a player who uses a Joker or 2 at the end of a sequence cannot move it to the other end of a sequence to help a later play.

However, a player who melds with a Joker can replace the Joker with the card it represents should he obtain that card on a future turn. He can then take the Joker back into his hand. (This applies to the Joker only and not wild 2s). By this means a player can take the discard pile. If the card his Joker represents appears on top of the discard pile on his turn, he can take it to replace his Joker.

A player can add only to his own melds, and the Joker can be replaced only by the player in whose meld it is.

A player may discard any card he pleases except a ♠Q, which can be discarded only if it is the only card remaining in the player's hand. A deal ends when a player goes out (i.e. has no further cards left) or when a player draws the last card of the stock and discards without going out.

A player must discard before going out. This means that a player holding less than three cards before he draws can go out only by adding to his existing melds. If, for example, after the draw his only cards were ♥7, ♠7, ♦7 he cannot go out, because if he lays them down in a meld he has no discard.

Scoring

When the deal ends, the cards in a player's melds are scored for him, those in hand against him, as follows:

Card	Melded	In hand
Joker	100	−200
♠Q	50	−100
Each Ace	20	−20
2 representing K, Q, J, 10, 9, 8 (including ♠Q)	10	−20
Each K, Q, J, 10, 9, 8 (excluding ♠Q)	10	−20
2 representing 7, 6, 5, 4, 3, 2	5	−20
Each 7, 6, 5, 4	5	−5

A player who goes out receives a bonus of 100 points, but not if he goes out on his first turn. A player who goes out on his second or later turn and who has not previously melded is said to go out *concealed* and scores an additional bonus of 250 points (which does not count towards reaching the game score).

The game score is 1,000 points, the game ending with the deal on which a player passes this score. The player who reaches game receives a bonus of 200 points, and if two or more players reach 1,000 points on the same deal, the player with the highest score receives the bonus.

For settling purposes, each player's score is rounded up or down to the nearest 100 points, and players settle separately with each other at a previously agreed rate per 100 points.

OLD MAID

Old Maid is a game for young children.

Players
Any reasonable number may play, the best being from four to eight.

Cards
The full pack is used, from which is removed and set aside one of the Queens.

Dealing
It does not matter who deals. Cards are dealt one at a time to each player, beginning with the player to dealer's left, until all the cards are dealt. It does not matter if some players receive more cards than others.

The play
Each player discards by putting down in front of him all pairs that he holds. Should a player hold three of a kind, he puts down a pair and keeps the odd card.

The player to dealer's left then shuffles the remaining cards in his hand and offers his hand face down to the player on his left, who draws a card from it. He adds it to his hand, and if it matches with a card he already holds he pairs the two cards and discards them before him as before. In any case he shuffles the cards left in his hand and offers them face down to the player on his left, and so on. As a player pairs all the cards in his hand he drops out.

Eventually, all the cards will be paired except the odd Queen, and the player holding it is Old Maid and the loser.

Children enjoy this game and show their relief when passing on the last queen, so the whereabouts of the damning card is known, but this seems to add to the enjoyment.

OMBRE

This old Spanish game dates back to the fourteenth century, and for 400 years was the favourite card game of Europe. It was introduced to England by Katherine of Braganza, who married Charles II in 1662, and a four-handed version of it, called Quadrille, was one of the three cards games mentioned by Edmond Hoyle in his famous book *Treatise on Games* in 1743. It was superseded by Whist, but is still played in Spain as Tresillo and in Latin America as Rocamber. In the United States a simplified version called Solo (not Solo Whist) is played.

Ombre is not a difficult game in itself, but the ranking of the cards is complex and unique, and for many not worth the bother of mastering. It is included here for those with a sense of history who want to try the game which 'reigned' for so long.

Players

Ombre is a game for three players.

Cards

The Spanish pack of 40 cards is used. This is the regular pack from which the 10s, 9s and 8s have been removed. In *plain* (non-trump) suits the cards in the *red* suits rank in the order K Q J A 2 3 4 5 6 7; those in the *black* suits rank in the normal order A K Q J 7 6 5 4 3 2.

In *trump* suits, if a *red* suit is trumps the cards rank in the order ♠A (*spadille*) 7 (*manille*) ♣A (*basto*) A (*punto*) K Q J 2 3 4 5 6. If a black suit is trumps the cards rank in the order ♠A (spadille) 2 (manille) ♣A (basto) K Q J 7 6 5 4 3.

The three top trumps (spadille, manille and basto) are called the *matadores*, the plural of *matador*.

When a red suit is trumps there are 12 trumps, when a black suit is trumps there are only 11.

Preliminaries

Any player takes the pack and deals a face-up card to each player in turn anti-clockwise, continuing until a black Ace appears. He who receives it is the first dealer. Before the deal each player puts an agreed stake into a pool. Each deal is a game in itself, and the cards are again dealt round to determine dealer, i.e. the deal does not pass in rotation.

Dealing

The dealer shuffles, and the player to his left cuts. Nine cards are dealt to each player in bundles of three, beginning with the player to dealer's right (in Spanish games play is anti-clockwise). The 13 cards remaining are placed face down in the centre of the table.

The play

One player (*ombre*) plays against the other two. The player to the right of dealer has the first choice of being ombre. Ombre names the trump suit, and he may exchange cards by discarding and drawing from the stock.

If the first player wishes to be ombre he says 'I play'. Otherwise he says 'I pass'. However, a player who wishes to become ombre might be overcalled by a succeeding player saying 'I play'. In this case the second player is announcing that he will be ombre without exchanging any of his cards. The first player to want to play now has the option of remaining ombre if he too is prepared to play without exchanging any of his cards.

If all three players pass the deal is abandoned, the cards are collected and shuffled and dealt round again to find the new dealer.

If a player is going ombre without exchanging cards he now names trumps and leads. If a player is playing ombre unopposed he first exchanges as many cards as he wishes by discarding and drawing from stock. The next player to his right does the same, then the third. Should there be any cards left in the stock after the draw the third player is entitled to look at them, but if he does he must show them to the other players too.

Ombre now announces the trump suit and leads to the first trick. The normal rules of trick-taking games apply: a player must follow suit to the card led, and if unable to may trump or discard as he wishes. There is one exception: the holder of a matador need not follow suit with it to a trump lead unless a higher matador is led, in which case, if he has no other trump to play, he must play it.

The winner of a trick leads to the next. The object of each player individually is to score the most tricks, and a secondary objective of ombre's opponents is to ensure that ombre does not win the most tricks.

Settlement

If ombre wins the most tricks, i.e. more than either of his opponents but not necessarily the majority of the tricks, he takes the pool. This is called *sacardo*.

If one of the opponents wins more tricks than ombre, then ombre pays him a sum equal to the amount in the pool and the pool is

---

The deal for the hand of Ombre described in the text.

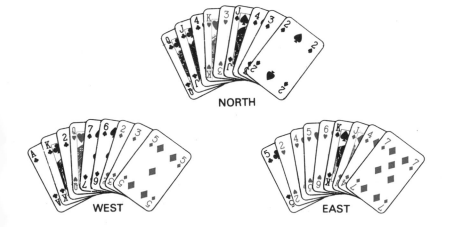

NORTH

WEST

EAST

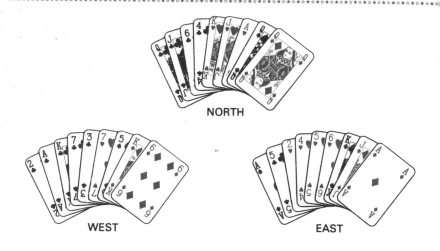

NORTH

WEST

EAST

The hands arranged in trump order for the trick-taking phase, after the draw and announcement of clubs as trumps.

carried forward to the next deal. This is called *codille*.

If one or both of the opponents wins an equal number of tricks as ombre, ombre doubles the amount in the pool and the doubled pool is carried forward to the next deal. This is called *puesta*.

Example hand

North is dealer and deals the hands as illustrated on page 173.

West likes his clubs, as he would be holding three of the top four clubs should clubs be trumps, so he says 'I play', intending to exchange all six of his other cards. Should another player want to play without exchanging, West will not want to be ombre. As it happens, East and North have poor hands and pass.

West discards all six of his non-

clubs and draws ♣7 3 ♥7 ♦K 6 ♠5. East suspects trumps will be a black suit and has such a poor hand that he decides to discard only ♦4 7, leaving five cards in the stock for North, whom he hopes will be able to foil West. He draws ♠A ♦A. North suspects trumps might be diamonds, and decides to discard his spade suit and the ♥3. He draws ♥J A ♦Q ♠Q ♣6.

West announces clubs as trumps, and the new hands are as in the second illustration, arranged with spadille, manilla and basto in their proper sequence in the trump suit.

West can now see that he will lose a trump trick to spadille but hopes to make three or four of them plus the ♦K to score sacardo.

He leads manille, which East takes with spadille. East decides his best policy is to make his ♠K and then lead a heart hoping that North is void and able to trump. The play proceeds as follows:

	West	East	North
1.	ma(♣2)	sp (♠A)	♣4
2.	♠5	♠K	♠Q
3.	♥7	♥6	♥K
4.	♣7	♥5	♥J
5.	ba(♣A)	♣5	♣6
6.	♣K	♥2	♣J
7.	♣3	♥4	♣Q
8.	♦6	♦A	♥A
9.	♠K	♦J	♦Q

West made his fourth trick at the last to score sacardo, East and North's tricks being split. It is interesting to try to work out what might have happened had East not taken his ♠A trick, but tried to discard instead, or if he had not drawn any cards at all and left spadille to North, or if he had discarded seven of his red cards and held the stronger opposing hand himself.

OMNIBUS HEARTS

Omnibus Hearts gets its name because it incorporates most of the features of the games of the Hearts and Black Maria family. It is also called Hit the Moon. Many players think it is the best version of the game, and this is true in so far as it presents a variety of tactics that a player may follow.

Players
Omnibus Hearts is best for four players, although any number from three to six may play satisfactorily.

Cards
The full pack of 52 cards is used. They rank from Ace (high) to 2 (low). If three or more than four people take part, a number of 2s are removed to ensure each player receives the same number of cards.

Preliminaries
Players draw cards to determine the first dealer. The lowest card deals. Dealer has the right to shuffle last and the player on his right cuts. Thereafter the deal moves to the left on each hand.

Dealing
The whole pack is dealt clockwise one at a time to each player beginning on dealer's left.

The play
Before the opening lead, each player passes on three cards from his hand to his left-hand neighbour, each player passing on before looking at the cards he is to receive.

The game is of the trick-taking kind. First lead is by eldest hand (to dealer's left), and each succeeding player must follow suit if able. If unable to follow suit he may discard whatever card he likes. The trick is won by the highest card in the suit led, and the winner of a trick leads to the next.

The object is to avoid taking penalty cards which are (a) all the hearts, which count as minus 1 point each to the player who takes them and (b) the ♠Q which counts minus 13 points to the player who takes it. However there is a further object, which is to capture the ♦10, a bonus card. This counts plus ten to the player who takes it.

Should a player manage to take all the counting cards (♠Q, ♦10 and all hearts) he scores plus 26 points, and the other players, of course, all score nothing. This is called *hitting the moon, take-all* or *slam*.

The game ends when one player reaches a score of minus 100, when the player with the highest plus score, or lowest minus score, is the winner. If playing for stakes, each player settles with each other separately, according to the difference between them.

Example hand
Cards are dealt as in the illustration.

All players have difficult choices in the passing on. North, who is on lead, decides he will

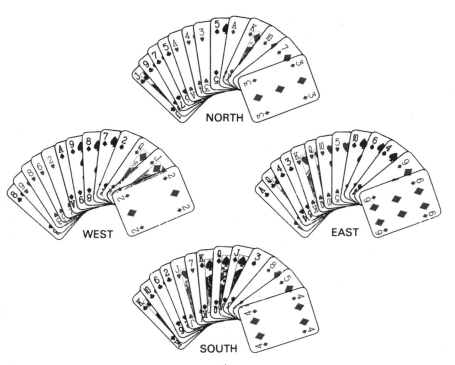

NORTH

WEST

EAST

SOUTH

attempt to win ♦10, which he holds, by trying to get the penalty cards played early and winning three rounds of diamonds at the end. He decides to keep his diamonds, his ♠5 (in case he is passed large spades) and his hearts which are reasonably safe, so passes on ♣J 9 7, feeling reasonably secure at the moment in all suits. East is most threatened by his high hearts, and passes ♥K Q ♣A. South has spade problems and passes on ♠K Q and ♥J. West is not at present worried about anything and passes on ♦Q J and ♣8.

The new hands are therefore as in the illustration overleaf.

Things have worked beautifully for North, who must now decide whether or not to risk leading ♦10, which will win the trick. He decides against it (although it was

The deal for the hand of Omnibus Hearts described in the text.

safe as it happened), on the grounds that West might well be holding a void, having passed him the ♦Q J. He decides to wait until diamonds are led through West to him, and leads ♠5. Play proceeds as follows:

	North	East	South	West
1.	♠5	♠10	♠J	♠A
2.	♦10	♦9	♦8	♦2
3.	♣8	♣7	♣A	♣Q
4.	♦A	♦6	♦4	♥J
5.	♥3	♥5	♥K	♥9
6.	♥A	♠6	♠3	♣7
7.	♥4	♥10	♥7	♥6
8.	♣5	♣4	♣6	♥8
9.	♦K	♣Q	♣2	♥2
10.	♦J	♣3	♣10	♠K

South cannot now lose the lead

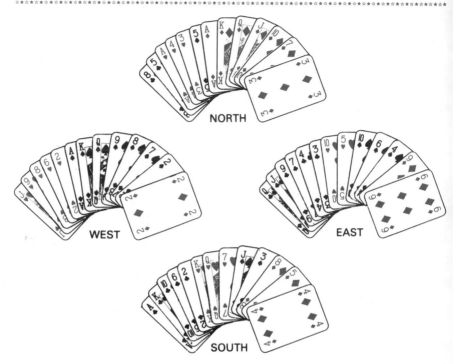

The hands after each player has passed on three cards.

and must make the ♥Q, the only penalty card outstanding. So at the end of the first deal North is plus 9, East minus 5, South minus 19 and West minus 1.

Strategy

As with all games in this family, where not being forced to win tricks is of the utmost importance, it is most important to recognize danger suits, which are suits short of low cards. A suit with three or four low cards, particularly if it includes the 2, is usually safe no matter what high cards are held. The danger in these games frequently comes from suits of three or four middling cards – by the third round cards like 7s or 6s are often forced to take a trick.

The introduction of a plus card in Omnibus Hearts makes the game more interesting. Only one of the suits, clubs, is now neutral.

A player should look at his hand, decide on an overall strategy, and discard accordingly. The usual strategy is to attempt to take no tricks whatever, as in the game Hearts. But the ♦10 offers other possibilities. A player is not going to discard the ♦10 while he might win with it himself, so a player with a good supply of high cards and low cards, particularly low hearts and spades, might choose a policy of trying to capture the ♦10. He will keep high cards to win harmless tricks, and lead low hearts and perhaps spades to force out the penalty cards. He then wins the ♦10 at the end with his remaining high cards. This strategy calls for nice judgement, of course.

A player dealt a very strong hand of high cards might go all out to hit the moon, but this is another chancy business. A couple of long, solid suits is the prime requirement. Such an objective must be approached with stealth. A player who during the play obviously embarks on winning everything must by then be in control of all suits he holds – after all, no other player *has* to discard his hearts or even the ♠Q, and if one penalty card escapes, the consequence is a huge minus score.

Variants

In some schools the ♦J or the ♦8 is used as the bonus scoring card, instead of the ♦10.

Some players prefer to play for an agreed number of deals each, instead of the game ending at a certain score.

The layout for the game of Paganini described in the text.

Paganini is a double-pack **patience** or **solitaire** in which all the cards are spread out on the table throughout the game. Clearly two packs of the small cards manufactured for such games would be useful for Paganini, which is included for those who derive pleasure from having all the cards spread out before them at once.

The play

The tableau is simple. All 104 cards are dealt face up in eight rows of 13 cards each. The object is to finish the game with all eight rows beginning with Aces on the left and running in suit sequences to the Kings on the right. There is no stipulated order for the suits; the player makes his own decisions, but having made them, cannot change them.

All Aces are immediately available for play, and the player begins by moving one of the Aces to the extreme left of one of the rows. It will be noticed therefore that when the game is finished the whole tableau will have moved one space to the left, so provision must be made for this.

When the Ace is moved the space it leaves is filled by a card of the same suit and next higher in rank to the card at the left of the space. As this is a double pack layout there are two cards which will fill each space, and the skill in the game comes with choosing which of the two will be moved. Filling a space creates another in the layout which is filled in the same way, and so on.

A space created to the right of a King, of course, cannot be filled, so that space is wasted until the King can be moved. With eight Aces immediately available for play, creating eight spaces into which 16 cards might go, there is clearly scope for careful play. The tableau should be studied at the beginning of the game to decide which Ace could most profitably be moved, and it also pays when moving an Ace to study which row it might be best to move it to. This will depend upon whether the card in the '2 space' can easily be moved, and so on.

The illustration shows a tableau.

The play can be started by moving the ♦A and the ♣A together in the second row to spaces in front of the ♦2 and ♣2, which will then be already in their right positions. The ♣6 in the first column can be moved to the space provided. The ♠A from the top row can be played to the front of the fourth row and the ♠2 from the extreme right of the fifth row can be played to the space beside it. This releases the ♠5 from the left of the seventh row to the space created. The ♥A from the middle of the third row can be played to the left of the seventh row and the ♥2 from the second row played beside it.

Now the ♣7 from the extreme right of the bottom row can be played to the space in the second row, allowing the ♥J from the seventh row to be played to the space, and the ♥3 from the fifth row can be played to its rightful space in the seventh row. This allows the ♠K from the fourth row to fill the space created, and the ♦7 from the left of the top row to go in the space provided. The ♠9 in the seventh row can now be played beside the ♠8 in the third, which allows the ♥7 in the seventh row to be played the ♥6 in the same row, making a space into which the ♣K from the second row can be played. Now the ♦3 can move along the space in the second row. The ♣A from the bottom row can be played to the top left position, followed by the ♣2 from the top row and the ♣3 from the right of the seventh row, and so on. It can be a long game and often a frustrating one.

PATIENCE

For games of Patience, or competitive Patience, see the following:

Accordion
Beleaguered Castle
La Belle Lucie
Bisley
Calculation
Clock
Cribbage Patience
Crossword
Demon

Golf
Klondike
Miss Milligan
Paganini
Pyramid
Russian Bank
Scorpion
St Helena
Windmill

PINOCHLE

Pinochle was originally a European game for two players, derived from Bézique (q.v.). It is now extremely popular in the United States, where it is played by three as Auction Pinochle. The name Pinochle possibly comes from the French *binocle*, meaning eye-glasses, and in England the name is often spelt without the 'h', i.e. Pinocle. This is the version the Oxford Dictionary approves, but as the game is now most widespread in America, where the 'h' is generally used, it is spelt Pinochle here. However, the first description will be of the older two-handed game as played in Europe.

Players
Pinochle is a game for two players, but can be played by three or more (as described under Auction Pinochle with other variants later).

Cards
Two standard packs are used, stripped of all cards of the rank of 8 or below, so that the pack consists of two cards each of A K Q J 10 9 in each suit, making 48 cards in all. The cards rank in the order A 10 K Q J 9.

Preliminaries
The two players cut, the lower being the dealer (cards rank as above). The dealer has the right to shuffle last and his opponent cuts. The deal thereafter alternates if the game is played to an agreed number of points (see scoring), or the winner of each hand deals the next, if each hand is played as a separate game.

Dealing
The dealer deals 12 cards to each player, beginning with his opponent, in bundles of four or three according to preference. The next card is turned face up to indicate the trump suit. The rest of the pack is placed face downwards on the table to half cover the turn-up. This is the *stock*.

Objects of the game
The objects of the game are to win tricks that include cards of scoring value and to meld certain combinations of cards that carry a scoring value.

When taken in tricks, each Ace scores 11 points, each 10 ten points, each King four points, each Queen three points and each Jack two points. Only 9s have no value. The player who wins the last trick scores 10 points.

The points values of the melds are:

Sequences (class A)
A 10 K Q J of the trump suit   150
K Q of the trump suit (royal
  marriage)   40
K Q of the plain suit (common
  marriage)   20

Groups (class B)
Four Aces, one of each suit   100
Four Kings, one of each suit   80
Four Queens, one of each suit   60
Four Jacks, one of each suit   40

Special (class C)

Pinochle (♠Q ♦J)	40
Dix (9 of the trump suit)	10

The play

Non-dealer leads to the first trick. Thereafter the winner of a trick leads to the next. The second player need not follow suit. The trick is won by the higher trump, or lacking a trump, by the higher card in the suit led. Of two identical cards, the one led is the higher.

After each trick both players bring their hands back to 12 cards by drawing from the top of the stock, the winner of the trick taking the top card, the loser the next.

Melding

A player can meld by placing the melding combinations face up on the table before him, but can do so only after winning a trick and before drawing from stock. He must also observe the following rules:

1. Only one meld is allowed at each turn.

2. For each meld, at least one card must be taken from hand, whether it is a fresh meld or a meld with cards already on the table.

3. A card may not be used twice in the same meld, nor in any two melds of the same class unless the second is higher scoring than the first. For example a player may meld K Q of trumps for a royal marriage for 40 points and later may add A 10 J for 150 points, but if he melds A 10 K Q J he cannot claim later for the royal marriage. A player may make two identical melds (as there are two of each card in the pack) but no one card can be used in each meld, i.e. each meld must be complete in itself.

However, a card may be used in two or more melds of different classes. For example, a player with four Kings melded can, on another turn, add a Queen to make a marriage.

Cards in melds are part of the hand, and once melded are played in tricks as normally.

A player holding dix may meld it whenever he wins a trick, or he can exchange it for the upcard, which is equivalent to melding it, and scores 10 points. Should the upcard be a dix, the dealer scores 10 points immediately.

The play continued

The player who wins the 12th trick may meld if he can, and then he draws the last card of the stock. He must show this to his opponent, who takes the upcard, which by now is probably a dix. When the last card is taken from the table there is no further melding.

The play of the last 12 tricks follows a different pattern. It is now obligatory to follow suit to the card led if able, to trump if possible when unable to follow suit, and when a trump is led to win the trick if possible. Otherwise any card may be played.

Scoring

Melds are scored when they are declared. Points for cards won in tricks are added after the hand is complete. Including the 10 points for the last trick the two totals for cards should add to 250. Scores are recorded in 10s, an odd 7, 8 or 9

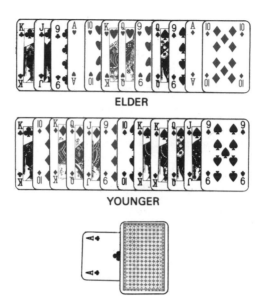

ELDER

YOUNGER

The deal for the hand of Pinochle described in the text.

being rounded upwards, 6 or below being disregarded.

Every deal may constitute a game, but it is more usual to play to 1,000 points. A player may *count himself out* by claiming 1,000 points at any time. Play stops and his count for cards won in tricks is added to his existing score (melds are already entered). If he has 1,000 points he wins, if not he loses. It is not necessary for a player to count himself out, he still wins if his opponent does not reach 1,000 on the deal. However, if neither player counts himself

out, and both are found to have passed 1,000 play continues to 1,250, and if necessary in further multiples of 250 until a winner is found.

Example hand

Younger hand dealt the two hands shown in the illustration. Neither player is within reach of a sequence of trumps, although elder can claim the turn-up Ace with his dix. Elder also has a common marriage in hearts. Younger has four Kings but not one of each suit, but has a pinochle and two common marriages to declare, and will probably decide to win tricks in order to meld them. Play proceeds:

	Elder	Meld	Draw	Younger	Meld	Draw
1.	♥9	♣9	♠J	♦9		♥9
2.	♠9		♣J	♦J	♠Q ♦J	♠A
3.	♠J	♥K Q	♠A	♠9		♣9
4.	♥Q		♥10	♥9		♦J
5.	♠Q		♣10	♠10	♠K (♠Q)	♣Q
6.	♥K		♣A	♦Q	♦K Q	♥J
7.	♦10	♣A ♥A ♠A ♦A	♥Q	♦J		♦K
8.	♥Q		♥J	♠K		♥K
9.	♥J		♣10	♣9	♣K ♥K ♦K ♠K	♣10
10.	♥10		♣Q	♥J		♦Q
11.	♣A	♣A 10 K Q J	♥A	♦J		♦9
12.	♣J		♣9	♣10	♣Q (♣K)	♠A

Cards in melds are now gathered up and Younger leads in the last phase as follows:

	Elder	Younger
13.	♦A	♦A
14.	♣9	♦9
15.	♣A	♣Q
16.	♣10	♣K
17.	♣K	♦10
18.	♣Q	♦Q
19.	♥A	♥K
20.	♥A	♦Q
21.	♥10	♦K
22.	♠A	♠K
23.	♠10	♠A
24.	♣J	♦K

After the first deal therefore Elder had made 280 in melds to Younger's 200. In tricks, including 10 for the last, Elder made 171 points, counting as 170, and Younger 79, counting as 80.

So after the first hand the scores were Elder 450, Younger 280.

Strategy

Play to the first 12 tricks is based mainly on the need to meld, since few games can be won with the tricks alone. So in the first stages cards which might make melds should be kept, even to the extent of losing tricks which could cheaply be won. At the same time a player should build his hand towards winning tricks in the later stages, when they might be worth more. An Ace led early is likely to draw a worthless 9, but later on might win a 10.

As the stock is diminished a player will be anxious to win a trick or two to get down any melds he holds in case he doesn't get another chance, and if holding a trump sequence will perhaps place them on the table as soon as he can, forgoing the extra points for royal marriage. By the same token, a player might think it worth using powerful cards to win the last two or three tricks, even if they do not draw high-scoring cards from his opponent, if he fears his opponent is about to make a meld.

In much of the early play players are not attempting to win the low-scoring tricks but are keeping valuable cards. In this phase it is best to lead from long suits and discard from short ones, other things being equal. A long suit is likely to be the opponent's short suit, where he might be forced to concede the trick rather than win it with a card valuable for melding.

At all times, of course, an ability to remember the cards played is useful, and the really expert player would know pretty well what cards his opponent holds when it comes to playing off the last 12 tricks.

Auction Pinochle

Auction Pinochle is a game for three players, using the same pack of 48 cards. It is also a popular game for four (or five), the dealer for each hand not dealing cards to himself (and if five play, the player to his left). In effect players sit out a hand in turn, but all participate in the settlement for each hand.

The dealer deals 15 cards to each of the three active players either in five bundles of 3 each or in three bundles of 4 and one of 3. After the first round of dealing he deals three cards face down to a *widow* in the centre of the table. There is therefore no stock and no turn-up for trumps.

After examining their hands, the players bid for the contract, a bid being an undertaking to score the number of points named. The high bidder is entitled to name the trump suit before play to the first trick.

The first active player to the left of dealer makes the first bid, which must be of at least 300. The following players may pass or bid a higher number (bids are in multiples of ten). The auction continues round the table provided each bid is higher than the last until two players have passed, when the last bidder wins the contract and plays against the other two players. Players can bid any number of times, but having once passed cannot re-enter the auction. If the enforced opening bid of 300 is passed by the other two players, the bidder may concede defeat without playing out the hand merely by throwing in his cards. However, he must not look at the widow, which commits him to playing. If he throws in his hand, he pays a forfeit of 3 units to a kitty (but nothing to the other players) and the deal passes to the next player to the left of the dealer.

Otherwise the bidder takes the widow, showing it face up to his opponents, and takes it into his hand. He then names the trump suit and places in front of him his melds. The melds, and the values for them are the same as for the two-handed game described. A card can be used in two or more melds of different classes (e.g. the ♠Q for a marriage and pinochle) but may be used only once in melds of the same class.

Only the bidder melds. Having done so, he *buries* (discards) three cards from his hand face down before him to bring his hand back to the 15 cards of the other players. The three buried cards belong to him as an extra trick at the end of the game.

When the bidder and his opponents have agreed on the value of the melds and how many further points he needs to make his contract, the bidder takes them back into his hand. The bidder leads to the first trick, and may change his mind about his melds and even the trump suit up until the time he leads.

Having acquired the widow, the bidder might discover it to be useless and might decide before leading to the first trick that he will not make his contract. If so, he can concede defeat and pay to the players (including any inactive ones) the value of his bid (see unit values under *settlement*). This is called *single bete*.

During the trick-taking phase a player must follow suit to the card led if he can, and if he cannot he must trump, if able. If he is third player and is void in the suit led, and the second player has trumped, he too must trump if able but need not overtrump. If trumps are led, succeeding players must, if able, play a higher trump than any in the trick. This is called *playing over*. Only if a player cannot follow suit to the card led and cannot trump is he allowed to discard.

A trick is won by the highest trump it contains, and if there are no trumps by the highest card in the suit led. If two identical cards qualify to win the trick, the first to be played wins the trick. The winner of a trick leads to the next.

The bidder adds all the cards he wins in tricks to those he buried, while one of his opponents collects the tricks for his side.

Cards won in tricks are valued as for the two-handed game, i.e. Aces 11, 10s ten, Kings 4, Queens 4 and Jacks 2. 10 points are won for taking the last trick, so the two sides' points for cards should add up to 250.

If the bidder has scored, with melds and points taken in tricks, the number of points of his contract he wins.

Settlement

Each deal is separate, and it is usual to reduce the contract to units for settlement as follows:

Contract	Unit value
300–340	3
350–390	5
400–440	10
450–490	15
500–540	20
550–590	25
600 plus	30

If the trump suit is spades, the values are doubled.

The successful bidder receives from all players, active or inactive, payment for his contract according to this scale. Any extra points he makes are immaterial. If his contract was for 350 or more he also receives payment from the kitty, which can be regarded as an extra player, and is the property of all players, active or inactive. So if the kitty does not contain sufficient funds to pay, all players must contribute to it equally so that sufficient funds are there.

If the bidder fails to make his contract he pays double the unit value to all players. This is called *double bete* and explains why it is sometimes profitable for a bidder to concede before leading to the first trick. If a player is faced with double bete and his contract was 350 or more he must also pay double to the kitty as well.

Any funds in the kitty at the end of the game are shared equally among the players, and a player leaving the game collects his share of the kitty on departure.

Auction Pinochle, of course, need not be played for stakes but scores can be kept on paper, the player with the most units in credit at the end being the winner.

Pinochle for four players

Four can play in partnerships of two, partners sitting opposite each other. The same 48-card pack is used with the same ranking of the cards.

The dealer deals each player 12 cards in bundles of three (i.e. the whole pack) and turns up his own last card to denote trumps. If he turns up dix he scores 10 points for his side. Otherwise, a player holding a dix (beginning with eldest, to dealer's left) can exchange it for the trump card, scoring 10 points himself, the dealer taking the dix into his hand. If no player wants to exchange a dix for the trump card, dealer takes the trump card into his hand. Each dix, except one exchanged for the trump card, scores 10 points for its holder, when it is played.

After the deal each player puts his melds on the table before him and scores for them according to the table given earlier. However, for the following melds a player scores extra points as shown:

Sequences (class A)
Double trump sequence
(A 10 K Q J)   1,500

Groups (class B)
All eight Aces   1,000
All eight Kings   800
All eight Queens   600
All eight Jacks   400

Special (class C)
Double pinochle (♠Q♦J)   300

These scores are very rare, except perhaps for double pinochle. Cards can be melded in separate melds, provided the melds are in different classes.

Players enter their scores for melds (one score is kept for each partnership) and the players take up their hands for the trick-taking phase. Eldest (to left of dealer) leads to the first trick. Throughout, a player must follow suit to the card led if able, and if not must trump, if able (it follows that a player must sometimes trump his partner's winner). If a suit has been trumped, and a following player must also trump, there is no obligation to overtrump. However, if a trump is led, each following player, if able, must play a higher trump than has been played already. A player may discard only if he cannot follow suit and holds no trumps.

The winner of a trick leads to the next. At the end of the trick-taking each partnership counts 10 points for each Ace and 10 won in tricks, 5 points for each King and Queen, and 10 points for winning the last trick (there are thus 250 points at stake in this phase but counted differently to the preceding games described). A partnership must win a trick to count the points recorded for melds, so if a partnership fails to make a trick, the points for melds are cancelled.

Game is to 1,000 points, and any player may count his side out as described under the two-handed game above – if his claim is wrong his side loses. As described earlier, if both sides pass 1,000 on the same deal, neither side having counted out, play continues to 1,250 and so on. It will be noticed that some of the new melds win a game immediately.

Pinochle for six or eight players

Pinochle can be played by six or eight players by playing in two sides of three or four a side. Partners sit alternately.

Two pinochle packs are used (i.e. the Aces to 9s of four standard packs) making 96 cards in all. With six players, each receives 16 cards, dealt in bundles of four. With eight players, each receives 12 cards, dealt in bundles of three.

The game is played in the same way as partnership *Pinochle for four* described above, except that triple and even quadruple melds are possible with the double pack. There are also now bonus scores for multiple marriages. The additional points scores to those in the table for two-handed Pinochle are as follows:

Sequences (class A)

Triple trump sequence (A 10 K Q J)	3,000
Double trump sequence (A 10 K Q J)	1,500
Four Kings and four Queens of the same suit	1,200
Three Kings and three Queens of the same suit	600
Two Kings and two Queens of the same suit	300

Groups (class B)

Fifteen Aces, Kings, Queens or Jacks	3,000
Twelve Aces	2,000
Twelve Kings	1,600
Twelve Queens	1,200
Twelve Jacks	800
Eight Aces	1,000
Eight Kings	800
Eight Queens	600
Eight Jacks	400

Special (class C)

Quadruple pinochle	1,200
Triple pinochle	600
Double pinochle	300

Again, a card may be used in more than one meld, provided the melds are in different classes.

Game is to 1,000, and the counting-out principle described earlier applies. Some melds win a game immediately (i.e.. a player can count out if he melds 15 Aces).

Firehouse Pinochle

Firehouse Pinochle is a form of Auction Pinochle for four players, two playing in partnership against the other two. The 48-card pack is used, and each player is dealt 12 cards. As in Auction Pinochle described above, the players bid to make the trump suit. However, each player, beginning with eldest (to dealer's left) has only one opportunity to bid. He may bid or pass. There is no obligation on the first player to bid, and the minimum bid is 200. Each bid must be higher than the previous bid. The high bidder makes the trump suit and all players make their melds. Both sides agree on how many points are required from tricks for the bidding side to make its contract and the hands are gathered up and played. The values of the cards are 10 for Aces and 10s and 5 for Kings and Queens.

A side making its contract scores the points it makes. If it fails to make its contract the amount of the bid is deducted from its score. In either case the opponents score the points they make. Game is to 1,000 points and the bidding side's points are taken first. *Variant* Some players prefer the bidding to be continuous, i.e. players can continue to bid in rotation until three have passed. A player who passes cannot re-enter the bidding. The high bidder must meld at least a royal marriage (i.e. a marriage or sequence in the trump suit). Eldest hand leads first no matter who is high bidder.

Check Pinochle

Check Pinochle is played by four, in partnerships of two. The 48-card pack is used and each player receives 12 cards.

Players bid for the trump suit, eldest (to dealer's left) bidding first. Bidding is continuous and a player may continue to bid on his turn until he passes, when he cannot re-enter the bidding. The minimum bid is 200, and to bid a player must hold a marriage. Should the first three players pass, the dealer must bid 200, whether he has a marriage or not. Bids are in multiples of 10, and the high bidder names the trump suit.

Each player then places on the table his melds, and scores for them are as listed in the main description, and with the extra melds listed in Pinochle for four players above (i.e. the double sequence, double pinochle and group of eight apply).

The melds are gathered up and the high bidder leads to the first trick. The rules for playing to tricks are as in *Pinochle for four players*, with the same values for the cards.

If the high bidder's side scores at least the amount of its bid, it is credited with all the points it has scored. If the high bidder's side fails to make its contract, the amount of its bid is deducted from its score. The opponents score, in either case, the points they make. Melds count whether a side wins a trick or not. An odd 5 points scored in the count for cards is ignored.

Game is to 1,000 points, and the score of the bidding side is taken first.

Settlement is made in *checks* (chips), hence the game's name. A check is won by a side for certain melds, for making or defeating a contract, for winning all the tricks and for winning the game, according to the following:

Melds	Checks
Sequence in trumps	2
Four Aces	2
Four Kings, Queens or Jacks	1
Double pinochle	1

Tricks	
For winning all 12 tricks	4

Contracts	
For making contracts as follows	
200–240	2
250–290	4
300–340	7
For each additional 50	3

For defeating contracts, the above scale is doubled

For winning the game   7
plus 1 check for each 100 points or fraction of 100 points in the difference between winners' and losers' scores, plus an extra 4 checks if the losers have a minus score.

Each time a check award is won, each player on the side to whom it is due collects it from the opponent to his right.

PIQUET

This very old game, known in Elizabethan England as Cent, Sand or Saint, is probably of Spanish or French origin, but is pronounced pi-ket, not as if it were a French word.

Players

Piquet is one of the best of all games for two players, but can be played by three or four as explained later.

Cards

The short pack of 32 is used, i.e. the standard pack from which the 6s, 5s, 4s, 3s and 2s have been removed. The cards rank from Ace (high) to 7 (low).

Preliminaries

The players draw for choice of deal. The higher card has the choice and would be advised to deal, as there is an advantage to dealing first and being non-dealer on the sixth and last hand.

Dealing

The dealer deals each player 12 cards in bundles of three or two. The remaining eight cards form the *talon*, which is placed face down between the two players. Some players think it a courtesy to separate the top five cards from the bottom three.

The play

Elder (non-dealer) is entitled to exchange from one to five of his cards by discarding to a waste pile and drawing an equal number from the talon (the reason for separating the five cards). He must exchange one, and if he exchanges less than five, he may look at those to which he was entitled. He does not show them to dealer.

Younger (dealer) is now entitled to exchange cards up to the number remaining in the talon (it might be any number between three and seven). He too must exchange at least one. Any cards remaining in the talon he may now turn face up for both players to see or leave face down at his discretion. Throughout the game each player may look at his own discards.

If either player is dealt a hand without a court card (King, Queen or Jack) he may claim *carte blanche* and score 10 points for it immediately. Elder must declare it on picking up his hand, Younger as soon as non-dealer has discarded and drawn from the talon. A player claiming carte blanche must show his hand to his opponent before drawing.

Object and scoring

Because scoring in Piquet is achieved in three ways, it is necessary to understand the objects from the beginning. Piquet is partly a trick-taking game, but points are scored in a count before the trick-taking phase, then during the trick-taking phase, and in extraordinary scores like carte blanche.

Before the trick-taking, the hands are compared and score in the following ways:

a) *Point* Points are scored for the longest suit. Elder announces the number of cards in his longest suit. If this beats Younger's suit, Younger says 'Good', and Elder scores 1 point for each card in the suit. If Younger has a longer suit, he will say 'Not good' and score himself. If Younger has an equal suit he will say 'Making?' which asks Elder for the pip value of his suit. For this purpose Ace counts 11 and court cards 10 each. Elder announces his total, and Younger says either 'Good' or 'Not good' and one of them scores accordingly. Younger might say 'Same', in which case neither player scores for point.

b) *Sequences* Points are scored for the longest sequence of cards in a suit. A sequence must be of at least three cards. Elder announces his longest sequence. The French terms are used: *tierce* (three), *quart* (four), *quint* (five), *sixième* (six), *septième* (seven) and *huitième* (eight). Younger replies with 'Good', 'Not good', or if his own sequence is equal, 'How high?'. This asks for the rank of the highest card in the sequence, which Elder announces. The answers now are 'Good', 'Not good' or 'Equal'. The player with the best sequence scores for it, but if the sequences are equal neither scores. The points scored are: tierce 3 points, quart 4 points, quint and better, 1 for each card plus 10 points. Thus sixième scores 16. The player with the best sequence may also declare other sequences and score for those, too.

c) *Quatorzes* and *trios*. Points are scored for the highest *quatorze* (four cards of the same rank) or, failing a quatorze, for highest *trio*

(three of a rank), provided the quatorze or trio is of the rank of 10 or above. Elder states his best, e.g. 'Quatorze of Jacks' and Younger says 'Good' or 'Not good'. Obviously there cannot be a tie, but if neither player holds a quatorze or trio neither scores. A quatorze scores 14 points and a trio 3. As with sequences, the player with the higher may also score for any lower quatorzes or trios that he holds. He must announce to his opponent what they are.

The points in these three categories are scored in the order given, and the points entered on the score-sheet as they are scored. A player is not under an obligation to declare any of them, but of course cannot score for them if he doesn't declare them. Either player can ask another to prove his claim, but this is hardly ever exercised, because each player can more or less infer which cards his opponent holds. A player can legitimately declare less than he holds in order to deceive, e.g. a player with four Aces might, if he wishes, declare three and score for trio, keeping the other concealed to mislead his opponent in the trick-taking phase. This is called *sinking*.

The trick-taking phase
Before leading to the first trick Elder announces his scores for the categories above. He then leads and announces another point, since the lead to a trick is worth a point. Before playing to the first trick Younger announces his score so far. Thereafter each player announces his score with each card

he plays, even if it is the same as the score he announced previously.

Players must follow suit to the card led if able, and if not must discard. There are no trumps. The higher card in the suit led wins the trick. The winner of a trick leads to the next. As stated, a player scores 1 point for each lead. He also scores 1 point for each trick he takes on his opponent's lead, so sometimes each player wins a point on the same trick.

The player who makes the majority of the tricks (seven or more) scores an extra 10 points (for *cards*). If the players take six tricks each, neither scores for cards. If a player takes all twelve tricks, he scores an extra 40 for *capot*, instead of 10 for cards.

Pique and repique

There are two further extraordinary scores. Should a player score 30 points in the combination categories alone before his opponent has scored a point, he scores a *repique* which gives him a bonus of 60 points. This is why points are scored in the order stated: carte blanche, point, sequences and lastly quatorzes and trios. For example, if Younger scores 7 for point, 17 for sequence and 14 for quatorze, total 38, he scores repique and his score becomes 98.

Should a player score 30 points in combinations and trick-taking before his opponent has scored, he scores a *pique*, which gives him a bonus of 30 points. Notice that Younger cannot score for pique, because Elder always scores the first point in the trick-taking phase by leading, so if Younger doesn't score 30 before the trick-taking, he cannot reach that figure before Elder has scored a point.

Partie

A game is called a *partie*, and consists of six deals, three by each

The deal for the hand of Piquet described in the text.

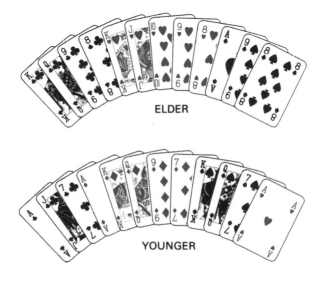

ELDER

YOUNGER

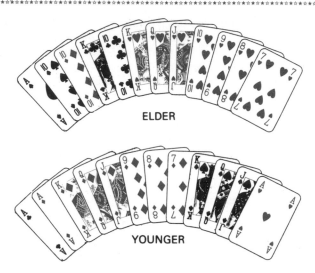

The two hands after the draw.

player. At the end of the partie the loser's total is deducted from the winner's, and 100 added to determine the winning margin. If one or both players fail to reach 100 however, then the two totals are added together and 100 added to determine the winning margin.

Example hand
The hands are dealt as in the illustration on page 195. Elder decides to keep his heart sequence, although realizing that Younger must have many diamonds. He decides to gamble and leave his ♣K unguarded (he might well pick up another club from the talon) and discards ♣Q 9 8 ♠9 8. He is very lucky. He picks up ♥Q 7 ♣10 ♠10 ♦10.

Younger has an easy choice. He can discard ♣J 7 ♠7. He has all four suits guarded, and whatever Elder leads he knows he must make the first or second trick and then his five diamonds, so is sure

to get the majority of tricks. Meanwhile with the right three cards in the talon he could make capot. He picks up ♦J 8 ♠J, which could have been worse.

The new hands are shown in the second illustration.

The scoring for combinations takes place as follows:

Elder: 'Point of seven.'
Younger: 'Making?'
Elder: 'Sixty-four.'
Younger: 'Not good.'

Younger's sequence makes 65. None of this was a surprise to either, and indeed Elder might have been tempted to sink his point, but he knew all would be revealed shortly however:

Elder: 'Septième.'
Younger: 'Good.'
Elder: 'Quatorze.'
Younger: 'Good.'

Elder was lucky to find the three 10s in the talon.

Elder now announces his score as follows: 'Septième, seventeen, quatorze, fourteen, I start with thirty-one'. He then leads and announces: 'Thirty-two'. He does not score for repique, because Younger scored for point.

Younger now announces his score as follows: 'Point of seven, seven'. He then plays to the first trick, and since he wins it, says: 'Eight'.

The play proceeds as follows:

	Elder	Younger
1.	♥K '32'	♥A 'Eight'
2.	♦10 '32'	♦A 'Nine'
3.	♣10 '32'	♦K 'Ten'
4.	♥7 '32'	♦Q '11'
5.	♥8 '32'	♦J '12'
6.	♥9 '32'	♦9 '13'
7.	♥10 '32'	♦8 '14'
8.	♥J '32'	♦7 '15'
9.	♠A '33'	♠K '16'
10.	♥Q '34'	♠J '16'
11.	♣K '35'	♣A '17'
12.	♣10 '35'	♣Q '18'

Younger wins the point for the last trick '19' and ten for cards '29'. Despite appearing to have the weaker hand, therefore, Elder won the first deal 35 to 29 (high scoring) and deals the second hands.

Strategy

Strategy in Piquet begins with the discarding, which is where a player can most improve his chances. In the trick-taking phase, of course, each player can guess at the hand of his opponent.

The philosophy of the two players differs in the discarding. Elder is on the offensive because (a) he is safe from pique, as mentioned earlier, (b) he has the first lead in the trick-taking, and (c) he can exchange five cards.

Therefore, he can attempt to build up a long suit. A suit of six or better headed by the Ace and King will almost certainly win him the majority of the tricks, and he can try for points for point and sequence.

Younger will have different objectives. A long suit to him is of less value in the trick-taking, because he might have to discard most of them before he gets the lead. (In the example hand, it was Elder who was forced to discard his long suit, but only because he lacked the Ace). Younger must keep stoppers in at least two suits, or he might easily suffer capot against him in the trick-taking.

Each player will try to build up a picture of his opponent's hand. For example a player void in a suit will know that it is likely that his opponent has a long suit, and might himself concentrate on quatorzes or trios. The score is important, too. If Elder knows on the last hand that only pique can win the game for him he will go all out for it and discard accordingly.

Elder and Younger might discard quite differently if holding the hand in the illustration.

Elder would concentrate on building his spade suit. One more

Elder and Younger might discard differently with this hand, as discussed in the text.

spade and he is certain to make the majority of tricks (he probably will anyway). His only awkward choice is whether or not to discard ♥K. His best play is probably to discard ♥K 10 ♦Q 9 8, but some players might keep ♥K and discard only the other four cards, hoping to pick up ♦K and make 14 for quatorze.

Younger, with this hand, might prefer to discard ♠J 8 7. This enables him to guard all four suits, and means that whatever he picks up, he can get the lead no later than the fourth trick. With a reasonable pick-up from talon he has a good chance of the majority of tricks. He has sacrificed point and sequence (but knows Elder can score more than 4 for sequence only by holding the small clubs, which is unlikely). He has the chance of quatorze, and unless Elder has four 10s must at least score for trio with his Kings.

It is a good hand for either player, but for different reasons.

Piquet Normand

This is a version of Piquet for three players. Each player is dealt ten cards, the remaining two forming the talon. The dealer may discard two cards and take the talon. The eldest player (to dealer's left) begins by announcing the number in his longest suit, the other players in turn responding with 'Good', 'Not good' or 'Making?' as in the parent game until the scorer for point is established. The same procedure is followed for the other categories. Only one player may score for each category – if there is a tie nobody scores. A player needs only 20 points (not 30) to score for pique or repique, although his score increases to 60 or 90 as in the parent game.

Eldest hand makes the opening lead, and the player winning the most tricks scores 10 points for cards; if two players tie each scores 5 points. A player winning all ten tricks scores 40 for capot, rather than 10 for cards; if two players make five tricks each, they score 20 points each. The first player to score 100 points is the winner.

Piquet Voleur

This version of Piquet is for four players, playing in two partnerships. Partners sit opposite each other.

Each player is dealt eight cards, there being no talon. Eldest hand announces how many cards he holds in his longest suit, the other players responding until the scorer for point is established. No point can be scored if the value of the cards is less than 30 (Ace 11, King, Queen, Jack 10 each, others at pip value). The other combinations are scored in the same manner.

A side which can score for a category (including point) may score for lesser combinations in that category, e.g. if a player scores for quatorze, both he and his partner can also score for other quatorzes or trios. If players from opposite sides tie in a category, neither side scores in that category, but if players on the same side tie, both score.

Pique and repique are scored if one player can score 20 before his opponents score: pique increases the side's score to 60 and repique to 90. Eldest hand makes the opening lead. The side taking most tricks scores 10 points, unless they take all eight, when they score 40 for capot. Game is to 100 points.

PITCH

Pitch is more properly called Auction Pitch. It is also called Setback and is of the All Fours family, and in the United States is probably the most popular of that type of game.

Players
Pitch is best as a game for four, each playing for himself. It can, however, be played by any number from two to seven.

Cards
The standard pack of 52 cards is used, with the cards ranking from Ace (high) to 2 (low).

Preliminaries
The players draw cards to determine the first dealer; the highest deals. Dealer shuffles last and the player on his right cuts.

Dealing
Six cards are dealt to each player, beginning with eldest hand (to dealer's left) in bundles of three.

The play
Pitch is a trick-taking game in which one player, the *pitcher* or *maker*, plays against the rest who are in temporary partnership, so play begins with a round of bidding to determine which player he is. There are four possible points to be won on each hand, and each player on his turn may either bid to win any number from one to four, or pass. A player is allowed only one bid and each bid must be higher than the previous one. Bidding begins with the eldest hand and ends with dealer.

The high bidder leads first (called *pitching*), and the suit he leads denotes the trump suit. A player who wishes to bid four (called a *smudge*) usually just pitches on his turn, since his bid cannot be overbid. A player who can follow suit to the card led in a trick can either follow suit or trump, but he cannot discard. A player who cannot follow suit may either trump or discard.

A trick is won by the highest trump it contains, or if there are no trumps in the trick by the highest card of the suit led. The winner of a trick leads to the next.

Scoring
The actual number of tricks won are not of significance. One point each is scored for taking certain cards as follows:

High	The highest trump card in play
Low	The lowest trump card in play
Jack	The Jack of trumps
Game	The highest total of points taken in tricks based on Ace counting as 4 points, King 3, Queen 2, Jack 1 and 10 ten.

There are thus 4 points at stake in a deal, but Jack will not be scored if the Jack of trumps is not in play, and game will not be scored if two or more players tie for it.

If a pitcher scores as many

points as he bid, or more, he scores all the points he made. If he scores fewer points than he bid the amount of his bid is subtracted from his previous score. If this gives him a minus score, the score is circled and he is said to be *in the hole*. The opponents of the pitcher always score any points they make individually.

A player who bid a *smudge* and makes all four tricks wins the game immediately, unless he was in the hole, when his four will count as 4 points as usual.

Players' scores are kept individually, and the winner is the first to score 7 points. If two players reach 7 on the same deal, the pitcher's points are counted first, and among the other players the points are scored in the order high, low, jack, game.

Example deal

South deals four hands as shown in the illustration.

West cannot bid. He is certain to make one trick in clubs, and might make high, low and jack if the ♣A is not in play, but if it is he is unlikely to make a point, and decides not to take the chance. North cannot bid. East bids two. He is sure to make a point for high with the ♥A, could score for low with ♥3 and might make the point for game, if he can make a trick with his ♦10. He does not bid one in case South overbids. South cannot overbid at either one or two level, and passes. The play proceeds as follows:

	East	South	West	North
1.	♥A	♥7	♥9	♥5
2.	♥Q	♣2	♥8	♥K
3.	♦J	♦Q	♦2	♦3
4.	♦10	♦8	♠7	♦5
5.	♠4	♠A	♣K	♠J
6.	♥3	♣10	♣Q	♦6

East therefore made the point for high and the point for low as anticipated. He also took both the 10s in play, so easily won the point for game. The Jack of trumps was not in play, so East was the only player to score, and is three ahead of all his opponents.

Strategy

The main requirement for bidding is length in the trump suit. Usually the lead of Ace and another will be sufficient to remove opposing trumps, and a third trump should win a trick. Only after drawing trumps can a pitcher be certain of making Aces in side suits, because his opponents need not follow suit and can trump if they wish. Since all players are playing basically for themselves they will all pay attention to the score. Although all other players are attempting to beat the pitcher on a particular hand, it might be more sensible to give him the point for Jack or low rather than another player who is much nearer the winning total.

Since many of the cards in Pitch are sleeping, players should have a basic knowledge of probabilities. With four players, for example, the odds are 7 to 6 against any particular card being in the deal, and a player well behind who needs an Ace to be sleeping to score a smudge might well regard the odds as sufficiently good.

Variants

Some players award the scorer of a smudge the game, even if he is in the hole.

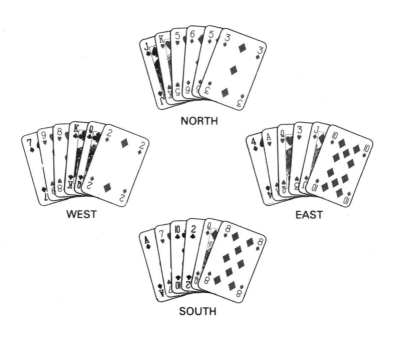

NORTH

WEST

EAST

SOUTH

The deal for the hand of Pitch described in the text.

In early forms of the game the dealer had the right to the contract merely by bidding as high as the previous highest bidder, i.e. he did not need to overbid to become pitcher or maker.

In some schools the lowest bid allowed is a bid of two, not one.

POKER ✓

Poker is an international card game of great popularity in the United States, where it is sometimes referred to as the national card game, and where annual 'world championships' are held. It is purely a gambling game, albeit one requiring considerable skill to play at the top levels. It developed from similar games like Brag (q.v.), and a German game Pochen, from which word Poker probably derives. It is a game with as many variants as people care to dream up, and outlandish 'house rules' in bars and clubs designed to fleece strangers are the subject of many jokes.

The original game did not allow players to change their cards. As in Brag, the cards dealt were the ones the players bet upon. This version is called Straight Poker. The game in which players improve their hands by discarding and drawing new cards is Draw Poker. This is the most popular version of the game, so it will be described first in its simplest form. Variants follow.

Players

Any reasonable number may play, five, six or seven being considered best.

Cards

The full pack of 52 is used, the cards ranking from Ace (high) to 2 (low). There is no ranking in the suits. As Poker is a gambling game in which stakes can mount rapidly, it is convenient to play the game with gambling chips, and it is assumed in this description that chips are used, but of course currency can be used.

Preliminaries

The first dealer may be determined by any player dealing the cards one at a time face up to each in turn, the first Jack dealt indicating the first dealer. The deal thereafter passes clockwise with each hand. It is best to agree when the game will end. All players can begin with equal stakes, the game to end when one player loses all, or until three players are left, or whatever else is preferred. Or play can end at an agreed time.

It is best to agree on minimum and maximum bets, and also to limit the number of raises of the stake which one player can make in each betting interval – a popular limit is three raises.

Before the deal the player to the left of the dealer puts one chip into a *pot*, or pool. This is known as the *ante*. The player to his left puts two chips into the pot. This is known as the *straddle*. These players are betting *blind* (i.e. before they have seen their cards), and this method of starting the betting is known as the 'blind opening'. It is widespread, but in the United States it is more popular to begin the betting with *Jackpots*, and this is described after the main description of the game.

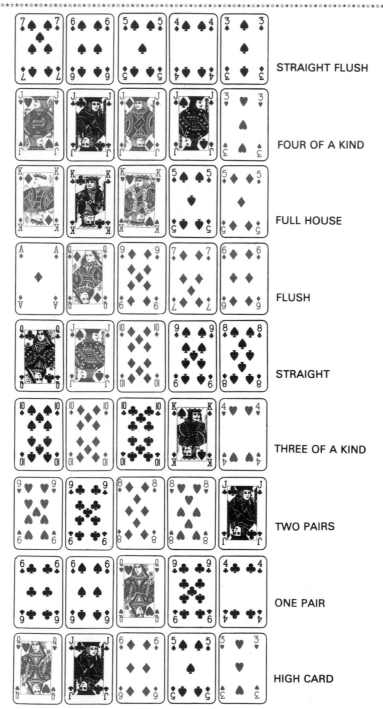

STRAIGHT FLUSH

FOUR OF A KIND

FULL HOUSE

FLUSH

STRAIGHT

THREE OF A KIND

TWO PAIRS

ONE PAIR

HIGH CARD

Dealing

The dealer deals five cards to each player, one at a time face down beginning with the player on his left and ending with himself. The remainder of the pack is placed face down before him. He will need it later.

The object

The object is to win the pot. This can be done in two ways. The first is to hold the best Poker hand at the *showdown*, the part of the game when hands are compared and the player with the best wins. The second method is to bet in such a way that other players will drop out before a showdown is reached. This is known as 'bluffing' and many a pot is won by a player who was not holding the best hand during the betting.

Examples of the ranks of Poker hands are shown in the illustration. They are in order of precedence:

a) *Straight flush* This is a sequence of five cards in the same suit. Ace may count as either high or low for this purpose. Competing straight flushes are ranked by the highest card in the sequence. Thus A K Q J 10 is the highest straight flush of all, and the highest Poker hand. It is called a *royal flush*.

b) *Four of a kind* This is a hand containing four cards of the same rank. Four Aces is highest and four 2s lowest.

c) *Full house* This is a hand con-

Examples of the ranks of Poker hand, highest at the top. They are also described in the text.

taining three cards of one rank and two of another. With competing full houses the rank of the set of three cards determines precedence.

d) *Flush* This is a hand containing five cards of the same suit, not in sequence. With competing flushes the rank of the highest card determines precedence, if equal the next and so on.

e) *Straight* This is a hand with five cards in sequence but not of the same suit. Again an Ace may be high or low. With competing straights the highest card determines precedence (i.e. that at the top of the straight).

f) *Three of a kind* This is a hand containing three cards of the same rank with two odd ones. With competing hands of the same type the rank of the three determines precedence.

g) *Two pairs* This is a hand with two cards of the same rank, another two of a different rank and an odd card. With competing hands of the same type, the rank of the higher pair determines precedence, if equal the rank of the second pair, if equal the odd card.

h) *One pair* This is a hand containing two cards of the same rank and three odd cards. With competing hands of the same type the rank of the pair determines precedence, if equal the highest odd card, then the next and so on.

i) *High card* This is a hand with five assorted cards not satisfying the requirements of any of the hands already noted. With competing hands of the same type, the rank of the highest card determines precedence, if equal the next and so on.

The play

The players examine the hands dealt them, and take part in a betting interval. The first two players to dealer's left have already bet with the ante and straddle, and the player to their left begins the 'voluntary' betting, which passes clockwise round the table. The first player to bet voluntarily must put in four chips. A player on his turn has three options:

Drop This means that he does not wish to bet, and he folds his cards, places them face down before him and takes no further part in the deal. A player who drops after already having bet does not recover his chips, which remain in the pot.

Call This means that he places in the pot enough chips to make his contribution to it equal to each of the preceding players but no higher.

Raise This means that he places in the pot enough chips to make his contribution equal to each of the preceding players plus a raise of one or more chips (up to the agreed maximum). Succeeding players, to stay in, must raise their stakes to the new level or drop out.

It follows that players, while putting chips into the pot, do not mix them, since the value of each player's contribution to the pot must be seen. In effect they push their chips towards the centre.

When the betting reaches ante and straddle the chips they have already contributed count, so if the level is 4 chips, they can call with 3 and 2 respectively.

When the stakes of all the players remaining in the game are equal the first betting interval ends.

The players now have the opportunity to improve their hands by discarding and drawing. The dealer takes up the pack, and beginning with the player still in who is nearest his left, deals with each in turn.

Each player may discard any number of cards (with six or more players, he is not allowed to discard more than three) by placing them face down before him, announcing how many. The dealer then deals him the same number of fresh cards to bring his hand back to five. If the dealer remains in he too must announce how many cards he is drawing, since this is valuable information to the other players. A player who is satisfied with his original five cards and does not draw is said to *stay pat*.

The discards are collected by the player to dealer's left. With seven or eight players it sometimes happens that the pack is exhausted before all players have drawn. When the undealt pack is reduced to one card, the dealer claims those already discarded, adds them to the one card remaining, and shuffles. The next player to be dealt with cuts the new pack and play proceeds. At no time must a card be exposed, of course.

When all players have drawn, the second betting interval takes place. Of the players remaining, the first to the left of straddle begins the betting. He has the same options as before but, since at the beginning of this betting round all bets are equal, he has a further option which is to *check*. This means he wishes to stay in, but not at the moment to raise the stake. Of course, if the stake is raised subsequently, on his turn he must call, raise or drop out. The second betting interval ends when all stakes are equal, and the showdown takes place.

All players left in now expose their cards, and the best hand wins. Should all except one player drop before the showdown, the remaining player takes the pot without being required to show his hand (it might be worthless!).

If a player runs out of chips during a hand, he may call for whatever chips he has. The other players still in equalize their stakes, and the pot is frozen. However the other players may con-

tinue raising and betting by means of a side pot. It is possible that the same thing could happen in the side pot, in which case a second side pot is started, and so on. At the showdown all players who have not dropped (except for running out of chips) compete for those pots to which they contributed, but not for the others.

Each hand is separate and the deal passes clockwise.

Example hand
Six players are dealt the hands in the illustration. A is dealer, so B has put 1 chip into the pot as ante,

---

The Poker hands dealt for the game described in the text.

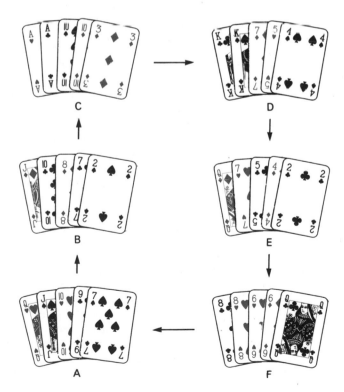

and C has put in 2 chips as straddle. D is the first to bet voluntarily.

D decides his pair of Kings is worth 4 chips, so bets. E, with a very poor hand, drops. F, with his two pairs, quickly decides to stay in. A, the dealer, decides it is worth 4 chips to remain in. He has four cards in sequence, and a K or 8 would give him a straight. B drops – he is happy to lose his ante and nothing else with his poor hand. C decides he probably has the strongest hand at the moment (he is right) and decides to raise the stakes by 2 chips. He already has 2 chips in the pot, so he adds 4, saying something like 'I call and raise by two'.

D now needs to add 2 chips to stay in, and with three players in opposition decides his pair is not good enough and drops. F suspects at least a hand of two pairs is against him, but he is brave and contributes 2 chips to stay in. A now works out that there are 17 chips to be won, and it will cost him another 2, making 6, to stay in. Are the odds of 17 to 6 worth the risk? From the accompanying table it can be seen that the odds against improving his hand are 5 to 1. He decides to drop.

The bets are now equal, so the draw takes place. Only two players remain in, C and F, and each draws one card, from which each can guess that it is likely that the other has two pairs. C draws ◆ K and F draws ♥ 4, so neither improves his hand. F bets first, and suspects he is beaten. He checks. C is confident now, and raises two. Had he raised, say, 4, F would probably drop, but F has now to decide whether it is worth 2 more chips just to make sure he hasn't been bluffed by C. He puts in 2 and calls. C wins the showdown and collects the pot of 25 chips, 17 of which are winnings.

Jackpots

This version of Draw Poker mentioned earlier is popular in America and was invented to encourage betting.

The idea of ante and straddle is abolished, each player putting in 1 chip to start the pool (some prefer that dealer puts in for all, which amounts to the same thing as the deal circulates).

The player to dealer's left has the first opportunity to bet, but no player may open the betting without a pair of Jacks or a higher-ranking hand. The first player's options are:

a) *Open* This means he has a hand of the minimum strength, and he bets by putting chips into the pool (maximum and minimum stakes as usual, should be agreed).
b) *Check* This means he wishes to stay in the game without yet betting further. He may, or may not, have a hand of the required strength.

If all players check, including dealer, the deal is abandoned. The pot remains for the next hand when it is doubled as the players again put in their stakes.

Once a player has bet, the options for succeeding players are to drop, call or raise as described above. Play proceeds as before except that the opener's discards are not collected up, because he may be required to show, after the hand, that he held the requisite strength to open.

Progressive jackpots

With this variant of Jackpots, when a deal is passed and all players have put in a second ante for the following deal, the minimum hand to open becomes a pair of Queens (a *Queenpot*). If this is passed, the minimum hand becomes *Kingpots*, then *Acepots*, where it usually remains until somebody bets and the stakes are won, when it reverts to Jackpots.

Wild cards

By arrangement any card or cards in Draw Poker may be used as wild. A wild card is one which its holder can use to represent any other card. Sometimes the Joker is added to the pack and becomes a wild card, sometimes as an ordinary wild card, sometimes as a limited wild card. In the latter case it can be used only as an Ace or to complete a flush or straight, and it is called the *bug*.

It is customary for the 2s to be used as wild cards. If all four are wild the game is known as *Deuces wild* or a *Freakpot*. In most schools a wild card cannot duplicate a card already held. This means one cannot hold 'five of a kind'. Some schools prefer only black 2s to be wild.

Variants

There are many variants of Poker, some weird and wonderful, and most adding complications for the sake of it, like the hand called a *blaze*, which contains five assorted court or face cards. A distinct and excellent game, however, is Stud Poker.

Stud Poker This is an interesting game for up to nine players, but is a better game than Draw Poker if there are only two or three players. It is the game played by Edward G. Robinson and Steve McQueen in the film *The Cincinnati Kid*.

Dealer is decided as before. The dealer gives one card to each player face down. This is his *hole-card*. He then deals a second face up – in fact all succeeding cards are face up. There is now the first betting interval.

Players look at their hole cards but do not expose them until the showdown. The player with the highest card showing opens the betting. If two or more players have equal cards showing, the one nearest dealer's left opens the betting. On each round the dealer announces who bets first. Subsequent players drop, call or raise as in Draw Poker. A player who drops must turn over his exposed cards.

When bets are equal the betting ends, and the dealer deals each player a second face-up card and indicates who bets. This is the player with the highest-ranking Poker hand, which with two cards showing, might be a pair. On this and subsequent rounds a further option is to check, as described earlier. In fact all players in the game may check, when the betting interval ends. If a player raises, of course, all must subsequently call to remain in.

Play proceeds thus till each player has five cards. On the third and fourth face-up card the dealer must point out possible straights and flushes as he deals the card, but this is not significant in deciding the first to bet. For instance, a player with a pair showing will bet first – even if other players have possible straights or flushes.

When all players have five cards, i.e. a hole-card and four face-up cards each, there is the fourth and last betting interval. All those remaining in the game when bets are equalized expose their hole cards and the player with the best hand takes the pot. If all but one player drop out, the winner does not have to show his hole-card.

Strategy

In all poker games a knowledge of the probabilities of certain hands and the chances of improving them is of great importance, as are nerve, the ability to bluff and the capacity to work out the likely hands of the opponents from their behaviour. The game is part mathematics and part psychology, and players cannot agree on the proportions. The two tables included here give some of the mathematical information.

The tables show the heavy odds against improving an inside straight (a straight with one of the inside cards missing) and the general advisability against keeping a *kicker* (an odd card, usually an Ace) when trying to improve three of a kind or a pair.

So far as psychology is concerned, good players will not be impatient enough to try desperately to improve bad hands. They will wait for the good ones. They will not keep betting when they think they are beaten. Players tend to do this either because 'it's the only decent hand they've held all night' or because 'most of the money in the pot was theirs anyway'. The really expensive hands are the good ones which prove to be second best. Good players will control their emotions, and will pay their opponents the compliment of not expecting them to be easily bluffed.

In Stud Poker it is usually best not to bet on a hand which, even with the hole-card, is not as good as a hand another player has exposed, and to realise that, with three of a suit and two cards to come, it is 23 to 1 against completing the flush, and a player showing a pair is in a much stronger position.

The incidence of Poker hands is as follows:

Hand	Number in pack	Approximate probability of being dealt
Straight flush	40	65,000 to 1
Four of a kind	624	4,166 to 1
Full house	3,744	693 to 1
Flush	5,108	508 to 1
Straight	10,200	254 to 1
Three of a kind	54,912	46 to 1
Two pairs	123,552	20 to 1
One pair	1,098,240	4 to 3
High card	1,302,540	evens

The chances of improving a Poker hand:

Holding before draw	Number of cards drawn	Improvement to	Odds against drawing	Odds against any improvement
One pair	3	Two pairs	5 to 1	5 to 2
		Three of a kind	8 to 1	
		Full house	97 to 1	
		Four of a kind	359 to 1	
One pair and a kicker	2	Two pairs	5 to 1	3 to 1
		Three of a kind	12 to 1	
		Full house	119 to 1	
		Four of a kind	1,080 to 1	
Two pairs	1	Full house	11 to 1	11 to 1
Three of a kind	2	Full house	$15\frac{1}{2}$ to 1	$8\frac{1}{2}$ to 1
		Four of a kind	$22\frac{1}{2}$ to 1	
Three of a kind and a kicker	1	Full house	15 to 1	11 to 1
		Four of a kind	46 to 1	
Open-ended four straight	1	Straight	5 to 1	5 to 1*
One-sided or inside straight	1	Straight	11 to 1	11 to 1*
Open-ended straight flush	1	Straight flush	$22\frac{1}{2}$ to 1	$22\frac{1}{2}$ to 1*
One-sided or inside straight flush	1	Straight flush	46 to 1	46 to 1
Four flush	1	Flush	$4\frac{1}{4}$ to 1	$4\frac{1}{4}$ to 1*
Three flush	2	Flush	23 to 1	23 to 1*

* The odds against improving to a pair, or in the case of a three flush to threes or two pairs are not considered.

POLIGNAC

Polignac is sometimes called Quatre Valets or Four Jacks, for reasons which the description of the game will make clear.

Players
Polignac is best for four players, each playing for himself, but can be satisfactorily played by five or six.

Cards
The 32-card pack is used, i.e. the standard pack stripped of the 6s, 5s, 4s, 3s, and 2s. If five or six play, the two black 7s are also taken out, reducing the pack to 30. Cards

---

The deal for the hand of Polignac described in the text.

rank in the order Ace (high) to 7 (low).

Dealing
The dealer is chosen by any agreed method, and he deals all the cards. When four play he deals in bundles of 3, 2 and 3, when five play in bundles of 3 and 3, when six play in bundles of 3 and 2.

The play
Polignac is a trick-taking game. Eldest hand (to dealer's left) makes the opening lead. Players must follow suit if able, and if they cannot they may discard any card. Each trick is won by the highest card in the suit led. The winner of a trick leads to the next.

The object is to avoid taking any

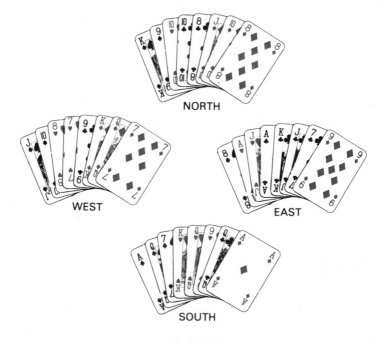

NORTH

WEST

EAST

SOUTH

of the four Jacks. The ♠J (polignac) counts 2 points against the player who takes it while the other Jacks count as 1 point each.

Scoring

There are two main methods of scoring. One is to supply each player with an agreed number of chips, and for each point conceded he must put one chip into the centre. The winner is the player holding the most chips when one player has lost all of his.

Another method is to agree on a number of deals, so that each player deals an equal number of times, the winner being he with the lowest minus score at the end.

Example hand

The hands are dealt by South as in the illustration and West leads. He leads his ♣9 and play proceeds as follows:

	West	North	East	South
1.	♣9	♣10	♣A	♣Q
2.	♦K	♦J	♦9	♦A
3.	♥8	♥10	♥A	♥9
4.	♠10	♦K	♣8	♣7
5.	♠J	♠9	♥J	♠Q

Since ♥A had been played, South must now take the remaining tricks which will include the ♣J, so he has made all 5 points in this opening hand.

Strategy

Skill lies in judging which card to lead when on lead, which to discard when unable to follow suit and when to take a trick, given the choice of playing high or low. The

other players' actions convey information. At trick 5 in the example hand, for instance, North had the choice of a diamond, spade or club to lead. He could guess by West's lead of ♣9 at trick one that West was probably void in clubs, and by South's play of the ♦A in second position in trick 2, when he hadn't the ♦J, that the ♦A was probably a singleton. The card which gave him the best chance of losing the trick, and opponents the least chance of discarding a Jack, was ♠9, which proved a successful lead.

Variant

As protection for a player with a very bad hand, a call of capot before the opening lead is announced. A player who calls capot is announcing that he will win all the tricks. If he succeeds all his opponents are debited 5 points; if he fails, he is debited 5 points, plus the penalty points for each Jack.

Slobberhannes

This game with its peculiar name is so similar to Polignac that it is convenient to describe them together. The rules of play are exactly the same, but the penalties are different. The only penalty card is the ♣Q, the taker of which loses 1 point, but there are also penalty points awarded against the taker of the first trick and the taker of the last. Should a player be unlucky enough to take all 3 points against him in the same deal, he is given a fourth penalty point.

POPE JOAN

Pope Joan is an ancient game, the forerunner of such as Newmarket and Michigan (q.v.). It was once very popular in Scotland. The Pope is the ◆9, and as the real Pope was the Antichrist of Scottish reformers the ◆9 became known as the Curse of Scotland, by which name it is still called by

---

A representation of an old Pope Joan board, now to be found in museums or antique shops.

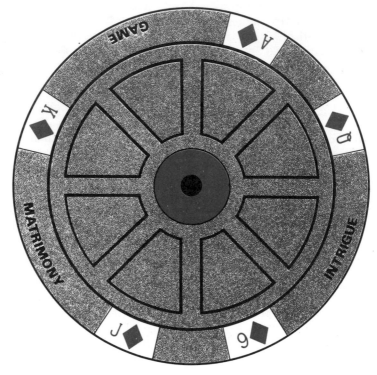

some card players. That is, at least, the most plausible reason for the card's nickname. At one time a special board in the form of an intricately decorated circular tray containing eight compartments for stake money was used for the game, as represented by the illustration. Nowadays players use eight saucers carrying the labels Pope, Ace, King, Queen, Jack, Matrimony, Intrigue, Game. Pope Joan is a gambling game.

Players
Three to eight may play, with four, five or six being the best numbers.

Cards
The standard pack of 52 cards is used, but the ♦8 is removed before play. The cards rank from Ace (high) to 2 (low).

Preliminaries
Cards are dealt face up one at a time to each player, and the first Jack turned up indicates the first dealer. He is entitled to shuffle and the player on his right cuts. Before the deal the dealer puts units of stake (chips, counters, currency) onto the board or into the saucers as follows: 6 units in that labelled Pope (♦9), 2 each in Matrimony and Intrigue, and 1 each in Ace, King, Queen, Jack and Game. This is known as dressing the board.

Dealing
Cards are dealt one at a time clockwise to each player, including dealer, beginning with eldest (to dealer's left). Each player must have the same number of cards and the odd cards go into a widow, left face down in the centre of the table. The number of cards dealt to each player and widow are as follows:

Players	Cards each	Widow
3	15	6
4	11	7
5	9	6
6	8	3
7	7	2
8	6	3

The last card of the widow is turned over to show the 'trump' suit. If it is the ♦9 or any Ace, King, Queen or Jack, the dealer wins the stakes in the appropriate place on the board or in the saucer.

The play
The player to the left of dealer makes a lead and announces it. He may lead from any suit he chooses, provided it is the lowest card he holds in that suit. Suppose he leads the ♣3, he announces 'Three of clubs' and the player with the ♣4 plays it, followed by the player with the ♣5 and so on. Any player may play a number of cards consecutively. The runs will be brought to a stop eventually either by a King being played, or the ♦7 (the ♦8 is missing) or because a card is in the widow.

When a run is brought to a stop the last player to play a card begins a new run. Again he can choose any suit, but must lead the lowest card he holds in that suit.

In the 'trump' suit, if a player lays the Ace, King, Queen or Jack he collects the stakes in the appropriate space on the board, or in the saucers. If he lays the Pope (♦9) he collects those stakes. Should he lay both the King and Queen of the 'trump' suit he also claims the stakes for matrimony, and if he lays the Jack and Queen of the suit he claims the stakes for intrigue.

The player who gets rid of all his cards first collects the stakes from the game space or saucer, and in addition each player pays him 1 unit for each card remaining in his hand. A player caught with the Pope ($\blacklozenge$ 9) in his hand, however, avoids paying the extra units. Once he lays the Pope he loses this benefit.

Any stakes left on the board or in the saucers at the end of a hand remain there and are added to by the new dealer. It is recommended that a game should be of an agreed number of deals, or until each player has dealt an equal number of times after an agreed time is reached.

Pyramid

Pyramid is a one-pack **patience** or **solitaire** with a very pleasing tableau. The full pack of 52 cards is used, of which 28 cards are built in a pyramid shape in seven rows as shown in the illustration.

The play

The remainder of the cards are held in the hand and turned over one at a time. The first card turned over is available to be matched with any of the seven cards in the bottom row. To match, two cards must have pips which add up to 13. An Ace counts as one, Jack 11, Queen 12 and other cards their

The layout for the game of Pyramid described in the text.

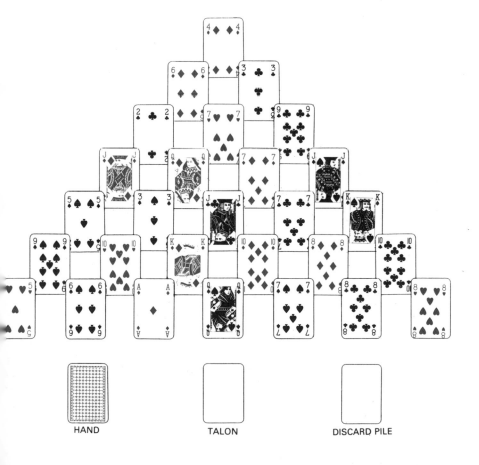

HAND   TALON   DISCARD PILE

pip value. Kings, counting 13, are single entities which do not need a match. When two cards match, they are set aside in a discard pile. Kings are set aside as soon as they become available. As cards are removed from the tableau, those on the next row become available for play. A card is available if no other card covers it.

A card turned from hand which cannot be matched in the tableau is placed onto a *talon* or waste pile. The top card of that pile is also available for matching, either with an available card in the tableau or with the next card turned over from hand.

Available cards in the tableau can be matched only with the card turned over from the hand or the top card of the talon; they cannot be matched with each other.

The object of the play is to clear away the pyramid before the cards in hand are exhausted. There is no re-deal allowed.

In the game illustrated the first card turned over was the ♠10. It does not match so is played to the talon. The next card is the ♣Q. This matches the ♦A, so the two are discarded onto the discard pile. The next card is the ♠8, which matches the ♦5. The next card is the ♥A, which matches the ♠Q, so they are discarded. The ♦K is now available and is discarded. The next card, the ♥J, goes onto the talon as does the next, the ♦9. The next, the ♣6, matches the ♠7, so they are discarded and the ♦10 is now available. The next card is the ♣4, which matches the ♦9 on the talon, so they are discarded. And so on.

Pyramid is not a game which is easy to get out, and is not one which can be influenced much by skilful play, but when a game lasting about five or ten minutes is required it is pleasing enough.

QUINTO

Quinto is a trick-taking game in which three of the suits can be used as trumps during any one deal, sometimes in one trick. It is an interesting game in which much skill can be used.

Players
Quinto is for four players, playing in two partnerships. It can be played by three, as noted later.

Cards
The standard pack of 52 cards is used to which is added the Joker. The cards rank from Ace (high) to 2 (low). The Joker itself has no trick-taking value, but is a useful card to win in a trick. The suits also rank, as follows: hearts, diamonds, clubs, spades. Each suit can be used as a trump suit to trump over a lower one. Thus only spades can never be used as trumps, and the most powerful card is the ♥A, and the least powerful the ♠2. The ♣2 is the lowest card which can be used as a trump.

Preliminaries
Players draw cards for partners, the two lowest playing against the two highest, and the lowest is first dealer (there cannot be any ties, since the cards rank from ♥A to ♠2). The dealer shuffles and the player to his right cuts. After the first deal the deal passes in rotation clockwise.

Dealing
The dealer places the first five cards from the top of the pack face down on the table in front of him. These five cards are known as the *cachette*. The remaining 48 cards are dealt one at a time to each player, beginning with eldest (the player on dealer's left).

The play
Players examine their cards, and beginning with eldest, each in turn has the option of deciding to double the value of each trick. Once the trick values have been doubled a succeeding player on the opposite side may, if he wishes, redouble, thereby quadrupling the value of each trick. However, a player may not redouble a double by his partner.

Eldest leads to the first trick. A player must follow suit if he can. If he cannot he may trump with any card from any of the higher ranking suits, or he may discard. Notice it is impossible to discard if a spade is led, since all the other suits are trumps over spades.

A trick is won by the highest value card in the trick, and it can be seen that this is true no matter what suit was led. The Joker has no trick-taking value, and can be played by its holder whenever he likes, irrespective of the suit led and whether or not he can follow suit. If the Joker is led there is no need to specify the suit it represents, since every trick is won by the highest-ranking card, and the suit led is immaterial.

The winner of a trick leads to the next. The winner of the last trick takes the cachette as an extra trick.

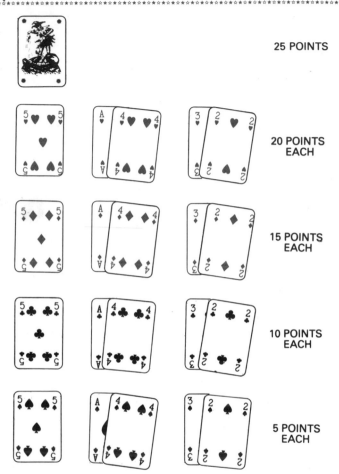

25 POINTS

20 POINTS EACH

15 POINTS EACH

10 POINTS EACH

5 POINTS EACH

The values of the quints in Quinto.

Scoring

A side scores 5 points for each trick that it wins. If doubled, this is increased to 10 points, and if redoubled to 20.

The Joker is worth 25 points to the side which takes it in a trick. It is known as the *quint royal*. The four fives are *quints* as are any two cards in a suit whose pip value is five (A 4 and 2 3). To score for a quint made up of a pair, the pair has to be taken in one trick. Scores for all quints are shown in the illustration.

The scores for quint royal and quints are entered as the tricks are won, and the scores for tricks at the end of a deal. Score is kept by partnership and the first to pass 250 points wins the game. A *rubber* is the best of three games, so might last two or three games. Each side's score for each game is added together, and the winner of the rubber adds a bonus of 100 points.

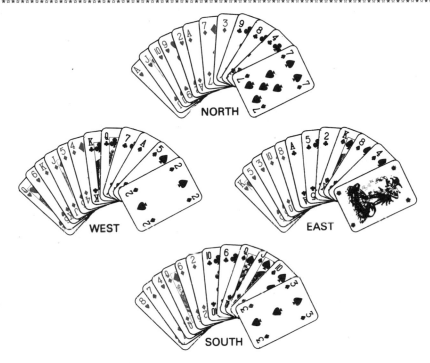

Example deal

South deals as in the illustration. North, on his turn, doubles. East does not redouble. West has the lead and tries to make his ♠A. His partner, holding the 4, plays it to give his side a quint. South holds up his ♠3. As his partner has a strong hand he might be able to make a quint for him later. Play proceeds as follows:

	West	North	East	South
1.	♠A	♠7	♠4	♠10
2.	♣K	♣4	♣A	♣6
3.	♣Q	♣8	♣5	♣10

East read his partner's lead of the ♣K as indicating he held the ♣Q also, so overtook with ♣A and led the quint. It was good play. West now decides to get off lead, and is unwilling to lead the ♠5 or ♠2.

The deal for the hand of Quinto described in the text.

4.	♣7	♣9	♣2	♠J
5.	♦K	♦7	♦8	♦Q
6.	♥6	♥9	♥K	♥7
7.	♦J	♦A	♦10	♦6

West gave up what would have been the master diamond rather than present North with a quint, since he guessed North held the Ace. North guesses (rightly) that the ♦3 would be a dangerous lead, and decides the time has come to draw the hearts. With the King played, he is likely to lose only one to the Queen, and as the cards lay he didn't lose that.

8.	♥Q	♥A	♥3	♥4
9.	♠2	♥J	♥5	♥8
10.	♦4	♥10	♠8	♠3
11.	♠5	♥2	♠K	♦2
12.	♦5	♦3	Joker	♣Q

West took the cachette as an extra trick. North's double was unlucky. Each of his opponents had a better hand than his partner.

The final scores in this deal were: North/South 60 for tricks, and 45 for quints (♥ 5, ♥ A 4, ♠5), total 105; East/West 70 for tricks, 65 for quints (Joker, ♦ 5, ♣5, ♣ A 4, ♠A 4).

Quinto for three players Quinto can be played by three players by two playing in partnership against another with a dummy hand. The player with the dummy has an advantage and so his opponents receive a start of 25 points towards game. The player with the dummy hand deals first in each game, and thereafter the deal passes to the left as usual. The player with dummy must look first at the hand which will have to play first to the first trick, and may double or redouble with it, but cannot look at his other hand before making this choice. He cannot double or redouble with his second hand, having seen both his hands.

Rubbers are not played. Each game is complete in itself, and the three players take turns in having the dummy hand.

Ranter Go Round

This is an old Cornish game which is also called Cuckoo. It is a very simple game for children of age about seven to twelve.

Players

The game is played by any reasonable number, five to 20 being best.

Cards

The standard pack of 52 cards is used, the cards ranking from King (high) to Ace (low).

The play

In this game the players have three 'lives', and all should begin the game with three counters. It is best to have a receptacle like a saucer in the centre of the table to receive the counters as lives are lost.

Any player may deal, and dealer deals one card to each player, including himself, face down. The object is to avoid being left with the lowest card.

Each player looks at his card and play begins with the player to dealer's left. He may keep his card if he considers it sufficiently high not to be the lowest, or he may command the player to his left to change cards with him. He does this by offering the card and saying 'Change'. This player must change unless he has a King, when he can reply 'King', forcing the first player (who wished to change) to keep his card. The play then carries on round the table to the player on his left.

When an exchange has been made, the player receiving the unwanted card may pass it on in his turn by asking his left-hand neighbour to change, and so on round the table. The card is finally brought to a halt either by a player calling 'King' or by a player not wishing to pass it on by virtue of having exchanged a card of inferior rank for it, and thus knowing he cannot hold the lowest card. In this case the player to his left has the chance of keeping his card or passing it on, and so on.

A player who, in obeying the command to change, passes to his right-hand neighbour an Ace, 2 or 3, must announce the rank of the card. This immediately tells succeeding players whether or not their own card is safe: they will only decide to change if the card they hold is lower or equal in rank to the card announced.

The dealer is the last to play, and if he wishes to change his card, he does so by cutting the rest of the pack and taking the top card of the cut. He must show the card he draws, and if it is a King he is the loser and must put one of his counters into the saucer.

Otherwise, all the players now show their cards and the player with the lowest loses a life and puts a counter into the centre. If two or more are equal lowest, all put a counter into the centre.

The deal passes clockwise, and a player who loses his three counters drops out of the game. The winner is the last player left in with a counter. Children do not mind dropping out, as it is a fast-moving game and the next game comes round quickly enough.

Red Dog

Red Dog is also called High-card Pool. It is a simple gambling game that is likely to appeal more to casual family groups playing for small stakes than to serious gamblers.

Players
Up to ten players may play.

Cards
The standard pack of 52 cards is used, the cards ranking from Ace (high) to 2 (low).

Preliminaries
Players bet against a pool rather than a bank or each other, so all must contribute equally to a pool before the game starts. The pool is the property of all players, to be shared equally at the end of the game or to be replenished equally should it run out. If there are ten players each might contribute 2 or 3 units of stake to the pool, if only three or four perhaps 5 or 6 units.

Any player shuffles the pack and deals a card to each player. The player receiving the highest card becomes first dealer; he may have the last shuffle and the player to his right cuts.

Dealing
The dealer deals five cards, one at a time, to each player face down, beginning on his left. If there are nine or ten players he deals only four cards. It is best if the dealer does not have a hand himself, but merely looks after the play for one round. After dealing, he places the remainder of the cards face down before him to form the *stock*.

The play
Each player, beginning with the player to dealer's left, examines his hand, and bets that he has a card to beat the top card of the stock. To beat it he must hold a card of higher rank in the same suit. His bet can be from a minimum of 1 unit to a maximum which is the equivalent of the amount in the pool at the time. He puts his stake halfway between himself and the pool and announces it. If he likes, he may merely pay 1 unit to the pool instead of betting. This might seem pointless, but it serves to keep his hand secret from the other players.

When the bet is made, dealer faces the top card of the stock. If the player has a card to beat it, he exposes it. The dealer then adds to his stake an equal amount from the pool and he withdraws it. If the player cannot beat the card exposed, he must show his entire hand face up for the other players to see. His stakes are then added to the pool. In each case the player's cards are collected up and set aside, and play passes to the next player clockwise.

When the pool is taken in its entirety by one of the players, it is replenished by each player contributing equally to a new pool. At the end of each deal, the deal passes to the next player to the left.

Variants

a) Some schools give each player the choice of betting to beat the top card or betting that he cannot beat the top card. If he bets that he will lose, he must show his entire hand after the card is turned, no matter what the result of his bet.

b) It is easy to work out the chances of a hand winning (see below) and a player or players who want to play seriously can spoil the game, since the optimum play is to bet the minimum stake when the odds are against winning and the whole pool when the odds are in favour. If some players play like this the pool will be found to need replenishing after every three or four bets, occasionally on two or three successive bets, and this gets tedious. It is suggested then that the game is played only for fun, and that only three bets are allowed: 1, 2 or 3 units. If the pool is made sufficiently large, it will therefore last a long time.

Strategy

Should the whereabouts of no other cards be known than the five in the hand, it is easy to calculate how many of the remaining 47 will beat the hand if turned up, and how many will not. If a player subtracts the rank of the top card he holds in each suit from 14 (counting Aces as 14, Kings as 13, Queens 12, Jacks 11 and a void as 1) and adds the four figures together, he will know how many cards will beat him, and by subtracting from 47 how many will not. As stated above, a serious gambler will bet the whole pool if the second number is the higher and the minimum if the first number is the higher. As the deal progresses, and some cards are exposed, the odds will fluctuate slightly. But this is not a game to be treated in this way.

A Red Dog hand with an almost equal chance of beating the turn-up or losing.

ROCKAWAY

Rockaway is a game for children aged between about eight and fourteen. It is also called Go Boom.

Players
Rockaway is for two to eight players.

The deal for the hand of Rockaway described in the text.

Cards
The standard pack of 52 cards is used for two to four players, the cards ranking from Ace (high) to 2 (low). Two packs shuffled together are used if more than four play.

Dealing
Any player may deal, and he deals each player seven cards, beginning with the player on his left,

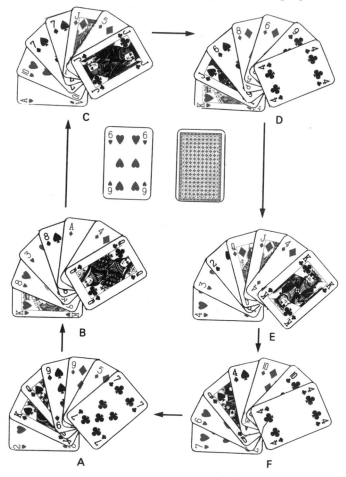

and including himself. He then turns over the next card, which is the *widow*, and places it face upwards in the centre. The rest of the cards are placed face down beside it to form the *stock*.

The play

The player to dealer's left must put on the widow a card of the same suit or rank as the widow, or an Ace. If he cannot, he must draw a card from the top of the stock and continue to draw cards until he is able to cover the widow. The next player must then play a card of the suit or rank of the new card at the top of the widow or an Ace, and so on round the table.

When the stock is exhausted, play continues with a player unable to lay a card merely missing his turn.

The hand ends when one player gets rid of all his cards (he *goes boom*). The other players expose their cards and are debited with a score against them according to the cards they hold: each Ace counts 15, a court card (K Q J) 10 and other cards their pip value.

The deal passes round the table in a clockwise direction, and when all players have dealt once the winner is the player with the lowest debit score.

Example hand

Six players A, B, C, D, E and F, are dealt the hands in the illustration. The widow is the ♥ 6 and A is to play first. Play proceeds as follow:

	A	B	C	D	E	F
1.	♥ 2	♥ K	♥ 10	♥ K	♣ K	♣ 10
2.	♣ 7	♣ Q	♣ J	♣ 9	?	

Player E must now draw from stock until he gets a club, a 9 or an Ace. He was anxious on the first round to play his high-scoring King rather than the low ♥ 4, but this was a mistake. Early on, when nobody is threatening to go boom, it is best to try to keep at least one card of each suit and as many ranks as possible. With a card of each suit a player is sure to be able to play a card on his next turn.

Variant

A variant which is more interesting is played with one pack and limited to six players. It introduces children to the principles of trick-taking games.

The widow is dispensed with, and the Ace has no special properties. The player to dealer's left makes the first lead and all players must follow by playing a card of the same suit or the same rank as the card led (note: not of the previous card played). If unable to play such a card a player draws from stock until he can. When each player has played to the card led, the cards played form a trick. The player who played the highest card of the suit led wins the trick. The trick itself is worthless and is gathered up and discarded to one side, but the winner of it has the right to lead to the next trick, and so on.

When the stock is exhausted, a player who cannot follow the suit or rank led merely misses a turn.

When a player gets rid of his cards the deal ends and other players are debited with the cards they hold: 10 points for court cards (K Q J) and other cards at their pip value, including Aces, which count as 1. Each player deals once, the player with the lowest score being the winner, or, if preferred, play continues until one player is debited with 100, when the lowest score wins.

RUMMY

Rummy is the name given to a family of card games which grew out of the old game of Conquian, now called Coon-Can (q.v.). Derivatives which are sufficiently different and popular to merit separate treatment in this book are Gin Rummy and Canasta. Its name is frequently shortened to Rum (hence Gin), and apart from Bridge is probably in all its forms the most widely played of card games. The simplest version of the game is described first, and variants and games based on it follow.

Players
From two to six may play, although two might prefer Gin Rummy (q.v.). More than six will probably prefer the double-pack Coon-Can (q.v.) or the variant Continental Rummy, a description of which follows later.

Cards
The full standard pack of 52 cards is used, cards ranking from King (high) to Ace (low).

Preliminaries
Each player draws a card, and the lowest deals first. Dealer has the last shuffle and the player to his right cuts. After the first deal the deal rotates to the left.

Dealing
Cards are dealt one at a time face down clockwise to dealer's left until each player has the following number of cards: with two players,

10 cards; with three or four, 7 cards; with five or six, 6 cards.

The dealer places the remainder of the pack face down in the centre to form the *stock*, and the top card of the stock is turned over and placed beside it to begin a discard pile.

The play
Each player in turn, beginning with the player on dealer's left, draws a card either from the top of the discard pile or from the top of the stock and discards a card from his hand to the discard pile.

The object of the game is to make sets of (meld) three or four cards of the same rank, or sequences of three or more cards of the same suit (Ace being low). Melds are made on a player's turn between drawing a card and discarding one. In this interval a player can lay down in front of him any melds he has in his hand, can add a card or cards to an existing meld of his own, or *lay off* cards onto melds of other players. He can do any or all of these things on the same turn.

The first player to get rid of all his cards wins the hand. On his last turn he need not make a discard, but can meld all the cards in his hand. Alternatively he can meld all but one card and discard as usual.

Should the stock become exhausted before a player has *gone out*, the discard pile is turned over and becomes the stock, play continuing as usual.

Scoring

When one player has gone out, the other players are debited with all the unmelded cards held in their hands, on the following count: court cards (K Q J) count as 10 points and all other cards their pip value (Aces one). The winner is the player with the lowest total when another passes 100.

If the game is played for stakes, it is usual for losers to pay the winner after each hand.

The Rummy hand described in the text.

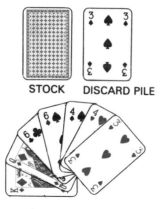

STOCK   DISCARD PILE

Strategy

A player should build a hand to give him as much chance as possible of melding. In the illustration the player should take up the ♠3 from the discard pile and discard ♦K. It gives him chances of melding ♠3 4 5 6, and also of picking up ♦3 or ♣3. The ♦K Q can only be melded with one card, ♦J, and since they count 10 points each if held at the end should be given up.

Of course, a player should carefully watch which cards have already been played to the discard

pile, and if in the example given ♦3 and ♣3 have already gone, he would be better advised to draw from stock.

Other players' discards can be used to gain information about the cards in their hands.

When discarding, keep adjacent cards which, with a draw, might provide opportunities to meld. In the second illustration it is better to discard ♠8 than any of the ten-count cards, since these would provide good opportunities to meld if ♦J, ♣Q, ♣10 or ♥J were drawn. However, high-count cards should not be held for more than two or three rounds.

The second Rummy hand described in the text.

One should also endeavour, when discarding, to discard cards which earlier discards show to be unlikely to be of use, such as a card of the rank of a previous discard by the left-hand opponent, or of a rank or in sequence with cards already discarded by others.

Generally, two cards in sequence are more valuable to hold than a pair, although each will meld with one of two cards, because should a sequence of three be achieved, there still remain two cards to improve it, whereas a set of three of the same rank can be improved by only one card.

When to declare melds is a nice decision. Holding them up to prevent opponents laying off is dangerous, since if an opponent goes out the cards become debits. Players should be aware of the state of the game, and if in doubt, meld.

Variants

a) In some schools a player who melds all his cards and goes out in one turn without having previously melded is said to have gone rummy, and opponents pay him double.

b) In some schools a player must make a discard in going out. This means that a player holding two cards cannot go out except by laying off.

c) In some schools laying off on opponents' melds in not permitted except when a player goes out, when other players are allowed to lay off on his melds as far as they can.

d) In some schools Ace can be melded in sequence with K Q. Sometimes 'round the corner' sequences are permitted, whereby the suit is considered circular, and 2 A K is regarded as a legitimate sequence.

d) In some schools play ends if the stock is exhausted, and the winner is the player with the lowest count in his hand. Players settle according to the difference in counts as before, and if there are two or more winners, the winnings are shared.

Knock Rummy

Knock Rummy is best for three to five players, each receiving 7 cards. It is played like the parent game, but players do not meld during the game. A player goes out on one turn by knocking on the table after making his draw. He then lays down his melds and discards.

In Knock Rummy a player is permitted to have an unmatched card. Usually the unmatched card must be a 3 or of lower rank, so the knocker comes up for three, two, one or nothing (all seven cards matched). The other players then lay down their melds and are allowed to lay off unmatched cards on the winner's melds. They are then debited with the count of their unmatched cards, with K Q J counting 10 each, and the others their pip value (Ace one). The knocker, if he had an odd card, is debited with its value. All players pay the knocker the difference in their counts.

It is possible that, after the laying off, another player, not the knocker, will have the lowest count. If so, he is the winner and the losers settle with him, not the knocker. Moreover, the knocker pays him the difference plus 10 units. If the knocker and another player tie, the other player is the winner, but the knocker does not pay the 10 units. Where two or more players tie, winnings are shared.

Variant This variant of Knock Rummy is sometimes called Poker Rum. The differences from the game just described are:

a) a player may knock at any time, with any number of unmatched cards;

b) there is no laying off;

c) if a knocker goes rum, i.e. has

all his cards melded, he receives a bonus of 25 points from each player. Should another player hold a completely melded hand, he must pay (this could happen only by mistake).

Boathouse Rummy

In Boathouse Rummy, the number of cards dealt to each player is nine minus the number of players. It is a game best for three to five players.

A player, on his turn, may take the top card of the stock or the top card of the discard pile as described above, but if he takes the top card of the discard pile he must also take either the second card in the discard pile or the top card of the stock. He discards only one card, so if he takes this course he increases his hand by one card.

The Ace is high, low or round-the-corner, i.e. can be matched in sequence with K Q, 2 3, or K 2.

Melds are not made during the play. To go out a player must make all his melds in one turn before discarding.

When a player goes out other players may lay down any melds they hold in their hands, and be debited only for the unmatched cards they hold. Ace now counts as 11, K Q J as 10, and other cards at their pip value.

Continental Rummy

Continental Rummy is suitable for any number of players up to 12. If two to five play, two packs are used, if six to eight play, three packs, and if nine to 12 play, four packs. Each pack must contain a Joker.

Each player is dealt 15 cards, the rest forming the stock. Play pro-ceeds as for the parent game with players drawing either from the discard pile or the stock. All melds are sequences – sets of cards of the same rank are of no value.

A player does not meld during play, and the winner has to go out with all 15 cards melded at one turn. He may have either five 3-card sequences; three 4-card sequences and one 3-card sequence; or one 5-card sequence, one 4-card sequence and two 3-card sequences. Other combinations are not allowed. A 6-card sequence can, of course, be regarded as two 3-card sequences and so on.

The Jokers can be used to represent any card the holder wishes.

The winner collects from all other players 1 unit for winning, plus 2 units for each Joker a player holds in his hand. Or the game can be played socially by totalling each player's debits, the winner being the player with the lowest total when another player reaches 11, or any number by previous agreement.

Gamblers Rummy

This version of the game is that favoured by serious gamblers. It is for four players, who are dealt seven cards each. It differs from the parent game in that:

a) A player cannot declare all his hand in one turn. He must meld on at least two turns, even if one turn is only laying off a card on an opponent's meld.
b) When the stock is exhausted, play continues while each player is content to draw the top card of the discard pile, and ends when one refuses it.

Players total the cards remaining in their hands at the end, cards having the same value as in the parent game, and the player with the lowest total receives payment from the others.

RUSSIAN BANK

Russian Bank is in the nature of a competitive **patience** or **solitaire**. It is also called Crapette and Stop!

Players

Russian Bank is for two players.

Cards

Two standard packs of 52 are used. Each player has his own pack, which for convenience of sorting after the game, should have different backs. The cards rank from King (high) to Ace (low).

Preliminaries

Players draw from one pack. The lower has choice of packs and plays first. The players sit facing each other. Each player shuffles his opponent's pack.

The play

The first player plays 11 cards face downwards in a pile to his right, covering it with the 12th card face upwards. This is his *depot*.

Then he deals four cards face up in a column towards his opponent. This is his *file*. He places the rest of his pack, face down to his left. This is his *stock*.

The first player now moves any Aces from his file to the space between them. The eight Aces are the *foundations*. A space in a player's file thus created is filled by the top card from his depot, and he turns the next card face up. He can then make further plays as follows.

The foundations are built on in suit-sequences from Ace to King.

The cards in the file are packed on in descending sequences of alternate colour. A player will pack onto his file outwards from the centre, i.e. each card packed on another will overlap it, so that the whole of the pack can be seen. The outwards direction is to avoid the foundation spaces in the centre.

All the cards in the initial file are available for play onto another card, as is the upturned card on top of the depot. Also, when a player has begun a waste heap the top card of that is available for play. A space created in the file is filled from the depot. When a card in the file has been built upon it can still be packed onto another card in the file, provided all the cards packed on it are transferred as well.

When all moves have been made the first player turns over the first card of his *stock* (the remainder of his pack). If he can build it to a foundation or pack onto a file, he does so, and turns over the next card, and so on. Readers familiar with the popular patience or solitaire called Demon or Canfield will realize he is playing a similar game.

When the first player comes to a halt, because the card he turned from stock will not go anywhere, he discards it face up to a waste heap and turns another card from stock onto his waste heap ready for his next turn, and the second player begins.

He deals himself a depot and a file as did the first player. He plays any Aces to foundations and fills the spaces. He then makes all the moves he can in the tableau, but now, and from here onwards each player is allowed to build on his opponent's foundations and pack on his opponent's files. He may also play cards from his own depot and file (but not his own stock and waste heap) to his opponent's waste heap, packing the top card in ascending or descending sequence, irrespective of suit and colour.

When a player's stock is exhausted, he turns over his waste heap, which becomes his new stock. He must not shuffle it. When his depot is exhausted he fills spaces in his file from his stock.

The game is won by the player who first gets rid of all the cards in his stock and waste heap.

The following rules of play must be observed:

1. A player must play a card to a foundation before he plays to a file.
2. A player must play a card to a file before he plays to his waste heap.
3. A player must play from his depot before he plays from his file or waste heap.
4. A space in a file must be filled before any other play is made.
5. When a card is played from the depot the next card must be turned over before the next play is made.

If a player violates any of these rules, or makes any other mistake such as packing on a file or building on a foundation with an ineligible card, or playing from his opponent's file, or ending his turn when a play is available to him, his opponent may cry 'Stop!' if he

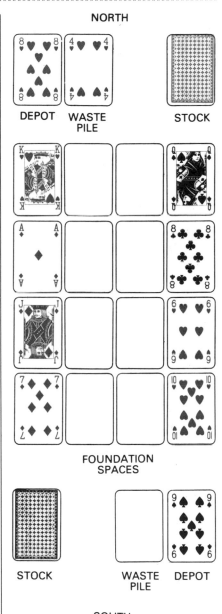

DEPOT   WASTE   STOCK
         PILE

FOUNDATION
SPACES

STOCK   WASTE   DEPOT
         PILE

SOUTH

Soon after the start of the game of Russian Bank. The next moves are described in the text.

wishes, thus bringing his opponent's turn to an end. To be effective, such a cry of 'Stop!' must be made before his opponent makes a further play after the offending one.

A player who cries 'Stop!' points out the offending play, makes the move his opponent failed to, and takes up the turn.

The illustration shows a game which has just started. North played first, and was unable to make any move, since none of his cards could be packed upon. South has just dealt. First he plays his ♦ A to the central foundation, replacing it with the ♦ 9 from the depot. He turns over the next card of the depot. Assuming it cannot be played, he plays his ♦ 7 to his opponent's ♣ 8, fills the space from the depot, turns over the new top card of the depot, and whether or not it is playable still has the ♦ J to pack on his opponent's ♣ Q before he needs to look at the first card of his stock.

ST HELENA

St Helena is a double-pack **patience** or **solitaire** also called Napoleon's Favourite. It is included because it is unusual in that the packs are not shuffled together but used one after another, and becuase it is simple enough to be played by young children, who like the idea of a game using two packs. Another far more difficult game has also been linked with Napoleon and St Helena.

The play

From the first pack the four Kings are arranged in a row with their four Aces below them. Then the first pack is shuffled and 12 cards are dealt clockwise in the order shown in the illustration. The object is to build on the Kings in suit sequence up to the Aces, and on the Aces in suit sequence up to the Kings.

There are restrictions. The cards in spaces 1, 2, 3, 4 can be built only to the Kings, while those in spaces 7, 8, 9, 10 only to the Aces. Those in 5, 6, 11, 12 can be built to either foundation row. When all the moves have been made with the first 12 cards dealt, the spaces around the foundations are filled by dealing from the pack, and the same procedure applies. This continues until all 12 spaces around the foundations are filled with cards which cannot be played

---

The layout for St Helena as described in the text.

legitimately to a foundation. A card once played to a foundation row cannot be moved to another.

Another 12 cards are then dealt, covering the cards in position. Further moves are then made, the top card in a pile always being available to play to a foundation. When all moves are complete, any space created is filled by a further deal from the pack. When no further moves are possible, another 12 cards are dealt all round. And so on, the second pack being taken up when the first is exhausted.

When the second pack is exhausted restrictions are lifted, and the top card of any of the 12 piles may be played to any foundation. Also the top card of each of the 12 piles may be played to another pile in descending or ascending suit-sequence.

When all these moves are completed as far as possible, the 12 packs are picked up as follows: pack 1 is put on pack 2, the two of them on pack 3, and so on round to pack 12, so that when the whole re-united pack is turned over the previous bottom card of pack 12 is now the new top card waiting to be dealt for a second round. Twelve cards are dealt round the now built-upon foundations and the process begins again.

A third deal is allowed, at the end of which one must admit defeat if all foundations are not fully built.

SCORPION

Scorpion is a single-pack **patience** or **solitaire**, with the property that a player can sometimes see fairly quickly from the tableau that it is impossible to get it out. This may make it a pointless game to some players, while others might appreciate knowing that something cannot be done before they 'waste time' attempting to do it. The game is included so that the reader can choose for himself.

The play

Seven cards are laid in a row, the first four face down and the last three face up. Two similar rows are dealt overlapping them, and then four rows of seven with all the cards face up. The tableau is like that illustrated. The remaining three cards, called the *merci*, are set aside face down for use later.

All building takes place in the tableau itself, the object being to build on the Kings descending suit-sequences to the Aces.

Cards available for building on are the seven at the foot of a column. They may be packed with the next lower card in suit sequence, which card may be taken from anywhere within the tableau, but all cards below it must be taken with it.

When the face-up cards in the first four columns have been moved, the face-down card which

---

The layout for the game of Scorpion described in the text.

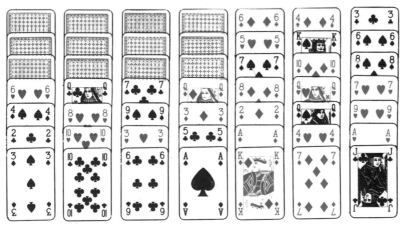

MERCI

is now at the bottom of a column is turned over and becomes available to be built upon. When a whole column is cleared, the space can be filled only by a King, which is moved there together with all the cards below it in the column.

When all moves in the tableau have come to a halt, the three cards forming the merci are dealt one each to the foot of the first three columns, and play resumes.

When a King has been played to a space, and its suit built on it down to the Ace, the whole suit is removed, and the object is to get all four suits removed thus.

In the layout illustrated, for example, the ♣10 can be built on the ♣J, the ♥9 (with the cards below it in the column ♥A ♣J ♣10) can be built on the ♥10. This allows the ♥6 in the first column, with the cards below it, to be built on the ♥7, so that the first face-down card is exposed.

The whole of the fifth column can be built on to the ♦7, thereby clearing a column. The ♦K can now be played to the space, and the ♦Q built upon it, thus freeing another face-down card to be exposed. And so on.

The combinations which can be spotted at the beginning of a game which make it impossible to get out are reverse sequences, such as ♠8, ♠6, ♠7, appearing in one column, with the 8 nearer the top. Clearly, the cards are blocking each other.

Another is the criss-cross. If, for example, the ♦10 appears below the ♣4 in one column, and the ♣3 below the ♦J in another, the ♦10 cannot be played to the ♦J before the ♣3 is played to the ♣4, which makes the arrangement impossible.

Should no such hazards be spotted, attempts should be made to uncover the face-down cards. With no adverse combinations visible, there is a good chance that the game be resolved, but there might be hidden impossibilities in the face-down cards. Care is still needed, as it is easy for a player to block himself.

SKAT

Skat is a German game which has been popular for nearly 200 years. It is complex and skilful.

Players

Skat is for three players.

Cards

The short pack of 32 is used, i.e. the standard pack stripped of 6s, 5s, 4s, 3s and 2s. Skat is a trick-taking game usually with a trump suit.

The four Jacks are part of the trump suit, and are the four strongest trumps.

Suits rank in the order: clubs (high), spades, hearts, diamonds. In each suit the 10 ranks between Ace and King.

In the trump suit, therefore, the cards rank:

♣J ♠J ♥J ♦J A 10 K Q 9 8 7

In the other three suits the rank is:

A 10 K Q 9 8 7

There are therefore 11 cards in the trump suit and seven in the three plain suits.

However there is also a contract in Skat (called *grand*) in which the four Jacks are in effect a trump suit of their own (making, as it were, five suits). In this contract the other four 'plain' suits have seven cards each, ranked as above.

Another contract, called *null* (a contract to make no tricks at all), is played without a trump suit. In this case, the four suits each have eight cards ranked in their usual order:

A K Q J 10 9 8 7

Preliminaries

One player picks up the cards, cuts, and begins to deal them one at a time face up to each player, the first player to be dealt a Jack becoming first dealer. The deal subsequently moves to the left with each hand.

Dealing

The dealer shuffles, and the player on his right cuts. Dealer deals ten cards to each player beginning on his left, in bundles of three, four and three. After the first round, he deals two cards face down to the table. These two cards are called the *skat*.

The next stage is the bidding, but to understand the bidding it is necessary to know how the game is played, the objects and the method of scoring.

The play

Skat is a trick-taking game in which one player (the winner of the auction) plays against the other two. Usually (but not always) he takes the skat into his hand and discards two cards. The winner of the auction (the *declarer*) announces the trumps.

The three players are known as *forehand* (the player to dealer's left), *middlehand* (the next player to his left) and *rearhand* (the dealer).

Forehand leads to the first trick, subsequently the winner of a trick leads to the next. Players must follow suit to the card led, if able, and if not may play any card they please. The four Jacks are regarded as ordinary members of the trump suit: if one is led the other players follow with a card of the trump suit, which of course includes the other Jacks.

Each trick is won by the highest trump it contains, unless the trick does not contain a trump, when it is won by the highest card of the suit led. Each player keeps the tricks won in front of him. The two cards in the skat, or the two discarded in their place, belong to the declarer, who adds them to his tricks. If he had not looked at the skat, and therefore not taken it up and discarded, he is said to play *in hand*.

The object

The object is to win tricks containing scoring cards. The scoring cards and their points values are as follows:

each Ace is worth 11
each 10 is worth 10
each King is worth 4
each Queen is worth 3
each Jack is worth 2

The 9s, 8s and 7s are therefore the only cards in play not worth a point.

The total of points in the pack is 120. The declarer wins when he gets the majority of the points (61). If he fails to get 61 he loses, i.e. he loses on 60 downwards.

The score

Whether the declarer gets 61 points or not determines only if he wins or loses – his actual score is determined by means of the *base value* of his contract and a *multiplier*.

The base value depends upon the trump suit as follows:

Diamonds = 9
Hearts   = 10
Spades   = 11
Clubs   = 12
Grand   = 20

The multiplier depends on the following:

a) If declarer holds the top trump (♣J) the first multiplier is the number of trumps he holds in sequence from the top (e.g. ♣J = 1, ♣J ♠J = 2 and so on).
b) If declarer does not hold the top trump, the first multiplier is the number of trumps missing before his top trump (e.g. if his top trump is ♠J the multiplier is 1, if it is the ♦J the multiplier is 3).
c) Declarer adds 1 to the multiplier for *game*, whether he wins or loses.
d) If declarer played in hand, i.e. without having looked at the skat, he adds another 1 to the multiplier.
e) If declarer takes 90 or more in card points, he is said to make *schneider*, and adds another 1 to the multiplier.
f) If declarer announced that he intended to make schneider at the beginning of the hand, he adds another 1 to the multiplier (in addition to the 1 for making it). However a declarer can only an-

nounce schneider when playing in hand. By announcing schneider the declarer is contracting to make 90 card points, so must make 90 (not 61) in order to win. If he fails the multipliers still apply, but he loses.

g) If declarer takes all the tricks he is said to make *schwartz*, and adds another 1 to the multiplier (in addition to the 1 for schneider).

h) If declarer announced schwartz at the beginning, he adds another 1 to the multiplier, in addition to the 2 for schneider and schwartz. Like schneider, he can only announce schwartz when playing in hand, and if he loses a trick the multipliers still apply, but he loses.

If declarer, having looked at skat, loses, then he loses double what he would have made had he won, so after adding all his multipliers, he must double them.

Here are some examples of scores:

1) A declarer plays in hearts, and his top trumps are ♣J ♠J ♥J ♥A (i.e. he is missing ♦ J). He makes 93 card points. The usual practice is to add the multipliers first, and then multiply by 10 (for hearts), so he would say: 'With 3, game 4, schneider 5, times 10, makes 50.'

2) A declarer plays in clubs, in hand, announces schneider, and he holds the top two trumps only. He makes only 87 card points. He announces: 'With 2, game 3, in hand 4, schneider 5, announced 6, times 12, loses 72.'

3) A declarer plays in diamonds, without the ♣J (i.e. his top trump is ♠J), and makes only 59 card

points. He announces: 'Without 1, game 2, off 4, times 9, loses 36.'

Null The above scoring is for trump contracts and there is a no-trump contract called null, as mentioned earlier. It is a contract to lose all the tricks. Here the cards revert to their normal ranking from A (high) to 7 (low) and there are no card points to consider. Winning or losing depends entirely on whether or not declarer takes a trick – if he does he has lost and the play for that hand ceases.

There are four null contracts. The declarer can play in hand or with the skat, and he can play with his hand concealed as usual, or he can play *null open*, in which he exposes his cards on the table at the beginning of the play.

These contracts score as follows:

Null makes 23
Null in hand makes 35
Null open makes 46
Null in hand open makes 59

As with the trump contracts, an unsuccessful declarer loses double if he has looked at skat.

Bidding
Middlehand bids first, in opposition to forehand only. Only when one of these has dropped out does rearhand (the dealer) enter the bidding. Middlehand begins by announcing the number of his bid, and forehand responds by saying 'Yes' if he is prepared to bid as high, whereupon middlehand increases his bid if he wishes. When one or other drops out by saying 'Pass', rearhand may also pass or enter the bidding by bidding a higher number. The procedure is

as before, with the remaining opponent either responding 'Yes' or 'Pass'. Eventually one bidder remains. An auction might proceed thus:

M: 20   F: Yes
M: 22   F: Yes
M: Pass   R:24
F: Yes   R: 27
F: Yes   R: Pass

Forehand has contracted to make 27 points.

Notice that the bidding relates to the final score a declarer expects to make from the hand, and not to the card points.

Bids can only be in numbers possible to score. Thus the smallest bid is 18 (diamonds, with or without one Jack), the next 20 (hearts, with or without one), then 22, then 23 (null), 24, 27 (diamonds with or without two), 30 (hearts with or without two) and so on.

Overbidding If declarer *overbids* and does not make the value of his bid, he loses, although he might have won the required number of card points in the play. It is possible for a player to overbid by 'accident', e.g. he might bid expecting to play 'without three jacks', and then is unlucky enough to find ♣J in the skat. Instead of being 'without three' he is 'with one'. Suppose his bid was 45, but he made only 'clubs with one', or 24. He loses the next higher multiple of his base value above his bid. With clubs as his trumps his base value is 12, and the next higher multiple of 12 over his bid of 45 is 48, so he loses 48.

Settlement

Skat is a game popular in bars and clubs and settlement is usually made after each hand. Whatever declarer makes he is paid by each player. When he loses he pays each player. Scores can, of course, be kept on paper for settlement later.

Strategy

Skat is a fascinating game because the most powerful cards in the trick-taking, the Jacks, are low in value when it comes to the card-point count. Jacks, the all-powerful, and Aces, the highest-valued of the ranks, are the most important cards, especially when bidding grand, when at least four are required by forehand, who leads first, and five by either of the other hands. With a long suit and three Jacks or Aces, one can usually compete in the bidding.

The decision to play in hand is usually taken with a hand strong in top cards, but the extra multiplier for 'in hand' can often be profitably sacrificed for the skat, which might add a multiplier for schneider while making the hand even stronger.

When taking the skat and discarding, declarer should attempt to make a void or to combine low cards in one suit. If he has to suffer two suits led in the play without being able to win the trick he is likely to lose many card points while his opponents unload high points-value cards, like 10s, on each other's winners.

It is sometimes profitable to discard valuable possible trick-taking cards like Aces and 10s into the skat. This is particularly true if declarer holds a bare 10. This is likely to lose to the Ace, whereas if safely put into the skat the declarer is certain to score 10 points for it.

When considering a bid of null, one needs long suits which include the 7s. A long suit without the 7 is dangerous, as one opponent can easily make himself void of the suit and the lead of the 7 by the other opponent then defeats the contract.

Example hand

The cards are dealt by rearhand as in the illustration. Let us consider each player's prospects: Forehand has a good hand, with two Aces, two Jacks and the lead to the first trick. He can bid up to 35 (spades without two) and need not fear finding a black Jack in the skat since that would make enough for Grand.

Middlehand also has a good hand. He would like to see the skat so as to get rid of either ♠K or ♥Q, but he decides to risk playing Diamonds in hand.

Rearhand's hand is a null or it is nothing. Some players would bid up to 46 on this hand, hoping to find a 7 or an 8 or two clubs in the skat and play null open. Others would consider this reckless.

The bidding goes:

M: 18	F: Yes
M: 20	F: Yes
M: 22	F: Yes
M: 23	F: Yes
M: 24	F: Yes
M: 27	F: Yes
M: 30	F: Yes
M: 33	F: Yes
M: 35	F: Pass
R: Pass	

The deal for the hand of Skat described in the text.

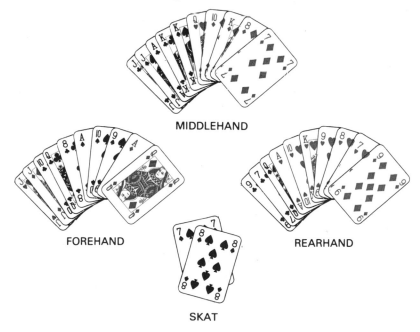

MIDDLEHAND

FOREHAND

REARHAND

SKAT

Actually with both Forehand and Middlehand bidding so vigorously it is likely from Rearhand's point of view that there are no Aces or Jacks in the Skat, so his bid to 46 becomes more reasonable. However, let us suppose he passes.

Middlehand therefore becomes declarer and now draws the skat towards himself and says: 'Diamonds, hand'.

The play proceeds:

Trick 1: Forehand has an obvious lead, the ♠A. Middlehand plays ♠K and Rearhand ♠Q.

score: M O; F and R 18

Trick 2: The purpose of Forehand's previous play was to set up this situation where he is leading into Middlehand and Rearhand's void suits. He plays ♠10. Middlehand trumps with ♦K (♦10 would be too risky, especially as the bidding indicated that Forehand had a lot of spades). Rearhand now undertrumps with ♦9. This is very important as it enables him to put his valuable cards (♥A and 10) on his partner's trump tricks. Rearhand now knows that ♠7 and 8 are in the skat.

score: M 14; F and R 18

Trick 3: Middlehand realizes that he is in trouble and may have to play for a trump or ♣10 to be in the skat. He leads ♦7 to see what happens. Rearhand contributes ♥A and Forehand wins with ♦Q (not the Ace, which is needed as a power card).

score: M 14; F and R 32

Trick 4: Forehand has no really good leads. He plays ♠9 hoping that Middlehand will decide to trump. Middlehand gratefully disposes of ♥Q and Rearhand plays the ♥10.

score: M 14; F and R 45

Trick 5: Now Forehand has no good leads at all. A trump means losing the Ace while a club means losing the 10. He plays ♣8. Middlehand plays ♣K – if this loses to ♣10 (had it been held by Rearhand) the defenders would have 59 and Middlehand would still win by finding a trump in the skat. Rearhand plays ♣7.

score: M 18; F and R 45

Trick 6: Middlehand has two chances left – either to find a trump in the skat (when he can win the remaining tricks) or to find Rearhand with nothing better than a Queen for the trump trick. He plays ♣J (nobody will be fooled by a lead of ♠J, the bidding proves he has both). Rearhand plays ♣9, Forehand ♦J.

score: M 22; F and R 45

Trick 7: More of the same. ♠J is followed by ♥7 and ♥J.

score: M 26; F and R 45

Trick 8: Middlehand plays ♦8 and prays. Rearhand contributes ♥K which looks like the last best chance and Forehand bangs the ♦A onto the trick with a triumphant flourish. (Bridge etiquette is not normal in Skat).

score: M 26; F and R 60

Tricks 9 and 10: Middlehand exposes his cards before Forehand has time to play, remarking ruefully as he does so 'Sixty'. The players recount to confirm that Middlehand loses. Middlehand announces "With two, game three, hand four, times nine, loses thirty-six". Middlehand loses 36 points.

SLIPPERY SAM

Slippery Sam is a simple gambling game also called Shoot. It is a banking game probably unique in that it heavily favours the players rather than the bank.

Players
Any number from three to about ten may play, but the game is best for about six.

Cards
The standard pack of 52 cards is used, cards ranking from Ace (high) to 2 (low).

Preliminaries
Players draw cards to decide on first banker. The highest deals (if there is a tie the tying players re-draw). Because the banker is at a disadvantage, it is necessary to agree beforehand that all players will hold the bank an equal number of times, and also to agree on a standard size of the bank that each player must put up on his turn. It is best also to agree on a minimum bet.

The banker puts the agreed amount to the centre as the bank, has the right to shuffle the cards last, and the player on his right cuts.

The play
The banker deals three cards one at a time to each player, beginning with the player to his left, and ending with the player on his right. He places the remainder of the cards face down before him.

The player on the banker's left examines his cards, and bets any amount between the agreed minimum and the total in the bank that he will beat the top card of the stock. To beat it he must hold a card of the same suit but higher in rank. When he has made his bet the banker exposes the top card of the stock. If the player has a card to beat it he shows it and he takes from the bank the amount of his bet. If he hasn't he adds the amount to the bank, without exposing his cards.

The four cards are collected by the banker and put aside face down, and if any of the bank remains play passes to the next player, who has the same options. To bet the whole amount of the bank is called *shooting*. No player may look at his cards until it is his turn to bet.

If the whole bank is taken, the bank passes to the next player to the left, who puts the same amount in the bank and begins again.

A banker holds the bank for three rounds. The cards are shuffled and cut between each round. Should there then be anything remaining in the bank after three rounds, the banker may, if he wishes, hold the bank for one more round (but one more only). Otherwise he takes the bank and passes the cards to the next player.

Strategy
As with Red Dog (q.v.) it is easy to calculate a hand's chances of beating the bank. The top card held in each suit held (counting

A good hand at Slippery Sam. The odds are exactly 4 to 3 on that it will win.

Aces as 14, Kings 13, Queens 12 and Jacks 11) is deducted from 14, and the numbers totalled. Thirteen is added for each void suit. The final number represents the number of cards in the stock and in other players' hands that will beat the hand. As there are 49 such cards, that number deducted from 49 gives the number of cards that will not beat it. The optimum play is to shoot whenever the odds are in favour and bet the minimum when they are not.

The odds will fluctuate, of course, as cards in earlier player's hands and those turned over by the banker become known.

Slippery Sam is a better game than Red Dog because each player has only three chances against each bank, and if the banker survives his three rounds he should make a good profit.

SOLITAIRE

For games of Solitaire, or competitive Solitaire, see the following:

Solo Whist

Solo Whist is a version of Whist which introduces a bidding principle and allows players to play for themselves. It is essentially a game played for stakes. It is usually just called Solo.

Players

Solo Whist is for four players.

Cards

The standard 52-card pack is used, the cards ranking from Ace (high) to 2 (low).

Preliminaries

Players draw cards for first dealer, the lowest being dealer (Ace is low for this purpose). Dealer shuffles and the player to his right cuts. Thereafter the deal passes in rotation to the left.

Dealing

The cards are dealt equally to all players in four bundles of three cards each, the last four cards being dealt singly. Dealer's last card is dealt face up to determine trumps. He announces the trump suit and takes the card into his hand. (The trump suit may later be changed).

Bidding

Beginning with the eldest (to dealer's left) each player must make a bid or pass. Each bid must be higher than the previous bids as the bidding progresses, but a player cannot bid again after he has passed (with one exception: eldest may accept a proposal after passing). Once three players have passed, the bidding ends, and the highest bidder (declarer) attempts to make his contract.

The bids are as follows, lowest first:

a) *Proposal* A player who proposes is asking for a partner to make eight tricks in partnership with him against the other two players, with the turn-up as trump. He states: 'I propose', and unless a higher bid intervenes any other player may accept by saying: 'I accept'. Or the two players might say 'Prop' and 'Cop', which is how the bid is sometimes known for short. If this is the highest bid the two players remain in their original seats, and do not move opposite each other.

b) *Solo* The bidder undertakes to win five tricks, playing alone, with the turn-up as trumps.

c) *Misère* The bidder undertakes not to win a trick. In this contract there are no trumps.

d) *Abondance* (or *abundance*) The bidder undertakes nine tricks naming his own trump suit.

e) *Royal abondance* This bid is used only over a call of abondance. It is an undertaking to win nine tricks with the turn-up card as trumps. It has no more value than abondance, but takes precedence in the bidding.

f) *Misère ouverte*, or open misère. The bidder undertakes not to win a trick, and after the first trick he exposes his hand on the table for the opponents to see. They must not discuss the hand, however. There are no trumps.

g) *Abondance déclarée* (or *abundance declared*) This is an undertaking to win all the tricks, the declarer naming the trump suit.

The play

If the contract is abondance or abondance déclarée, the declarer names trumps. Eldest hand leads to the first trick, except when the contract is abondance déclarée, when the declarer leads himself.

On all tricks a player must follow suit to the card led. If unable to, he may trump or discard. A trick is won by the highest trump it contains, and if it contains no trumps by the highest card in the

---

The hand of Solo discussed in the text.

suit led. The object of the declarer is to make his contract, of the others to defeat it.

Settlement

Settlement is usually made after each deal and the declarer pays each of his opponents or is paid by each of them according to the following scale of units;

a) proposal and acceptance: 2
b) solo: 2
c) misère: 3
d) abondance: 4
e) misère ouverte: 6
f) abondance déclarée: 8

Notice that in proposal and acceptance each of two players pays or receives 2 units from one of the other two, so the bid is not as high as solo, where three players pay or receive from one.

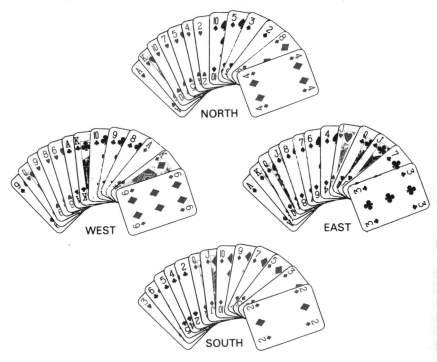

Example hand

Hands are dealt by South as in the illustration. Clubs are trumps. The bidding proceeds:

West	North	East	South
solo	misère	abondance	misère ouverte

West's bid of solo was safe. By leading trumps he was sure to make three, and, having cleared them would make his ♦A K. North's misère would have been interesting. West would probably lead ♣9, which East would make while South threw the ♦Q. If East had led three more spades, West could throw away his diamonds. South could now beat the contract by leading a low diamond, but he cannot be given the lead. The contract can be defeated by the very best play, but it would be almost impossible to find.

East's abondance would be made if he could make a club, which he would if West led a club at the first trick. If West led any other card, he would probably fail.

South is in the happy position of playing last to his contract, and he is safe. It is possible to work out a way in which he could lose, but it involves him foolishly keeping his ♥3 while East leads four rounds of spades. East then gives the lead to West with a club, who leads ♦6, taken by North's ♦8 while East discards ♥J, for North to lead ♥2. But South would have to be a very bad player to fall for that.

Strategy

There is little skill to be employed except in the misère contracts as the above example hand suggests. With solo and abondance contracts normally the tricks are safe before the lead, and rarely can an extra trick and thus a contract be won by skill rather than force. A principle which new players frequently fail to appreciate is that it is dangerous to bid misère with a long suit which does not contain the 2. Clever opponents will discard in that suit until between them they hold the 2 only, which when led will defeat the contract.

Variants

The main variations are as follows:

a) Most schools do not allow the 'prop and cop' bid, which contract is nearly always made.

b) Instead of using a turn-up to indicate trumps, some schools prefer a rota of hearts, clubs, diamonds, spades.

c) On an abondance contract, the declarer does not announce his trumps until the second round, the first round being with the up-turn as trumps. This gives eldest the chance of guessing declarer's trump suit and leading it. Frequently one of the other defenders is void and can trump with the original suit, thus depriving declarer of a trick.

d) After a deal has been passed, many schools have a *goulash* deal in which the hands, sorted into suits by the players, are collected into a pile which is cut but not shuffled before the next deal. This provides more hands of the misère and abondance type, which otherwise are rare, and although purists dislike the practice, it does lead to more interesting hands. Some schools do not shuffle after any hand.

Auction Solo

Auction is played in exactly the same manner as Solo Whist, but permits many more bids, and is a more interesting game in that more of the contracts are competitive. In Solo a player frequently cannot be beaten in a contract of solo, but cannot bid abondance, so the actual play is either a lay-down or is no more than going through the motions. The bids in ascending order are:

1. proposal and acceptance
2. solo of five in own suit
3. solo of five in trump suit
4. solo of six in own suit
5. solo of six in trump suit
6. solo of seven in own suit
7. solo of seven in trump suit
8. solo of eight in own suit
9. solo of eight in trump suit
10. misère
11. abondance of nine in own suit
12. abondance of nine in trump suit
13. abondance of ten in own suit
14. abondance of ten in trump suit
15. abondance of 11 in own suit
16. abondance of 11 in trump suit
17. abondance of 12 in own suit
18. abondance of 12 in trump suit
19. misère ouverte
20. abondance déclarée in own suit
21. abondance déclarée in trump suit

Only in abondance déclarée in his own suit does declarer, and not eldest, have the opening lead.

Settlement is made as follows:

a) For proposal and acceptance, 6 units per player, plus 1 for each overtrick (if made) or 1 for each undertrick (if not made). Each partner pays or receives from one opponent only.

b) For solo, 6 units per player plus 3 for each overtrick (if made) or 3 for each undertrick (if not made).

c) For misère, 12 units per player.

d) For abondance, 18 units per player plus 3 for each overtrick (if made) or 3 for each undertrick (if not made).

e) For misère ouverte, 24 units per player

f) For abondance déclarée, 36 units per player.

The stake values for solo and abondance do not change with the number of tricks contracted. Overtricks and undertricks count from the number of tricks contracted.

It would follow that there would be sense in underbidding, making the contract easier, and the bonus for overtricks greater, but there is always the danger that a subsequent player will bid one more, so to get the contract a bidder must advance his previous bid by two, when perhaps a higher bid in the first place would have sealed the contract at a lower level.

Variant Most schools will not bother with the first two bids and the last one in the list above.

SPINADO

The names of card games are never precise. Spinado or Spin is a name often applied to any game of the Newmarket, Michigan or Boodle variety, but the game that goes under the name here is a simplified version of Pope Joan (q.v.). Three saucers, trays or cards are required marked *Matrimony*, *Intrigue* and *Game*.

Players

Any number from two to seven may play. The game is best for four or five.

Cards

The standard pack is used from which are stripped the four 2s and the ♦8. Cards rank from King (high) to Ace (low).

Preliminaries

Any player may deal the cards round face up to each player, the first Jack denoting the first dealer. Thereafter the deal passes clockwise. It is best to agree that the game will not end before all players have dealt an equal number of times. The dealer contributes 12 units of stake to the matrimony pool, and 6 each to the intrigue and game pools. The other players each contribute 3 units to the game pool. The dealer shuffles last, and the player to his right cuts.

Dealing

The dealer deals the cards one at a time face down to each player, including himself, and to a *widow*, which is the first hand to his left. Players must have an equal number of cards, any overs going to the widow. Therefore players receive cards as follows:

Number of players	Cards received	Widow
2	15	17
3	11	14
4	9	11
5	7	12
6	6	11
7	5	12

The play

The player to the left of dealer starts the game by playing any card he chooses, announcing its rank and suit, and the player with the next higher card in the suit follows, needing to announce only the rank while that suit continues. Players holding a sequence play them all. Eventually the run will come to a stop, either because a King is reached, or the ♦7 (the ♦8 is withdrawn) or because the next card needed is in the widow. All Aces are stops, because there are no 2s.

The player who plays the last card before a stop continues the game by playing any card from his hand and beginning a new run.

The player who gets rid of all his cards first wins the stakes in the game pool, and is exempt from the requirement to contribute to the pool on the next round, unless on the next round he is dealer. He also receives 1 unit from each of the other players for every card each player still holds in his hand.

During the game, stakes are won from other players for playing certain cards. The ◆A, known as Spinado or spin, is one of them. A player who plays it collects 3 units from each of the other players.

Spinado also has other properties. It can be played any time its holder likes, provided he is also playing a card which he is entitled to play because of the run, e.g. if the run reaches ♥10, a player can play ♥J *and* spinado. Spinado also constitutes a stop, so the player who plays it then begins another run.

During the game the player who plays the ◆K receives 2 units from each of the other players. If he plays the ◆Q as well, he receives the stakes in the matrimony pool. A player who plays both the ◆Q as well as the ◆J wins the intrigue pool. Players who play the other three Kings receive 1 unit from each other player.

If a player with spinado is caught with it in his hand at the end of the game he pays the winner 2 units for each card he holds in his hand instead of the usual 1 unit.

Any cards remaining in the matrimony or intrigue pool after a deal remain for the next, and are added to by the next dealer.

Strategy
Players should be aware of the stop

SPINADO

MARRIAGE

INTRIGUE

The special cards or combinations in Spinado.

cards. When a run is begun, the card below it becomes a stop card in a future run. It pays to begin a run with a suit in which one holds alternate cards – one must either be able to play them or one achieves a stop.

In this respect it is wise not to be in too much of a hurry to play spinado. If, for instance, one has a run of alternate cards to a King, such as ♠9 J K, it is pointless to play spinado on any of them, since if the 9 and Jack aren't stops, the King will be. Better to play spinado on a card of which one is otherwise void in a suit, in order to stop that suit and start another.

SPOIL FIVE

Spoil Five is a game of the Euchre family, and sometimes thought of as the national card game of Ireland. It is certainly played there more than anywhere else, perhaps because of the eccentric ranking of the cards!

Players

Any number of players up to ten can play, but the game is best for five or six.

Cards

The standard pack of 52 cards is used. The cards within a suit rank in a different order if the suit is trumps. The 5 of the trump suit is always the highest trump, the Jack the next. The third trump is always the ♥A, whatever suit is trumped. The rank of the cards in a *trump* suit is as follows:

hearts:
  5 (high) J A K Q 10 9 8 7 6 4 3 2

diamonds:
  5 (high) J ♥ A A K Q 10 9 8 7 6 4 3 2

clubs and spades:
  5 (high) J ♥ A A K Q 2 3 4 6 7 8 9 10

The rank of the cards in a *plain* suit is as follows:

hearts and diamonds:
  K (high) Q J 10 9 8 7 6 5 4 3 2 A (♦)

clubs and spades:
  K (high) Q J A 2 3 4 5 6 7 8 9 10

The rank of the cards below the court cards (K Q J) in the suits is expressed by 'highest in red, lowest in black'.

Preliminaries

Any player may deal cards round the table face up to each player, the first to receive a Jack being first dealer. The dealer may shuffle last, and the player to his right cuts. Before the deal, each player puts 1 unit of stake into a pool. If the pool is not won, the new dealer adds another unit to it before he deals, but if the pool is won, all players contribute 1 unit to a fresh pool. The deal passes clockwise.

Dealing

The dealer deals each player five cards begining with the player to his left, in bundles of three and two or two and three. The dealer turns up the next card to indicate trumps.

Robbing

If the turn-up is an Ace, the dealer may, before the opening lead, take it into his hand and discard. In practice it is customary to leave the Ace where it is until he plays it.

If any other player holds the Ace of trumps he may take the turn-up and discard. He does so on his turn, by passing his discard face down to dealer, who exchanges the turn-up for it. The turn-up need not be played at once, and is taken into hand. If the Ace is held by dealer he puts his discard under the stock on his turn and takes the upcard into his hand.

The play

The primary object of each player

is to win three tricks. A secondary object is to win all five. If neither can be achieved, his object is to prevent another player doing so.

Eldest hand (on dealer's left) makes the opening lead. Subsequent players, if able to follow suit, must follow suit or trump. If unable to follow suit a player may play any card.

An exception to the above rules concerns the three highest trumps: the 5 J ♥ A. The holders of these cards need not play them to a trump lead; if they hold no other trump they may discard. It is called *reneging*. However, a player cannot renege if a superior trump is led, i.e. if the 5 is led a player must follow with J or ♥ A if he has no other trump, and if J is led he must follow with ♥ A if he has no other.

If no player wins three tricks the game is *spoiled*, and the deal passes to the next player who, as stated, adds 1 unit to the pool.

If a player wins three tricks, he takes the pool. If he wins five tricks he wins an additional unit from each other player. Play ends as soon as one player wins three tricks, unless they are the first three tricks. In this case the player either throws in his cards or announces that he will *jink it*. This is an undertaking to win the remaining two tricks. If he does not do so, the game is spoiled and he loses his entitlement to the pool.

The deal for the hand of Spoil Five described in the text.

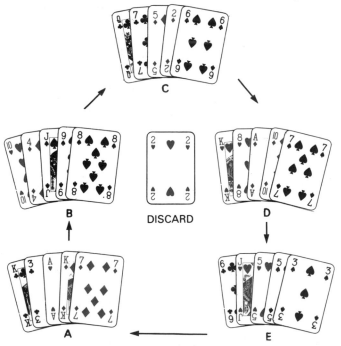

Example deal

Five hands are dealt as in the illustration. It is A's lead. Diamonds are trumps, and D on his turn, exchanges the ♥2 for the ♦10, the turn-up. A sees a chance to take three tricks. By leading his two highest trumps he hopes to make at least one, to regain the lead with his third trump (other players being void by then) and to make the ♣K. He leads ♥A, which is allowed to make by C, who is hoping to make the third trick with ♦5 and perhaps ♣Q 7 to follow. A then leads his ♦K. The first two tricks are as follows:

	A	B	C	D	E
1.	♥A	♦4	♦2	♦10	♣6
2.	♦K	♣8	♣6	♦A	♠5

C, following his plan, reneges. He knows D has ♦A and that A will lose the trick. He is hoping now that trumps are cleared, and that he will make the last three tricks. D sees the possibility for three tricks himself if all trumps are gone and no player holds two hearts. He leads his King, but, putting their plans into operation, A trumps, and C overtrumps. Play proceeds:

	A	B	C	D	E
3.	♦7	♥10	♦5	♥K	♥5
4.	♣K	♣9	♣Q	♥8	♠3

C has presented A with his three tricks, because his ♣3 now wins the last trick.

	A	B	C	D	E
5.	♣3	♠J	♣7	♠7	♥J

A could have been more sure of his contract by discarding ♣3 at trick 3, which would have left him with the last trump and the master

club. As it was, he could not have won had C not led back a club. However, this play would have failed if C had not used his trump on that trick.

Strategy

Many Spoil Five hands are won by a player dealt such strong trumps that he can lead them and clear his opponents of them, himself making an extra or side suit winner later, the plan adopted by A in the example hand.

However, sometimes stealth might pay – the policy of C, who attempted to win the last three tricks having lulled A into a false sense of security.

Players more often are intent on spoiling, as their own hands offer little chance of success. It is then a good plan to renege if possible to use the high trump against the player going for the pool. A might have thought this was C's policy in the example hand. If it had been C's policy it would have worked had he held his ♦5 for one more round, allowing A to win with his ♦7 and trumping A's ♣K. C's ♣Q would then have won the last trick. There was no possibility in the example hand of a player jinking it, but it is often good policy to renege against a strong hand, which is leading trumps, hoping that the player might jink it, and be thwarted. But, of course, if he doesn't jink it he might have been presented with his third trick.

Forty-five

Forty-five is a way of playing Spoil Five in teams, without hands being spoiled. It is played by two teams, so is suitable for two, four or six players. The teams sit alternately. A side that wins three tricks scores 5 points, that wins all five tricks scores 10 points. The game gets its name because 45 points is the winning score.

TABLANETTE

This simple game provides scope for skill and is enjoyable to play.

Players
Tablanette is for two players.

Cards
The standard pack of 52 cards is used.

Preliminaries
Players draw cards and higher deals first (for this purpose Ace is high, 2 low). It is convenient if players can sit opposite each other.

Dealing
The dealer deals six cards face downwards to each player, and the next four cards face up in a row to the centre of the table. If any Jacks are dealt to the table they are removed and placed on the bottom of the pack, their places being filled from the top of the pack, which is then set aside temporarily.

The play
Non-dealer plays first. If he plays a card of the same rank as one or more cards on the table, he claims the card or cards on the table. If he plays a card whose rank is the sum of two or more of the cards on the table, he claims both or all. In other words, he can claim all cards or combinations of cards of equal value to the card he plays. For this purpose a King counts 14, a Queen 13 and an Ace either 11 or 1. Non-court cards have their pip values.

Jacks have a special function, as will be seen.

The card played by the player and those taken by him he keeps together in a pile face downwards, and they will later contribute to his score.

If, however, he cannot play a card that will claim any from the table, the card he plays is added to the row on the table, and the dealer has his turn.

If at any time a player clears the table by taking all the remaining cards (there might, in fact, be only one) he announces 'Tablanette', and scores a bonus of the total value of the cards he takes plus the card he played.

Playing a Jack allows a player to claim all the cards from the table, but does not allow him the bonus score for tablanette.

When the table is cleared the next player is forced to play his next card to the table, beginning a new row, since there aren't any cards he can claim.

Players play in turn until all six cards in their hands have been played, whereupon dealer deals each six more cards (but none to the table) and play continues thus until the pack is exhausted. A dealer, therefore, will deal four times during a hand. When the last six cards have been played by both players the cards remaining on the table belong to the player who last took a card from the table.

Players then add to their scores for tablenettes according to the cards they have collected as

The deal for the hand of Tablanette described in the text.

NORTH

SOUTH

follows: for the ◆10 two points, for the ♣2 one point, for every Ace, King, Queen, Jack and 10 (except ◆10), one point. The player who takes the majority of the cards (i.e. 27 or more) scores three points.

The deal passes in rotation, and the game is won by the first player to reach 251 points.

Example hand

Cards are dealt as in the illustration.

North dealt, so South immediately plays ♠Q taking the ♣2, ◆5, ♥6, thus ensuring himself a point for ♣2 and another for ♠Q. (He could have played ♥8 and claimed ♣8 plus ♣2 and ♥6). North plays ♥4, as South cannot then make tablanette, as no card has a value of 12. South now claims ♣8 with ♥8. North plays ◆7, intending to take the two cards now on the table, ◆7 ♥4, with his ♣A. South plays ◆9. North claims ◆7 ♥4 with ♣A. South plays ♥9, claiming ◆9 and scoring 18 points for tablanette. North now plays ◆6 to the empty table, South ♥2 and North ♣5. South now plays his ♣J and clears the table. North is forced to play his last card ♠10 to the bare table.

North now deals six more cards each, and if South is dealt a 10, he can clear the table, claiming 20 points for tablanette and adding two 10s to his scoring cards. He is already well on his way to the majority of cards.

TOWIE

Towie is a game for Bridge-lovers who cannot raise a fourth. It is an excellent game, and is sometimes preferred to Bridge by four or five players, who take turns in sitting out, taking part in the settling of each hand as if they were the defenders. Waiting players replace the declarer of the previous deal in rotation, except that a non-vulnerable waiting player takes precedence over a vulnerable player (see Scoring).

Players
Towie is for three players (but see above).

Cards
The standard pack of 52 cards is used, the cards ranking from Ace (high) to 2 (low).

Preliminaries
The players draw to determine the first dealer, the player drawing the highest card being dealer.

Dealing
The dealer deals 13 cards, one at a time, to each player beginning with the player to his left, and including 13 cards (face down) to a dummy hand in the position opposite himself, i.e. between his two opponents. He then chooses six of dummy's cards at random and faces them.

The play
Beginning with dealer, the players bid, as in Bridge, for the contract (readers not familiar with Bridge will find the principles of the bidding in that section). Part scores are not considered in Towie, so there is little point in making a bid below a game score (i.e. a bid worth 100 points or more). If no player makes a bid of the level of game, there is a goulash deal.

In a goulash deal the players sort their cards into suits (dealer sorting the dummy hand) and the hands are collected and piled, the pile being cut but not shuffled. The same dealer then deals the cards in bundles of five, five and three instead of one at a time. This, of course, ensures that the hands are not random but will tend to be strong in certain suits.

The same dealer continues to deal, with further goulashes if necessary, until finally one of the players bids a game.

The highest bidder becomes declarer, and the dummy belongs to him. The dummy hand might need to be moved now, since it must be opposite declarer, of course. If it is convenient for the players to move seats, they must take care that the order in which they sit does not change (i.e. ignoring dummy, the players to their right and left remain the same).

The player to the left of the declarer makes the opening lead. Now the declarer exposes the remaining seven cards in the dummy and arranges them as the dummy is usually arranged in Bridge. The game is now identical with Bridge so far as the play of the cards is concerned, with the

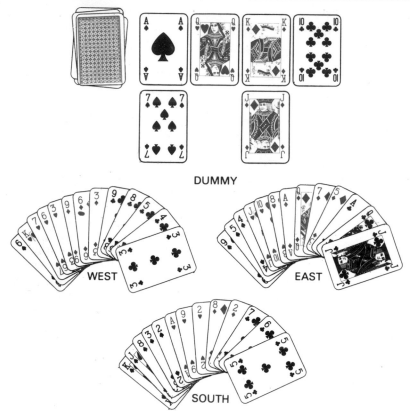

DUMMY

WEST

EAST

SOUTH

The deal for the hand of Towie described in the text.

declarer attempting to make his contract and the defenders attempting to prevent him.

The scoring is the same as in Bridge, with the following alterations:

1. In no-trump contracts each trick is worth 35 points.
2. For winning a first game a declarer scores a bonus of 500 points and becomes vulnerable. For winning a second game, and the rubber, a player scores 1,000 points.

3. A declarer who makes a doubled or redoubled contract scores a bonus of 50 points if not vulnerable, and 100 points if vulnerable.
4. For undoubled overtricks the declarer scores 50 points each. If doubled or redoubled he scores them as in Bridge.
5. Penalties for undertricks are:

Not vulnerable
undoubled: 50 points per trick
doubled: 100 points for the first and second tricks, 200 points for the third and fourth tricks, 400 points for the fifth and subsequent tricks

Vulnerable
undoubled: 100 points for the first trick, 200 points for the second and subsequent tricks
doubled: 200 points for the first trick, 400 points for the second and subsequent tricks.

If the contract is redoubled, the penalties are twice those of doubled contracts.

The game is played in rubbers, and when a declarer wins two games a fresh rubber starts.

Strategy
The bidding is, of course, largely a matter of guesswork, since there is no partner to help reach a contract, and seven of a potential declarer's 26 cards are unknown (some might think this six fewer than in Bridge itself). The game cannot be won, however, by defending alone, and bidders must take a few chances.

In the play the game is similiar to Bridge, but less information has been passed in the bidding. However, there is plenty of scope for the same sorts of skills as Bridge requires.

In the illustration, South, dealer, might well bid four spades, West will pass, and East will probably rightly decide he is not brave enough for five diamonds. As the cards lie, South will fail, whereas East might just make five diamonds.

VINGT-ET-UN

Vingt-et-un is the old French game from which sprang Blackjack (q.v.), the most popular card game played in gambling casinos. In the United States the casino rules governing Blackjack have caused the private game played in houses to follow them, so the game there is more restricted than it is in Great Britain. In Britain the name of the game became corrupted from the French to Van John, but for many years it has been known throughout the country as Pontoon. There is doubt as to whether Pontoon is a further corruption of Van John, or merely a corruption of the word 'punting'. In any case, for social play it is a much better game than Blackjack, with more options for the player. The most popular British version is described first.

Players
Any reasonable number may play, but if there are more than ten, two packs must be used. About five to eight is best.

Cards
The standard pack of 52 cards is used.

Preliminaries
One player shuffles the pack and deals face-up cards one at a time to each player until a Jack turns up to denote first dealer.

The play
The dealer, who is in effect a banker, deals one card face downwards to each player including himself. The players, but not the dealer, look at their cards and stake any amount they wish between an agreed minimum and an agreed maximum.

The object of the game is to build a hand with a pip total of 21, or as near to it as possible without exceeding it. An Ace counts 11 or one at the holder's discretion, a court card (K Q J) ten, and other cards at their pip value.

When the players have stated their stakes and placed them before them, the banker deals another card face down to all players. If a player holds a *pontoon*, or *natural* (an Ace and a ten-count card), he exposes it. This is the highest hand and can be beaten only by the dealer also holding one.

The dealer then deals with each of the players in turn, beginning with the player on his left. A player who has been dealt a pair of Aces may *split* them. He separates the cards and puts the same stake as his original stake on the second. Each card is now regarded as the first card of a separate hand, and the dealer deals a second card to each, and deals with each hand separately.

Each player has three choices when the dealer comes to deal with his hand. He may:

a) *Stand* or *Stick*, i.e. he takes no more cards, being happy with his total. He may not stand if his count is 15 or less (except for a five-card hand, as will be explained).

b) *Buy*, i.e. he may buy a further card, face down, for a stake not exceeding his original stake. He can then buy further cards, if he wishes, but not for a stake exceeding his previous one, until he has five cards, which is the maximum hand. He cannot buy a fifth card if his total count with four is 11 or lower but may *twist* one (see below).

c) *Twist*, i.e. he asks the dealer to twist him a card face up for which he does not pay with an extra stake. A player may twist at any time, whether or not he had previously bought cards.

As previously stated, a pontoon (Ace and ten-count) is the highest hand. A second special hand, which can be beaten only by a pontoon, is a five-card hand (the pip count, of course, not exceeding 21).

If during the play a player's count, either on buying a card or twisting, exceeds 21, he *busts* and throws in his hand (the dealer puts it on the bottom of the pack) and the dealer collects the stake.

When all players have been dealt with, the banker exposes his two cards. If they represent a pontoon, he takes all the players' stakes, including those of any player with a pontoon. Otherwise he may stand, or deal himself extra cards, standing when he wishes. Should his count exceed 21, however, be pays all the players still in the game.

When the dealer stands, he pays all players whose totals are nearer 21, and collects from all players whose totals are equal to or lower than his. Unless he himself has a pontoon or five-card hand he pays any player with a five-card hand. If both dealer and player hold five-card hands, dealer wins, irrespective of the count.

A player who holds pontoon is paid double by the dealer, except when the pontoon was one of a split hand. The dealer who holds pontoon is not paid double. A dealer is not permitted to split a pair of Aces.

Cards are shuffled between each deal.

The dealer holds the bank until a player holds a pontoon, when that player takes it for the next deal. However, should the dealer also hold a pontoon, or the player's pontoon was from a pair of split Aces, the dealer keeps the bank. Should two or more players hold pontoons on the same deal, the one nearest to dealer's left takes the bank.

Although players have the advantage of determining their stakes, the bank is usually very profitable, because the dealer wins on tied hands, and because he wins from all players who bust.

The illustration shows a game in progress.

Variants
The main variants to the game as played in Britain are:

a) There is a third special category of hand, which beats all: 7 7 7. When held by a player, dealer pays triple, but not vice versa.

b) The dealer looks at his first card after the first round of the deal, and if he wishes can double, which means all players must double their stakes. This is not recommended as it serves to increase

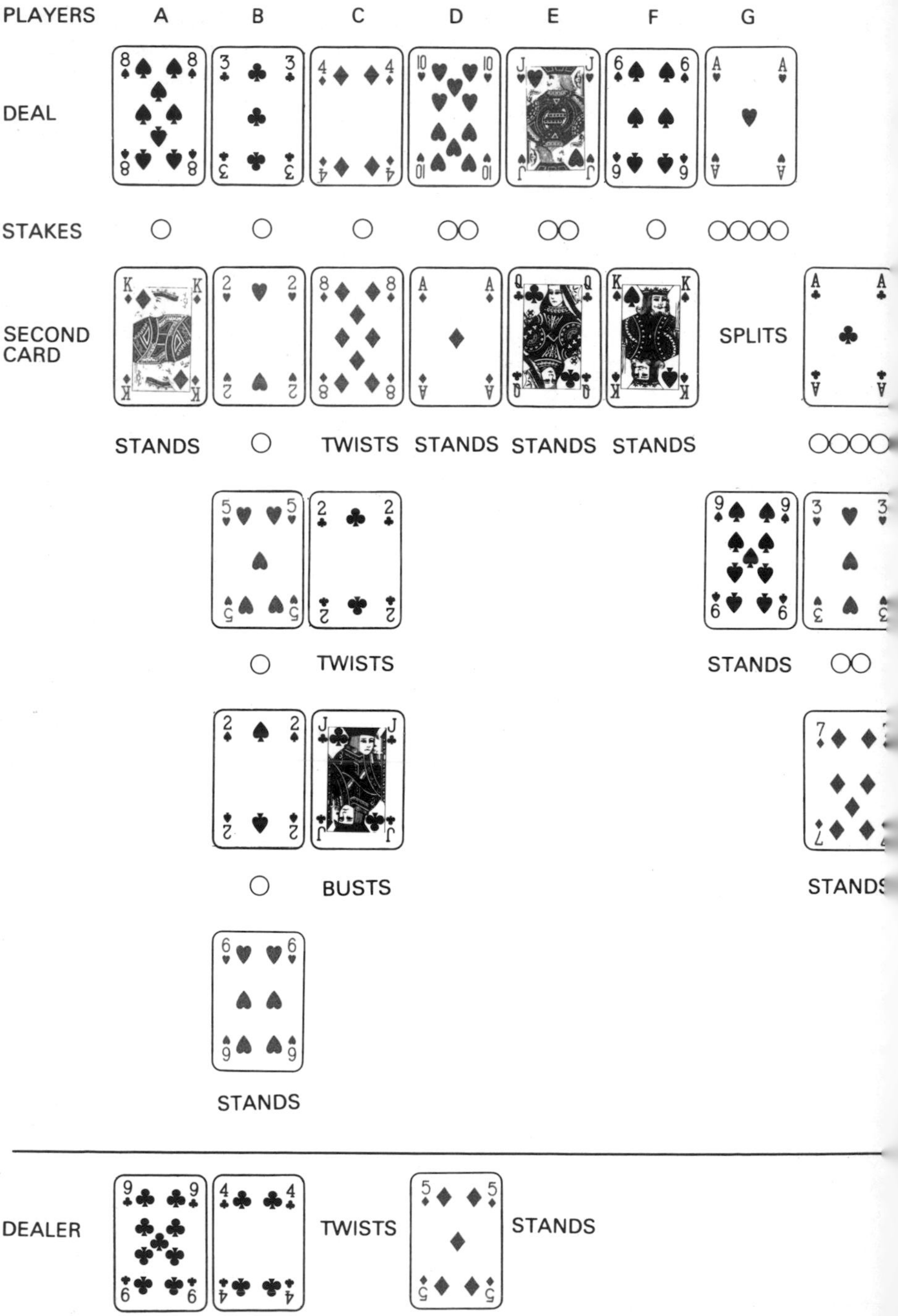

PLAYERS	A	B	C	D	E	F	G

DEAL

| 8♠ | 3♣ | 4♦ | 10♥ | J♣ | 6♠ | A♥ |

STAKES ○   ○   ○   ○○   ○○   ○   ○○○○

SECOND CARD

| K♦ | 2♥ | 8♦ | A♦ | Q♣ | K♠ | SPLITS A♣ |

STANDS ○   TWISTS   STANDS   STANDS   STANDS

| | | | | | | | OOOO |

| 5♥ | 2♣ |

○   TWISTS

| 9♠ | 3♥ |

STANDS   ○○

| 2♠ | J♣ |

○   BUSTS

| 7♦ |

STANDS

| 6♥ |

STANDS

DEALER

| 9♣ | 4♣ | TWISTS | 5♦ | STANDS

further the dealer's already substantial advantage.

c) If the dealer holds a pontoon,
he is paid double by all players
except a player who also holds a
pontoon, who loses only his original stake. This is not recommended for the same reasons as
above.

d) The dealer looks at his hand
immediately the second card is
dealt, and if he holds a pontoon he
exposes it and collects all stakes
immediately. This is to the
player's advantage, since it prevents them buying in a hopeless
cause.

e) Any pair may be split, not only
Aces. A pair must be of equal rank,
i.e. two differing ten-count cards,
like a Queen and a Jack, do not
constitute a pair. When it is
allowed, it is not a good play to
split any pair other than Aces, so
not allowing it does not hinder the
game. (For the same reason about
the advisability of splitting pairs,
in some United States' schools the
reverse will be true – any pair may
be split except Aces. (Never give a
sucker an even break).

Blackjack in the United States
In the United States the game will
be called Blackjack or Black Jack.

---

*A hand of Vingt-et-Un, or Pontoon.
Player C has bust and lost his stake.
All others are in contention when
dealer exposes his cards. He twists
and stands on 18, paying 19 or better.
A loses 1 unit; B, with a five-card
hand, wins 4; C loses 1; D, with a pontoon, wins 4 and takes the bank; E wins
2; F loses 1; and G, who split his Aces,
wins 10. A bad hand for dealer, who
lost 17 units and his bank.*

If there is a fixed dealer/banker
the game will resemble that
played in a casino and described
under Blackjack (q.v.). If it is
played socially, with a changing
dealer, the main differences to the
game described above are as
follows:

1) the dealer may look at his first
card and double all bets. If he
does any player may redouble.

2) the dealer's second card is
dealt face up.

3) if the dealer's face-up card is
an Ace or ten-count card, he must
look at his face down card and
settle immediately if he has a
natural (also called a *blackjack*).

4) the dealer is paid double for a
natural.

5) players say 'Hit me' rather
than 'Twist'.

6) players may split any pair.

7) if a player's first two cards
total 11, he may face them, double
his bet, and take one more card,
face down. That ends his turn – he
may not have another card.

8) players do not buy extra
cards. A player wishing another
card or cards may have them by
saying 'Hit me' but he may not increase his stake.

9) a player who completes a
five-card hand may then double
his stake.

10) a six-card hand is recognized.
A player who completes a six-
card hand may quadruple his
stake. Five-card hands and six-
card hands beat hands with fewer
cards (except naturals), whatever
the count.

11) a player who completes a
hand of 7 7 7 may triple his stake,
and a player with 8 7 6 may

double it. These are not widely played and may be regarded as variants.

12) should the dealer have a hand described in (9) (10) and (11) above, it does not affect the stakes of the player, i.e. the dealer does not win double or triple etc.

WHIST

Whist arose from an English game called Triumph, played nearly 500 years ago and commemorated in the word 'trump'. Triumph was played in the same way as Whist is today, but until 1718 it was largely a game for 'below stairs'. In that year it became popular at the Crown Coffee House in London and was taken up by society. It was by then called Whisk, probably because the tricks as won were 'whisked' up. This became Whist, presumably because the players liked to play in silence, and 'Whist!' was a plea for such. In 1743 Edmond Hoyle, one of the players, wrote his famous book *A Short Treatise on Whist*, thereby making the game universally popular and his own name a byword both as an authority on card games and as the symbol of 'playing by the rules'.

The game became the most popular in the world for about 200 years, when it was supplanted by a game which grew from it, Bridge (q.v.). Strangely, while still very popular it slipped down the social scale again; and while the upper classes would have their Bridge parties in their country houses, the middle classes in Britain, until soon after the Second World War, enjoyed their Whist 'drives' – social evenings held in such as village halls, where each partnership would play each other and there were prizes and booby prizes.

Whist has given its name to the family of games which employ the same trick-taking principle.

Players
Whist is for four players, playing as two partnerships.

Cards
The standard pack of 52 cards is used, the cards ranking from Ace (high) to 2 (low).

Preliminaries
Unless otherwise agreed, the players draw for partners, the two lowest (Ace for this purpose counting low) playing together, and the lowest dealing first. Partners sit opposite each other.

Dealing
The dealer deals the cards round one at a time to his left, and his own last card he exposes to determine the trump suit. It is customary to leave the card on the table until he has played to the first trick (unless he wants to play it).

The play
Eldest hand (to dealer's left) leads to the first trick. Other players must follow suit to the card led if they can; if they cannot they may play a trump or discard. The trick is won by the highest trump played, or, if none is played, by the highest card of the suit led. The winner of the trick leads to the next. The object is to score more tricks than the opponents. One player from each side gathers the tricks for his side.

The deal passes clockwise.

Scoring

There are many methods of scoring. Most of them use the principle of counting the winning side's score by the number of tricks made in excess of six, e.g. if it made nine tricks to four it would score 3. The first six tricks a side makes are known as the *book*.

A game is to 5 points, and a rubber is the best of three games. The Ace, King, Queen and Jack of the trump suit are known as *honours*, and a side dealt all four of them scores 4 points, a side dealt three of them 2 points. A side with a score of 4 points before the deal cannot score for honours. Points for honours are taken on each deal after the points for tricks, so if a side passes 5 points with its score for tricks, it cannot lose the game because of its opponents' honours.

Alternatively, instead of playing rubbers, a game can be played to as many points as the players choose, and they might decide to ignore the points for honours.

Example hand

The cards are dealt as in the illustration. South dealt and his last card was the ♠5, making spades trumps. West has lead and decides to lead his ♦K. The play proceeds:

	West	North	East	South
1.	♦K	♦5	♦4	♦A
2.	♣10	♣4	♣3	♣A
3.	♣K	♣5	♣2	♣Q
4.	♦J	♦6	♦8	♦2

The deal for the hand of Whist described in the text.

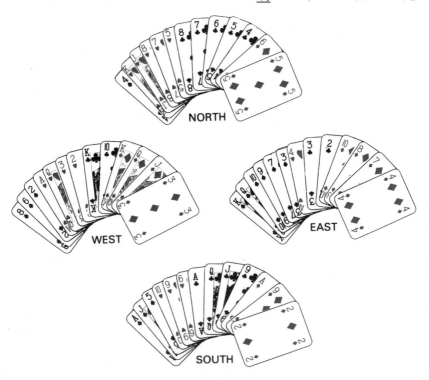

NORTH

WEST

EAST

SOUTH

5.	♠2	♠4	♠K	♠A
6.	♠6	♣6	♥4	♣J
7.	♠8	♣7	♣Q	♠5
8.	♦Q	♥5	♦7	♦9
9.	♦3	♥7	♦10	♥6
10.	♥2	♥8	♠3	♠J

East wins the remaining tricks with his spades, so East/West won nine tricks to North/South's four. There were no points for honours, so East/West lead 3–0 in the first game.

Strategy

Skill lies in remembering the cards played, attempting to form pictures of the other players' hands from the cards played, and trying to give partner information about one's hand, and to interpret information received from him.

There are some 'rules' which tend to receive too much attention (they are also advocated in Bridge) but they are based on sound principles. The best-known is perhaps 'second player plays low, third player plays high', the precept being that a player leads a suit in order to establish it, and wants his partner to help drive out the high cards. Following from this, it is recognized as sound play to return partner's lead when able.

Not finessing against partner is another sound principle. A finesse is the play that is effected in Bridge when, for example, dummy contains the A Q of a suit, and declarer leads that suit. If the player between the declarer and dummy has the King, he will not play it, since it will lose to dummy's Ace and establish the Queen. So he plays a low card instead, and declarer plays the Queen from dummy, thus making both Ace and Queen. This is finessing. However, in Whist, if a player holds Ace and Queen and his partner leads the suit, he should play Ace. Not to do so is known as 'finessing against partner' and it is considered bad play (in some circles, bad form).

An honour played by an opponent is usually best covered by a higher honour if possible.

Experienced players have drawn up a table of first and second leads which are considered profitable. They convey useful information to partner about one's holding in a strong suit. These are shown on page 274

Advised leads with special holdings:

In the trump suit

Holding	1st lead	2nd lead
A K Q J	J	Q
A K Q	Q	K
A K x x x x x and more	K	A
A K x x x x	4th best	

In plain suits:

A K Q J	K	J
A K Q	K	Q
A K x and more	K	A
A K	A	K
K Q J x	K	J
K Q J x x	J	K
K Q J x x x and more	J	Q
A x x x and more	A	4th best of remainder
K Q x and more	K	4th best of remainder
A Q J	A	Q
A Q J x	A	Q
A Q J x x and more	A	J
K J 10 9	9	K (if A or Q falls)
Q J x	Q	
Q J x x and more	4th best	

Without any of these holdings one should lead one's fourth highest card in one's longest suit.

WINDMILL

Windmill is a double-pack **patience** or **solitaire** which gets its name from its layout. It is also called Propeller.

The play

Any King is placed face up in the centre of the table, and two cards are dealt above it, two below it, and two on each side of it to form a cross, as illustrated. The first four Aces that are dealt, whether to the cross or as the game progresses, are played to the angles of the cross.

The object of the game is to build on the King in the centre a round-the-corner descending sequence of 52 cards irrespective of suit or colour, i.e. from King to Ace, then King to Ace again and so on. Meanwhile, on each Ace is built an ascending sequence to King irrespective of suit or colour.

Any card from the layout is available for play. The stock is turned one card at a time and that card is also available for play. If it cannot be played to a foundation it

---

The layout for the game of Windmill described in the text.

FOUNDATIONS

is played face up to a waste heap and the top card of the waste heap is also available for play.

When a space in the layout becomes vacant, it is filled immediately by the top card of the waste heap (or if there is no waste heap, by the top card of the stock). During play a card may be moved from an Ace foundation to the King foundation, but only one card can be taken from each Ace foundation during any one King-to-Ace sequence on the central King.

Should the stock become exhausted and the game not won, there is one further chance. The waste heap is turned over and dealt again, but this time there is no second waste heap started – as soon as a card cannot be played to a foundation the game is lost.

In the layout illustrated, the ♥ A can be played to a foundation space, and the ♠2 built upon it. The ♠Q can be built on the ♦ K, and the ♣J on the ♠Q. This leaves four spaces to be filled from stock. When the layout is complete again, and no further moves can be made, the top card of the stock is turned to the waste heap and so on.

General Index

CLASSIFIED INDEX

In this index games are classified according to the number of players for which they are suited. Gambling games and children's games are also listed separately.

Gambling games

All games can be played for stakes. The following games are those which lose their point without it:

Children's games

The following games are simple ones suitable for children: